PETRARCH

THE REVOLUTION
OF
COLA DI RIENZO

PETRARCH

THE REVOLUTION
OF
COLA DI RIENZO

EDITED BY
MARIO EMILIO COSENZA

THIRD EDITION
WITH NEW INTRODUCTION,
NOTES AND BIBLIOGRAPHY BY
RONALD G. MUSTO

ITALICA PRESS
NEW YORK
1996

First Published 1913
Copyright University of Chicago Press
Third Edition
Copyright © 1996 by Italica Press

ITALICA PRESS, INC.
595 Main Street
New York, New York 10044

Library of Congress Cataloging-in-Publication Data
Petrarca, Francesco, 1304-1374.
    The revolution of Cola di Rienzo.

    Bibliography: p.
    Includes index.
    1. Rienzo, Cola di, d. 1354. 2. Rome (Italy)—History—475-1420-
Sources. I. Cosenza, Mario Emilio, 1880-1966. II. Title.
DG811.6.P39 1986   945.05   86-80577
ISBN 978-0-934977-00-5 (pbk.)

Cover Art: Bronze statue of Cola di Rienzo, Capitoline. Girolamo
Masini, 1887. Italica Press Archive.

For a Complete List of Titles on Rome and
Other Titles in Historical Studies
Visit our Web Site at:
www.ItalicaPress.com

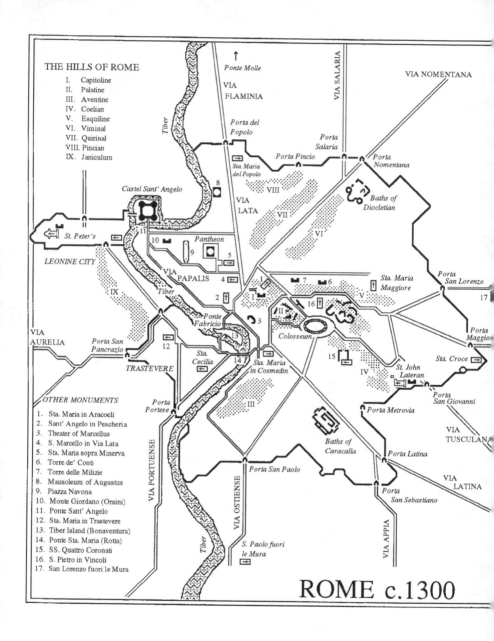

THE HILLS OF ROME

I. Capitoline
II. Palatine
III. Aventine
IV. Coelian
V. Esquiline
VI. Viminal
VII. Quirinal
VIII. Pincian
IX. Janiculum

Ponte Molle

VIA FLAMINIA

VIA SALARIA

VIA NOMENTANA

Tiber

Porta del Popolo

Porta Salaria

Porta Pincio

Porta Nomentana

Sta. Maria del Popolo

Castel Sant' Angelo

VIII

VIA LATA

VII

Baths of Diocletian

St. Peter's

LEONINE CITY

11

10

Pantheon

9

5

VI

VIA PAPALIS

4

IX

Tiber

2

1

Sta. Maria Maggiore

Porta San Lorenzo

17

V

16

II

VIA AURELIA

Porta San Pancrazio

Ponte Fabricio

3

13

Colosseum

Porta Maggio

12

Sta. Cecilia

14

Sta. Maria in Cosmedin

15

IV

St. John Lateran

Sta. Croce

TRASTEVERE

Porta Portese

III

Porta Metrovia

Porta San Giovanni

VIA TUSCULANA

OTHER MONUMENTS

1. Sta. Maria in Aracoeli
2. Sant' Angelo in Pescheria
3. Theater of Marcellus
4. S. Marcello in Via Lata
5. Sta. Maria sopra Minerva
6. Torre de' Conti
7. Torre delle Milizie
8. Mausoleum of Augustus
9. Piazza Navona
10. Monte Giordano (Orsini)
11. Ponte Sant' Angelo
12. Sta. Maria in Trastevere
13. Tiber Island (Bonaventura)
14. Ponte Sta. Maria (Rotta)
15. SS. Quattro Coronati
16. S. Pietro in Vincoli
17. San Lorenzo fuori le Mura

VIA PORTUENSE

VIA OSTIENSE

Porta San Paolo

Baths of Caracalla

Porta Latina

Porta San Sebastiano

VIA LATINA

VIA APPIA

Tiber

S. Paolo fuori le Mura

ROME c.1300

CONTENTS

PREFACE

The present text is a third edition of Mario E. Cosenza's *Francesco Petrarca and the Revolution of Cola di Rienzo*, presented to celebrate the tenth anniversary of Italica Press. It revises Italica's first publication, the second edition of Cosenza's book, originally published by the University of Chicago Press in 1913. This edition has again been completely reset, newly edited and provided with updated notes and bibliography to reflect the past decade of research.

While Cosenza's original edition served two generations of students, certain aspects of his language have invited revision to contemporary standards. These fall into two general categories: the deliberate archaisms of his English translations of Petrarch's Latin, and several early twentieth-century English usages now considered awkward or themselves archaic. In the first category, the most obvious revisions have been to Cosenza's use of the second-person singular: "thee" and "thy," where modern usage, in fact even the normal usage of the turn of the century, would use singular "you" undistinguished from the plural "you." The same applies to Cosenza's use of the second-person forms of verbs: "wouldst" and "canst," for example. Translating Petrarch's very complicated, and also very public, letters may have tempted Cosenza to use what was still in his day considered a formal and elevated style of language, but one that today seems quaint or stilted. The same is true of his many direct translations of the Latin passive and of complex sentences with many modifying clauses. In Petrarch's Latin these would read fairly clearly once their syntax had been determined and Petrarch's stylistics understood. In modern English, however, even the most elegant attempt to approach Petrarch's high style would have to employ a simplicity of structure and clarity of meaning.

We have therefore streamlined Cosenza's sentences and some of his vocabulary but without, we hope, altering the sense of his commentary, his translation, or of the original Latin. In doubtful cases we have rechecked Cosenza's English against the original Latin of Fracassetti's edition, as well as against other available English translations. We hope that the result is in the spirit of Cosenza's original and conveys Petrarch's meaning to a contemporary audience.

We have also retained Cosenza's original numbering system for the letters. While Cosenza's notes are still authoritative in most cases, we have added new research, editions, and translations where relevant and have annotated additional passages of the letters where recent research has presented new findings. This new research is often embedded into Cosenza's original notes, but the dates of the cited works should make identifying the new material an easy matter. In only a few instances, usually involving Cosenza's own editorial statements on the relations of Italy and the Italians to the rest of Europe, have we deleted text. In one instance in Chapter 3 we have deleted a lengthy discussion on the translation of the second-person plural from Latin to English, no longer of any practical interest for contemporary speakers. One major change that will be immediately apparent is the substitution of "Petrarch" for Cosenza's "Petrarca" throughout the text. While we have retained Cosenza's original preface verbatim, we have also deleted the section where he explained his decision to retain the Italian form of the name on nationalistic grounds. Contemporary English usage is moving away from this form. We have made no attempt to edit Cosenza's often highly rhetorical prose in regard to Rome and Italian unity.

Readers will note that the Bibliography has been expanded to include all new editions of works cited by Cosenza in his notes, as well as English translations and secondary studies on Cola and Petrarch, or related topics, published since 1913 or not included in Cosenza's original edition. Modern editions and translations of quoted texts have been cited along with Cosenza's original references in the notes, but most citations remain those to Cosenza's original sources. We have substituted modern readings in only a few cases, such as translations from *Spirto gentil* or selections of the *Africa* that were not Cosenza's original or where good contemporary translations are readily available. Classical references, abbreviated in Cosenza's original according to the familiar usage of his time, have been expanded for the contemporary reader and follow today's standard usage.

– Ronald G. Musto
New York City
September 1995

PREFACE
TO THE FIRST EDITION
(Abridged)

The present volume is the outcome of those notes that were taken during the preparation of my previous work, *Petrarch's Letters to Classical Authors*. In the pages which are now offered to the reader, I have endeavored to draw a picture of Petrarca as a statesman; for I firmly believe that, even if Petrarca had never sung a single sonnet in honor of Laura, he would still have been dear to endless generations of Italians for having been the first real Italian patriot – a man whose horizon was not bounded by narrow party lines, and whose heart, throughout his three score years and ten of busy life, was wholly devoted to the cause of *Italia una*.

It is evident that the material thus offered for research study was too abundant to be included within the covers of a single volume. In fact, it soon became necessary to concentrate upon only one period of Petrarca's political activities, and out of three or more possible choices, I have chosen to treat of Petrarca's relations with Cola di Rienzo. The reasons for this choice are such as would have appealed most strongly to Petrarca himself. In the first place, Cola and the revolution which he successfully accomplished were more nearly connected with the City of the Seven Hills than were the Popes or Charles IV, Emperor of the Holy Roman Empire; secondly, Petrarca's relations with Cola form a unit, a story that is easily understood; and thirdly, this story practically constitutes a chapter in the history of Rome during the Middle Ages.

The material of the present volume is drawn chiefly from Petrarca's letters, from the extremely important correspondence of Cola di Rienzo, and from the equally important archives of the Roman church. Nearly all the material of both the text and the commentary is new to the English language. Such passages and portions as have already been translated into English are called to the attention of the reader in the notes, where also criticism and comment thereon will be found. The notes have been made as detailed as seemed necessary, in order that the many allusions of Petrarca might become perfectly clear.

As formerly, the Latin edition and the complete Italian translation of Petrarca's letters, *De rebus familiaribus,* both by Fracassetti, have been indispensable. It is from these editions that I make all quotations from the letters. Passages from the other works of Petrarca are cited from the Basle edition of the Opera omnia, except those from the *De remediis utriusque fortunae,* for which the 1649 edition has been used. Biblical quotations have been taken from the Vulgate and from the Catholic (Douay) version of the Bible, for the convincing reason that it was from a Catholic Bible that Petrarca quoted, and that only by adopting such readings do certain passages of Petrarca's correspondence become clear. All other titles have been abbreviated in such manner as to be readily identified by consulting the Bibliography.

The contents of this volume breathe forth...an atmosphere of Rome and of Italy, and the poet battles and preaches and sings with...inspiration for the political liberty of the capital of the Caesars and for the re-establishment of the ancient *imperium*.... I acknowledge that nothing would have pleased me more than to cite the canzone *Spirto gentil* in the original Italian, which gives much of the fire and the pathos that are lost in translation. But, considering the nature of this volume, such course was impossible.

The difficulties of preparing this volume have been greater than they may appear at first sight. I have been encouraged throughout by a constant interest in the subject matter and by an increasing love for the patriot Petrarca. I now offer to the public these results of my labors, hoping that it too may be stirred by the prematurely national efforts of Francesco Petrarca and of Cola di Rienzo.

– Mario E. Cosenza

INTRODUCTION

In Rome on May 20, 1347 Cola di Rienzo, a young visionary with a gift for oratory, overthrew the rule of the barons and the pope. Cola's revolution then attempted to restore the greatness of the city, revive the ancient Roman Republic, and usher in a new age of liberty and peace. The bright hope for Rome and Italy soon changed to disillusionment, however, as Cola's rule turned first to tyranny and then to disgrace and exile only seven months later. After a period of wandering in Italy and to the court of Emperor Charles IV in Prague, Cola was eventually imprisoned at the papal court in Avignon and tried for heresy in 1352. In a bizarre turn of events he was freed and returned to Rome as a papal agent in 1354 in order to restore the republic. On October 8, 1354, however, the Roman people rose up and slew him on the steps of the Capitoline near where the statue of him now stands.

The following book tells the story of the relationship between Cola di Rienzo and Francesco Petrarch, the poet and first Renaissance humanist.[1] Using Petrarch's letters to and about the Roman tribune, it traces his friendship from their first encounter in Avignon in 1343 and the poet's enthusiastic embrace of Cola's revolution in 1347, through his growing doubts and first criticisms, to his bitter disappointment at Cola's fall.

The letters trace Petrarch's attempts to distance himself from the fallen leader and then follow the poet's final attempt to free Cola from his Avignon prison and his trial for heresy. They also help trace his continuing fascination with the revival of Rome's own liberty and its role as capital of a revived empire. The collection concludes with a series of poignant excerpts from Petrarch's letters that show that, even after Cola's death, he continued to fascinate and to haunt the poet and to conjure up memories of the deep bond between the two once beloved friends.

Cosenza's edition has become a standard reference since its publication in 1913. At that time it was one of the few English translations of Petrarch's letters, in fact of any of his works.[2] Cosenza's approach to Petrarch and di Rienzo was, in fact, among the first of the new classicist treatments of the tribune's revolution. Throughout the nineteenth century Rienzo's revolt had been seen in various romantic lights: the man of the people and patriot born ahead of his times, the hero of Wagner's *Rienzi*, of Byron's *Childe Harold*, or most especially of Bulwer Lytton's *Rienzi, The Last of the Roman Tribunes*. Here was the champion of the oppressed Italian people rising up against the haughty and foreign nobles, the star-crossed prophet of an Italian nationalism that could find its true folk expression only in the revival of its ancient heritage. While Cosenza certainly shared the enthusiasm of the first generation after Garibaldi, his training and previous scholarship brought him to the topic with a classicist's interest in the revival of Roman antiquity. Thus Cola's romanticism and Petrarch's Italian patriotism rest firmly together on the foundation of Cosenza's classical learning. His notes are full of references to classical mythology, literature, and the ancient historians, as well as to Petrarch's own classicizing works, especially the *Africa*. His edition thus appealed to the classical training and temperament of his contemporaries at the turn of the century and fit into the prevailing view of the Renaissance as the rationalist revival of ancient civilization, a break from the superstition and ignorance of the Dark Ages and its domination by the forces of religion and narrow party interest. Political independence, rational government, and self-determination went hand in hand with this return to ancient values.

Since Cosenza's day, however, the "revolt of the medievalists"[3] has tended to focus on the Middle Ages as a period worth studying in its own right, one with its own unique and valid culture that has contributed as much as antiquity or Renaissance to the modern West. Rienzo has, in fact, been seen as the symbol of the medieval roots of the Renaissance: all the spiritual and political forces for renewal and reform present in medieval civilization were themselves the impetus for the later movements that we call Renaissance and Reformation.[4] Many medievalists have also approached Italy and its cities as examples of the unique civilization of the age. Cola di Rienzo himself has been seen less as an isolated genius or nationalist born ahead of his time than as an example of the growth of secular political aspirations and class conflicts that characterized the new communes from the twelfth through the fifteenth centuries.[5] The wake of World War II also brought comparisons to Mussolini's rise and fall.[6] With the new interest in popular religion and heresy that marked the 1960s, Cola became a prime example of the chiliastic and violent capacities of the millennial tradition of the late Middle Ages or of its expectations of a new age of truth and light.[7] The new interest in psycho-history during the period also brought some students to expand on the Romantics' view of the tormented soul to see Cola's rise and sudden fall as the result of a paranoid-schizophrenia.[8]

It seems fair to say that, since the 1960s and the decline in "revolutionary" studies, interest in Petrarch and Cola's relationship has faded to a large degree. While several new studies have appeared in Italy,[9] as well as two new Italian editions of Cola's *Vita*; only one work, John Wright's translation of the *Vita*,[10] has appeared in English. In few of these studies has the relationship between Petrarch and Cola been examined, and none has equaled Cosenza's work of bringing together all the source materials and assembling the background notes. Other recent studies have focused on Roman social structures in the early fourteenth century, on the *Romanesco* dialect, or on the political program of Cola's now lost cycle of prophetic paintings.[11]

Thus Cosenza's edition has retained its usefulness since its first publication, and while no new edition or printings have appeared, it continues to appear in scholarly notes and bibliographies, most recently in 1994.[12] Yet why examine the poet and the political visionary together at all? What valid historical questions can such a collection possibly answer? Every age seems to have had its own fascination with Rienzo, and the nineteenth and early twentieth centuries' interest can easily be explained. Yet for the late twentieth century, considerably cooled in political fire and personal commitment, such a friendship can still yield considerable insight into the relationship between the ideal and the practical, between the world of the intellectual and that of politics. This collection also tells an exciting and emotionally satisfying story in itself. It provides excellent insight into Petrarch's deepest personal and public emotions and into his views of political effectiveness and of social justice. Cosenza's notes also help paint a vivid picture of late medieval Rome and its relationship to the popes at Avignon and to give vivid individual case studies of the problems of communication, distance, and time that the works of Braudel and the Annales school present in broad outline and statistic. It is also, as Cosenza himself claimed, a document of the emergence of early Renaissance views of renewal and reform.

Cosenza's chief interest in Cola di Rienzo lay in his relationship to Petrarch. He therefore picks up the story of Cola's life in 1343 when the two first meet at Avignon. It would be worthwhile, then, to briefly sketch Cola's early life to help fill in some of the background.[13] Nicholas Laurentii,[14] called Cola di Rienzo, was born in the spring of 1314 in the Regola *rione* of Rome, the section just below the Capitoline toward the Tiber Island, in fact near the Tiber mills. His father, Lorenzo, was an innkeeper; his mother Matalena, a wash woman and water bearer. After returning from Anagni in the Campagna where he had lived with relatives, "a peasant among peasants" as he himself said, he began his own education and before long was fully versed in the Christian and pagan classics, including Livy, Seneca, Cicero, Caesar, and Valerius Maximus. Cola could also read the many inscriptions that lay strewn all across medieval Rome and by 1333 had started a career there as a notary.

Rienzo soon gained a solid reputation as an orator and as an interpreter of these ancient inscriptions. This, and his opposition to the noble Colonna, Orsini, and Savelli families, won him a place among the republican elements of the city. In 1342, after the revolt of the Thirteen Good Men had overthrown the nobles,[15] Cola was named part of the delegation sent to Avignon to gain Clement VI's approval of the new government. It was on this embassy that he first met Petrarch.[16] Appointed Notary of the City Chamber by the pope on April 13, 1344, Cola returned to Rome and began to lay the groundwork for revolution in a series of fiery speeches against the barons, evocations of the glories of ancient Rome, and a series of political lectures on allegorical and apocalyptic paintings that he had arranged to appear on walls throughout the city.[17] Cola built his power base gradually among the *popoli minuti* – the city's poor and working classes – among the merchants and the lower nobility. After forming a conspiracy for the establishment of the *buono stato*,[18] Cola finally took advantage of the Colonnas' absence from the city to launch his revolution. After midnight on Pentecost day, May 20, 1347, he offered thirty masses to the Holy Spirit at the church of Sant' Angelo in Pescheria. Emerging the next morning fully armed, he then led a solemn procession of the citizens, along with the papal vicar, Raymond of Chameyrac, up to the Capitoline. Here he proclaimed the Roman Republic restored and took the title Tribune of the People.

A NOTE ON THE EDITOR AND TRANSLATOR

Mario Emilio Cosenza was born in Naples on November 21, 1880,[19] the son of Professor Giuseppe Cosenza, a Knight of the Order of the Crown of Italy, and of the former Emilia Contreras. Educated in the New York City public schools, he graduated class valedictorian with a B.A. from City College in 1901, then went on to Columbia University, where he earned a doctorate in Classics in 1905. His dissertation was published that year as *Official Positions After the Time of Constantine*.[20] During his graduate studies he also did field work in archaeology in Italy and in Latin literature at the then American School of Classical Studies, later to become the American Academy in Rome. In 1906 he was appointed instructor of Latin literature and language at the City College, assistant professor in 1913, deputy director of the Townsend Harris Hall High School, the prep school for the college, in 1916; and in 1917 he was named associate professor of Classical Languages at the City College. In 1919 he became director of the Townsend School, and in 1926 professor of Classical Languages and chairman of the department at the Brooklyn Center of the college, and chairman when this became Brooklyn College in 1931. In 1932 Cosenza was named Dean of Brooklyn College.

Cosenza's teaching and language work brought his pen into many areas of research. He completed several biographical studies of City College founder Townsend Harris[21] and works on the teaching of Latin and Italian in America.[22] Cosenza's classical and historical work gradually drew him away from antiquity to the reemergence of classical literature in the Italian Renaissance. In addition to the present volume of Petrarch's letters, Cosenza was also the translator of Ettore Pais' *Ancient Legends of Roman History*,[23] translator and editor of *Petrarch's Letters to Classical Authors*,[24] and the translator of Amerigo Vespucci's *Quatuor Americi Vesputii navigationes*,[25] a scholarly progress that gradually followed his own journey from the shores of the ancient Mediterranean to those of modern America.

Professor Cosenza is perhaps best known to Renaissance scholars as the author of several of the most important bibliographical tools still available to researchers. These include his *Biographical and Bibliographical Dictionary of the Italian Humanists,*[26] his *Checklist of Non-Italian Humanists 1300-1800,*[27] and his *Biographical and Bibliographical Dictionary of the Italian Printers and of Foreign Printers in Italy,*[28] all complied over long years of research and writing in the field of classical and Renaissance literature.

Mario Cosenza was also active in many community and civic groups. Among these were the Order of the Sons of Italy, the Italian Teachers Association, the High School Principals Association, and the Order of the Crown of Italy, of which he was made Cavaliere and Commendatore. He was active in the Dante Alighieri Society, Phi Beta Kappa, the American Philological Association, and the New York Classical Club. He married Verena Bostroem in 1914, with whom he had three daughters. He died at Rockville Center, NY, on October 22, 1966.

NOTES

1. Born July 20, 1304 in Arezzo, died July 19, 1374 at Arquà, Petrarch was brought up in Avignon and Carpentras in southern France, studied law at Montpellier and Bologna, and returned to Avignon in 1325 on the death of his father, already determined on a career as a lyric poet and writer. His sonnets begun in 1327 in honor of Laura, the wife of another man, earned him fame throughout Italy and Europe. Petrarch was an avid collector of manuscripts of the Latin classics and is credited with having launched the revival of classical studies central to the Renaissance. His work on Augustine and Livy brought him a solid reputation as a scholar.

In 1330 he accepted minor orders in the church and entered the Avignon household of Cardinal Giovanni Colonna, a member of the powerful Roman family with whom he was already well connected. Petrarch traveled throughout northern Europe in 1333, and in 1337 finally visited Rome for the first time. There on the Capitoline, on April 8, 1341, he was crowned poet laureate of Rome by King Robert the Wise of Naples. By the 1340s Petrarch was the acknowledged master of vernacular poetry in Italy and in Europe, a leader of the revival of ancient learning and a well-known critic, if also a somewhat independent courtier, of the Roman Colonna and of the popes at Avignon. Cosenza picks up his life at this point. The best account remains Ernest Hatch Wilkins, *Life of Petrarch* (Chicago: University of Chicago Press, 1963). For a general review of Petrarch scholarship see, for example, Marcello Aurigemma, "Recenti studi sul Petrarca," *Cultura e scuola* 23.92 (1984): 7-14; Ugo Dotti, *Vita di Petrarca*

(Rome: Laterza, 1987); and Giuseppe Mazzotta, *The Worlds of Petrarch*, Duke Monographs in Medieval and Renaissance Studies 14 (Durham, NC: Duke University Press, 1994), See also the notes below.

2. The only other one frequently cited was James H. Robinson and Henry W. Rolfe, *Petrarch, the First Modern Scholar and Man of Letters* (New York: Putnam, 1898). See the notes below.

3. The phrase is Wallace Ferguson's. See his *The Renaissance in Historical Thought* (Boston: Houghton Mifflin, 1948), 329-85.

4. See Konrad Burdach and Paul Piur, *Briefwechsel des Cola di Rienzo*, vol. 2 of *Vom Mittelalter zur Reformation*, 5 parts (Berlin: Weidmann, 1913-1929); Karl Brandi, *Cola di Rienzo und sein Verhältnis zu Renaissance und Humanismus* (Darmstadt: Wissenschaftliche Buchgesellschaft, 1965); and Karl Höfele, *Rienzi, das abenteuerliche Vorspiel der Renaissance* (Munich: R. Oldenbourg, 1958). For an analysis see Ferguson, *Renaissance*, pp. 307-9.

5. See, for example, Edward P. Cheyney, *The Dawn of a New Era 1250-1453* (New York: Harper & Row, 1936; rev. ed., 1957); Josef Macek, "Les racines sociales de l'insurrection de Cola di Rienzo," *Historica* 6 (1963): 45-107; and "Pétrarch et Cola di Rienzo," *Historica* 8 (1965): 5-51; Michel Mollat and Philippe Wolff, *The Popular Revolutions of the Late Middle Ages* (London: Allen & Unwin, 1973); and John Larner, *Italy in the Age of Dante and Petrarch 1216-1380* (New York: Longman, 1980).

6. See V. Fleisher, *Rienzo: The Rise and Fall of a Dictator* (London: Aigion Press, 1948). For another recent interpretation of Rienzo as a proto-fascist and forerunner of Mussolini see Nicholas Mann, *Petrarch*, Past Masters Series (New York: Oxford University Press, 1984), 36-37. In this light, compare Iris Origo, *Tribune of Rome: A Biography of Cola di Rienzo* (London: Hogarth Press, 1938).

7. See *Letters* 49 and 58, in *Visions of the End. Apocalyptic Traditions in the Middle Ages,* ed. Bernard McGinn (New York: Columbia University Press, 1979), 241-44. For eschatological expectations during the period see Eugenio Duprè-Theseider, "L'attesa escatologica durante il periodo avignonese," in *L'Attesa dell'età nuova nella spiritualità della fine del medioevo,* Convegni del Centro di Studi sulla Spiritualità Medievale (Todi: CSSM, 1962), 65-126; Massimo Miglio, "Gli ideali di pace e di giustizia in Roma a metà del Trecento," in *La pace nel pensiero, nella politica, negli ideali del Trecento,* Convegni del Centro di Studi sulla Spiritualità Medievale 15 (Todi: CSSM, 1975), 175-97; and "'Et rerum facta est pulcherrima Roma.' Attualità della tradizione e proposte di innovazione," in *Aspetti culturali della società italiana nel periodo del papato avignonese,* Convegni del Centro di Studi sulla Spiritualità Medievale 19 (Todi: CSSM, 1981), 311-69.

8. The contemporary Florentine historian Giovanni Villani had already dismissed Cola as a madman in his *Cronica* 12.90. See *Cronica, con le continuazioni di Matteo e Filippo* (Turin: Einaudi, 1979), 276-79. This evidence was summarized in Marisa Mariani, "Cola di Rienzo nel giudizio dei contemporanei fiorentini," *Studi romani* 8 (1960): 647-66. It is a charge that has been repeated quite often in the general literature since. See for example, Mann, pp. 35-37, cited below; and C.W. Previté-

Orton, *The Shorter Cambridge Medieval History,* 2 vols. (New York: Cambridge University Press, 1966), 2: 864.

9. See Giuseppe D'Arrigo, "Ricordo di due grandi: Francesco Petrarca e Cola di Rienzo," in *Fatti e figure del Lazio medievale, Gruppo culturale di Roma e di Lazio* (Rome: Fratelli Palombi Editori, 1979), 511-16; Massimo Miglio, "Gruppi sociali e azione politica nella Roma di Cola di Rienzo," *Studi romani* 23.4 (1975): 442-61; Innocente Toppani, "Petrarca, Cola di Rienzo e il mito di Roma," *Atti dell' Istituto Veneto di scienze, lettere ed arti. Classe di scienze morali, lettere ed arti* 135 (1977): 155-72; and Carmelo Musumarra, "Petrarca e Roma," *Critica Letteraria* 18.1 (1990): 155-67.

10. English in John Wright, trans. and ed., *The Life of Cola di Rienzo* (Toronto: Pontifical Institute of Mediaeval Studies, 1975); and Italian in Giuseppe Porta, ed., *Vita di Cola di Rienzo. Cronaca di anonimo romano* (Milan: Adelphi, 1979); and Anonimo romano, *Cronica, Vita di Cola di Rienzo,* Ettone Mazzali, ed. (Milan: Rizzoli, 1991).

11. On Roman society and economy see, for example, Étienne Hubert, *Rome aux XIIIe et XIVe siècles. Collection de l'École française de Rome* 170 (Rome: EFR, 1993), especially Sandro Carocci, "Baroni in città: Considerazioni sull' insediamento e i diritti urbani della grande nobiltà," 137-73; Clara Gennaro, "Mercanti e bovattieri nella Roma della seconda metà del Trecento," *Bullettino dell'Istituto storico italiano per il medioevo e Archivio Muratoriano* 78 (1967): 155-203; Carola M. Small, "The District of Rome in the Early Fourteenth Century, 1300 to 1347," *Canadian Journal of History/Annales Canadiennes d'Histoire* 16 (1981): 193-213. Many studies have appeared on the use of *romanesco* in the *Vita* of Cola by the Anonimo romano. Among these are Gian Mario Anselmi, "Il tempo della storia e quello della vita nella *Cronica* dell' Anonimo romano," *Studi e problemi di critica testuale* 21 (Oct. 1980): 181-94; idem, "La *Cronica* dell'Anonimo romano," *Bullettino dell'Istituto storico italiano per il medioevo e Archivio Muratoriano* 91 (1984): 423-40; Arrigo Castellani, "Note di lettura: La 'Cronica' d'Anonimo romano," *Studi linguistici italiani* 13 (1987): 66-84; Paolo D'Achille and Claudio Giovanardi, *La letteratura volgare e i dialetti di Roma e del Lazio. Bibliografia dei testi e degli studi.* Vol. 1: *Dalle origini al 1550* (Rome: Bonacci Editore, 1984), no. 17, pp. 28-30; Maurizio Dardano, "L'articolazione e il confine della frase nella 'Cronica' di Anonimo romano," in Federica Albani Leoni, ed., *Italia linguistica: Idee, storia, strutture* (Bologna: Il Mulino, 1983), 203-22; Gianfranco Folena, "Varia fortuna del romanesco," *Lingua nostra* 52.1 (1991): 7-10; Giuseppe Porta, "La lingua della 'Cronica' di Anonimo romano," in Tullio de Mauro, ed., *Il romanesco ieri e oggi* (Rome: Bulzoni, 1989), 13-26; idem, "Un nuovo manoscritto della 'Cronica' di Anonimo romano," *Studi medievali,* ser. 3, 25.1 (1984): 445-48; Mario Pozzi, "Appunti sulla 'Cronica' di Anonimo romano," *Giornale storico della letteratura italiana* 99 (1982): 481-504; Mario Sanfilippo, "Dell' Anonimo e della sua e altrui nobiltà," *Quaderni medievali* 9 (1980): 121-28; Gustav Seibt, *Anonimo romano: Geschichtsschreibung in Rom an der Schwelle Renaissance* (Stuttgart: Klett-Cotta, 1992); Giuliano Tanturli,

"La *Cronica* di Anonimo romano," *Paragone* 31.368 (Oct. 1980): 84-93; and Pietro Trifone, "Aspetti dello stile nominale nella *Cronica* trecentesca di Anonimo romano," *Studi linguistici italiani* 12 (1986): 217-39. On the role of art in Cola's revolution, see n. 17 below.

12. Benjamin G. Kohl's review of a similar collection of letters by Petrarch, *Babylon on the Rhone: A Translation of the Letters by Dante, Petrarch and Catherine of Siena on the Avignon Papacy,* Robert Coogan, trans. and ed. (Madrid: José Porrua Turanzas; Potomac, MD: Studia Humanitatis, 1983), in *Speculum* 60.2 (April 1985): 476, notes that Cosenza's notes are still superior. Mazzotta, *Worlds,* pp. 111-22, uses the second edition of the present book to trace Petrarch's political and cultural views of Rome's revival under Cola. See the brief summary of "Rienzi's mad scheme," provided by Donald R. Kelley, *Renaissance Humanism,* Twayne's Studies in Intellectual and Cultural History 2 (Boston: G.K. Hall, 1991), 11-13, and 149 n. 18.

13. The best sources for this are the *Vita di Cola di Rienzo,* in numerous editions. See bibliography below, and in the English translation in Wright, *Life,* pp. 15-20, 31-39. A good, brief account is Guillaume Mollat, *The Popes at Avignon 1305-1378* (New York: Thomas Nelson, 1963), 146-54; and Ferdinand Gregorovius, *History of the City of Rome in the Middle Ages,* English trans. Annie Hamilton, 8 vols. in 13 (London: George Bell and Sons, 1984-1900; rpt. ed., New York: AMS, 1967), 6.1: 227-376; abridged ed. by Karl F. Morrison as *Rome and Medieval Culture. Selections from History of the City of Rome in the Middle Ages* (Chicago: University of Chicago Press, 1971), 269-307. See also the notes to letters below. Other useful biographies and treatments include Jules S. Zeller, *Les tribuns et les revolutions en Italie* (Paris: Didier, 1874); Emmanuel Rodocanachi, *Cola di Rienzo* (Paris: A. Lahure, 1888); Paul Piur, *Cola di Rienzo* (Vienna: L. W. Seidel, 1931), Italian trans. Jeanne Chabod Rohr, 1934; Raffaello Morghen, *Cola di Rienzo Senatore,* L. Gatto, ed. (Rome: Ateneo, 1956); Luigi Barzini, "Cola di Rienzo or the Obsession of Antiquity," in *The Italians* (New York: Atheneum, 1967), 117-32; and Thomas G. Bergin, *Petrarch,* Twayne's World Authors 81 (New York: Twayne, 1970), 68-73; and Origo. See also the collection *Cola di Rienzo nel sesto centenario della morte* (Rome: Unione storia ed arte. Memorie e conferenze romane, vol. 1, 1955). Italian biographies of interest include Jean Claude Maire-Vigueur, "Cola di Rienzo," *Dizionario Biografico degli Italiani* 16 (Rome: DBI, 1982), 662-75; Francesco Mazzei, *Cola di Rienzo: La fantastica vita e l'orribile morte del tribuno del popolo romano* (Milan: Rusconi, 1980); Ugo Reale, *Vita di Cola di Rienzo* (Rome: Editori Riuniti, 1982); and idem, *Cola di Rienzo: La straordinario vita del tribuno che sogno riportare Roma all'antico valore...* (Rome: Newton Compton, 1991).

14. Of which Cola di Rienzo is merely the Roman nickname, in fact, "Nick, Larry's Son," by which he was known. The other form, "Rienzi," seems to have been the fabrication of later French historians. See Rodocanachi, p. 29. On the usage of the *Romanesco* dialect in this context see the works cited in n.11 above.

15. See Heinrich Schmidinger, "Die Antwort Clemens' VI. an die Gesandschaft der Stadt Rom vom Jahre 1343," in *Miscellanea in onore di Monsignor Martino Giusti*, 2 vols. (Vatican City: BAV, 1978), 2: 323-65; and below, Chapter 1, p. 1-2.
16. See below, Chapter 1, pp. 2-4.
17. See Jean-Philippe Antoine, *"Ad perpetuam memoriam*. Les nouvelles fonctions de l'image peinte en Italie, 1250-1400," *Mélanges de l'École Française de Rome. Moyen Age et Temps Modernes* 100.2 (1988): 541-615; Hans Belting, "Langage et réalité dans la peinture monumentale publique en Italie au Trecento," in Xavier Barral i Altet, ed., *Artistes, artisans et production artistique au Moyen Age*, Actes du Colloque internationale de Rennes, 1983 (Paris: Picard, 1990), 3: 491-511; and Philippe Sonnay, "La politique artistique de Cola di Rienzo (1313-1354)," *Revue de l'art* 55 (1982): 35-43. Most recently see Amy Schwarz, "Images and Illusions of Power in Trecento Art: Cola di Rienzo and the Ancient Roman Republic," (Ph.D. Diss. Binghamton: SUNY, 1994).
18. See Fritz Kühn, *Die Entwicklung der Bündnispläne Cola di Rienzos im Jahre 1347* (Berlin: Denter & Nicolas, 1905). On Cola's ancient models see also Marta Sordi, "Cola di Rienzo e le Clausole mancanti della 'lex de imperio Vespasiani,'" in *Studi in onore di Edoardo Volterrra* 2 (Milan: A. Giuffre 1971), 303-11.
19. See *Who Was Who in America*, vol. 4, 1961-1968 (Chicago: Marquis Who's Who, 1968), 205; and *Who Was Who Among North American Authors, 1921-1939*, vol. 1, A-J (Detroit: Gale Research Co., 1976), 356-57. The New York Public Library has extensive holdings on Cosenza.
20. Lancaster, PA: New Era Publications, 1905.
21. Including *The Establishment of the College of the City of New York as the Free Academy. Townsend Harris, Founder* (New York: Associated Alumni of the College of the City of New York, 1925); and *The Complete Journal of Townsend Harris, First American Consul General and Minister to Japan* (Garden City, NY: Doubleday and Japan Society, 1930; rev. ed., 1959).
22. These include *Instruction Book and Syllabus, Latin I* (1909); *Syllabus of a Course in Caesar, Latin II* (1910); and *The Study of Italian in the United States* (New York: Italy America Society, 1924).
23. New York: Dodd Mead, 1905.
24. *Petrarch's Letters to Classical Authors*, Mario E. Cosenza, trans. and ed. (Chicago: University of Chicago Press, 1910).
25. Washington, DC: U.S. Catholic Historical Society, 1907, 82-151.
26. *Biographical and Bibliographical Dictionary of the Italian Humanists and the World of Classical Scholarship in Italy 1300-1800*, 5 vols. with supplement, (Boston: G.K. Hall, 1962-67).
27. Boston: G.K. Hall, 1969.
28. Boston: G.K. Hall, 1968.

CHAPTER 1

AVIGNON 1343

On May 19, 1342 Clement VI was crowned pope at Avignon.[1] Pope John XXII and Pope Benedict XII, his predecessors, had offered the Romans hopes that were never realized. When Clement ascended the Sacred Chair, therefore, the hopeful Romans dispatched an embassy to their new lord. This embassy, consisting of eighteen men and representing the three classes of the Roman people, was headed by Stefano Colonna the Younger, Francesco di Vico, and Lello di Pietro di Stefano dei Cosecchi (or Tosetti). With all due humility the ambassadors made the following three requests: that the newly crowned pope should assume supreme power over Rome; that he should withdraw from Avignon and restore the church of Rome to its rightful seat in the city by the Tiber; and that he should decree the celebration of the Jubilee every fifty, instead of one hundred, years. The pontiff accepted the powers offered to him, granted the request concerning the Jubilee for Rome's financial advantage, but alleged that the Roman church could not be restored to Rome just at that time because of the unpleasant relations between England and France. Petrarch himself addressed a poem to the pope, likewise urging him to return to Rome. But it was all in vain, and the only tangible result of this audience was Clement's appointment of two nobles to represent him in the Roman Senate.

The medieval Romans lived in an atmosphere of eternal war. With the nominal ruler living a life of ease and splendor on the banks of the Rhone, the real control of the city lay in the hands of the Colonna and the Orsini. These powerful baronial houses made the city itself the spoils of their factional strife, and their daily encounters helped to hasten the depopulation of the Urbs.[2] Either in December 1342 or in January 1343 a revolt resulted in the overthrow of the senators and in placing the governing power in the hands of the Thirteen Good Men, who ruled in the name of the pope. A second embassy was dispatched to Avignon without delay to acquaint the pope with these changes and to justify the revolt. The Romans chose as leader of this embassy the low-born Cola di Rienzo, who was endowed, however, with wonderful powers of oratory. A kind reception awaited the envoys; and when the requests of the Roman citizens were made known to the pontiff, the same answers were given as on the occasion of the former embassy.

During the course of this, his first political mission, Cola di Rienzo met Francesco Petrarch. Cola, the son of an inn-keeper, took special delight in the writings of the ancient historians of the city. To this he added a passionate fondness for deciphering the time-worn and neglected inscriptions that he beheld on every side. There gradually grew up before him the image of an ideal Rome, a Rome powerful and revered as in the days of Augustus, peaceful and not torn apart by the foreign barons of his day. It is possible that Cola was present on the occasion of Petrarch's coronation on the Capitol in 1341. If so, we can well imagine the impression that that Easter spectacle must have made on his poetic nature. He may well have thought it a vision of the ancient days, a wondrous staging of a page from his beloved Livy. As for Petrarch, the coronation for which he had so ardently yearned formed only an interlude in the composition of his epic, the *Africa*.[3] It was the reputation of this unseen and unpublished poem that had so influenced King Robert of Sicily during his examination of Petrarch at Naples; and to this poem Petrarch returned with redoubled vigor after his triumph on the Capitol.

We must emphasize a well known fact here. Petrarch intended the *Africa*, whose hero was P. Cornelius Scipio, to be the national epic of Italy. His object was to offer a medieval *Aeneid* to the Italian world. He felt with all the deep feeling of a patriotic Italian the full force of the Virgilian command to the Augustan Romans: to dictate the conditions of peace, to spare the conquered, and to subdue the proud. Petrarch wept at the disunited condition of his Italy; at the internecine strife of the princes and potentates; but above all at the presence of the foreign barbarians, who ruthlessly trod under foot the ashes of their former conquerors. Can we wonder that Scipio Africanus had become the special object of Petrarch's veneration? Had not Scipio, at a most critical time, emerged as the champion of his country's liberty? Had he not roused the drooping spirits of the Romans? Had he not driven from Italian soil the most dreaded of all Rome's countless enemies, Hannibal?

CHAPTER I, AVIGNON 1343

Thus, in love with Rome's ancient grandeur and equally despondent at her present widowed state, both Cola and Petrarch were inflamed with thoughts of her future and with vague – very vague – dreams of a restoration. Chance or destiny brought them face to face in the papal palace at Avignon.

It does not matter whether Petrarch met Cola on the first, or on the second, or on any other particular day of the latter's stay at Avignon. But we can readily imagine their desire for friendship. Cola must surely have known of Petrarch's presence in the papal capital. The Roman envoy himself had eloquently portrayed the ruined state of the Queen of Cities, the fallen shrines and sanctuaries, the hatred of the Orsini for the Colonna greater than that of Romulus and Remus, the arrogant barbarians swaggering about on the soil that had been drenched with the blood of martyrs. Cola's dreams and hopes of a "single, harmonious, peaceful, holy, and indissoluble union" must have struck quite a responsive chord in Petrarch's heart. We may well imagine that to the Poet Laureate Cola must have appeared the reincarnation of his hero Scipio Africanus, who first freed Italian soil from the foot of the barbarian; or as the embodiment of Dante's Greyhound, who was to be the savior of that low Italy "on whose account the maid Camilla died."[4]

Clement VI was soon fascinated by Cola's eloquence, but not so the powerful and influential Cardinal Giovanni Colonna. It would have been superhuman for the cardinal to maintain a passive attitude when he heard Cola's fiery denunciations of the barons at Rome, of whom the Colonna formed so great a part. His influence with the pope was so great that Cola fell into disfavor, finally reentering the good graces of His Holiness only through Petrarch's intervention. Petrarch, we must recall, was an intimate member of the cardinal's household. The first beginnings, therefore, of that coldness between him and the house of the Colonna – a coldness that was to reach its climax with the battle of November 20, 1347 – must be ascribed to this period of Cola's disfavor.

Petrarch must have had many long meetings with Cola. It is quite possible that the more learned poet recited to the youthful envoy passages from his epic of liberation – passages that he had scrupulously guarded from the world; that he filled Cola's mind with countless examples of Roman greatness and patriotism drawn from the pages of his adored classics; and that Cola's own ideas, vague and misty at first, may have taken more definite shape from these inspired conversations. Indeed, today's world knows Petrarch's ideas and dreams so well and knows Cola's future actions so thoroughly, that it would be an easy and pleasant task to reconstruct some of these conversations. But as usual, Petrarch has anticipated the ideas of future generations. It seems that his meetings with Cola became somewhat more guarded than at first; they usually met somewhere beyond the confines of the papal residence and would saunter through the noisy, crowded streets of Avignon, earnestly discussing the ways and means for the realization of their hopes.

On one such occasion, perhaps after praying together in the church of St. Agricola to obtain the comfort both their distracted souls so badly needed, they stood outside the portals of that church. There they engaged in an inspired conversation that may have owed its origin to a belief strengthened by the devout prayer just offered. This conversation, and the feelings that it subsequently aroused in Petrarch, the poet himself relates in the following letter.

PETRARCH TO COLA DI RIENZO
(SINE NOMINE 7)

As I recall that most inspired and earnest conversation we had two days ago as we stood before the portals of that famous and ancient sanctuary, I glow with such zeal that I consider your words those of an oracle issuing from the innermost recesses of that temple.[5] I seem to have been listening to a god, not to a man. You bemoaned the present conditions – no, the very fall and ruin of the republic – in words of such divine inspiration, and you probed our wounds with the shafts of your eloquence to such depths that whenever I recall the sound and the meaning of your words, tears leap to my eyes, and grief again grips my soul.[6] My heart was all inflamed as you spoke. But now, as I recall the words and ponder them, as I anticipate the future, I melt into tears – not effeminate, but manly and bold – tears that, if the occasion offered, would dare accomplish some patriotic deed and would gush forth in the defense of justice, as befits a man. Therefore, though I had often communicated with you, since that day I have done so more than ever. Despair seizes me one moment, hope the next; and with my soul wavering between the two, I often murmur to myself: "Oh! if ever.... oh! if it would only happen in my day.... oh! if I could only share in so noble, so glorious an enterprise!"

Then I turn to that crucifix that is my solace and exclaim with sad tones and moistened eyes:

> O Christ, you are too good and merciful. What does this mean? Awake! Why are you asleep, O Lord? Arise and do not cast us off forever! Why do you hide your face, forgetting our woe and our oppression?[7] O Lord, our defender, look on us.[8] Behold our sufferings and their causes. Behold what deeds are done by your enemies under the shield of your name. Behold, and take vengeance. If not, help us before the power of the deadly poison wastes away the life of our body, before we are crushed by the insufferable weight of evils.
>
> What are you doing, O salvation of those who trust in you?[9] What are you planning, Savior? Why do you delay? How long will you avert your gaze? How long will you remain untouched by our trials, how long will you refrain from putting an end to such great distress? Don't you see our woes, you whom neither the vast expanse of heaven can escape, nor the unfathomable depths, nor the drops of the ocean, nor the leaves of the forest, nor the sands of the sea, nor the number of the stars, nor the multitude of living creatures, nor the countless plants and shrubs? Have we, then, become hateful to you, we whom you once loved so, we for love of whom you, our Lord ruling in heaven, descended to earth and, even as a mortal man, did suffer the Cross? Perhaps you both see and cherish us but are held back by your lack of power? But are you not omnipotent? And if not, what hope remains? Does your enemies' power make you fear? But the insolent pride of our age has not yet made men equal to their creator.[10] Or, finally, is it mercy that checks the thunderbolt of your judgment? But see to it, infallible judge, see to it that in sparing the few you do not destroy the many. See to it that your mercy, extended to the wicked, does not prove cruelty to the upright and destruction to the innocent.

But what am I saying, insignificant mortal that I am! Who am I to argue with you like this? We entrust ourselves and all our belongings to you, O Lord. Your will be done, you who created us. But remember that our frailty can no longer endure beneath the weight of such great calamities. Bring us your timely aid while life still remains in us, so that, if you permit us to die, you may not be obliged to resurrect those whom you might have spared. Come, our hope. Make haste, make haste to deliver us.[11] This is our daily prayer. And we beseech you, O Lord, either destroy the countless evils of this world, or destroy the world itself.[12]

NOTES

1. On the death of Benedict XI (1303-4), who had been forced out of Rome to Perugia by the interference of the local barons, it took several months before the election of his successor, Bertrand de Got, as Clement V. A Frenchman, Clement had every intention of traveling back to Rome, but the new war between England and France and anarchic conditions at Rome compelled him to remain on at the site of his coronation, at Vienne in southern France. Events soon persuaded him to move his see to papal possessions in nearby Avignon until conditions were right for a return to Italy. From 1305 until 1378 seven popes made their homes at Avignon, developing their own court and complex administrative system, ever promising and hoping for conditions in Italy to improve enough for their return to Rome. This period has been called the Avignon Papacy. To many, however, the absence of the bishops of Rome from their see was a scandal, attributed either to the scheming of the French kings or the French sympathies of these popes. Dante, St. Catherine of Siena, Bridget of Sweden, and Petrarch himself all harshly criticized the popes for their decision. Petrarch called the papal stay in southern France the "Babylonian Captivity," and later historians have come to adopt his phrase. The best account remains Mollat, *Popes*. See also Yves Renouard, *The Avignon Papacy 1305-1403*, Denis Bethell, trans. (Hamden, CT: Archon, 1970); Geoffrey Barraclough, *The Medieval Papacy* (New York: W.W. Norton, 1979), 140-64. For a collection of contemporary criticisms see Coogan, *Babylon on the Rhone*; and McGinn, pp. 239-45. On Avignon and Rome see Eugenio Duprè-Theseider, *I papi di Avignone e la questione romana* (Florence: Le Monnier, 1939). On the city and its life see *Avignon au temps de Pétrarque: 1304-1374* (Avignon: Direction des Services d'Archives de Vaucluse, 1974).

2. Only a very small portion of the city within the ancient walls remained inhabited. This lay largely in the bend of the Tiber between the Ponte Sant' Angelo and the Tiber Island, the medieval *abitato;* as well as the Leonine City around St. Peter's and the Vatican; and Trastevere, the district across the Tiber

opposite the Island. Many of the ancient monuments, theaters, and stadiums had been turned into the private bastions of the competing noble families; while beyond the *abitato*, but still within the walls, vast sections of the ancient city were now vineyards, country estates, and grazing lands for sheep and cattle. On the condition of the city and its territory in the thirteenth and fourteenth centuries see Hubert, *Rome*; V. De Caprio, "La cultura romana nel periodo avignonese 1305-1377," in Roberto Antonelli, Angelo Cicchetti and Giorgio Inglese, eds., *Letteratura italiana: Storia e geografia* (Turin: Einaudi, 1987), 495-505; Small, "District"; Richard Krautheimer, *Rome. Profile of a City, 312-1308* (Princeton: Princeton University Press, 1980); Peter Partner, *The Lands of St. Peter. The Papal State in the Middle Ages and the Early Renaissance* (London: Methuen; Berkeley: University of California Press, 1972); Robert Brentano, *Rome before Avignon. A Social History of Thirteenth-Century Rome* (New York: Basic Books, 1974); Gennaro, "Mercanti"; Macek, "Racines"; Daniel Waley, *The Papal State in the Thirteenth Century*, (New York: St. Martin's Press, 1961); and Eugenio Duprè-Theseider, *Roma dal comune di popolo alla signoria pontificia 1272-1377* (Bologna: C. Cappelli, 1952). On Rome as symbol and myth for Petrarch and Cola see Toppani, "Il mito"; Arturo Graf, *Roma nella memoria e nella immaginazione del Medio Evo* (Turin: E. Loescher, 1915); and Charles T. Davis, *Dante and the Idea of Rome* (Oxford: Oxford University Press, 1957).

3. Edited by Francisco Corradini (Padua: Premiata Tipografia del Seminario, 1874). See also the English translation in *Petrarch's Africa*, Thomas G. Bergin and Alice S. Wilson, trans. and ed. (New Haven: Yale University Press, 1977). For a study see Aldo S. Bernardo, *Scipio and the Africa, The Birth of Humanism's Dream* (Baltimore: Johns Hopkins University Press, 1962).

4. *Inferno* 1.107.

5. The church of St. Agricola, at Avignon. While the two enthusiasts discussed the ancient grandeur and the present widowed state of the Queen of Cities, we can readily picture the populace passing back and forth "on solid gain intent" *(la turba al vil guadagno intesa*, from the sonnet, *La gola e'l sonno)*, among whom, perhaps, as Adolfo Bartoli, *Il Petrarca e Cola di Rienzo*, in *Storia della letteratura italiana* 3. 110, says, there may have mingled some bishop or some cardinal, *cupidinis veteranus, Baccho sacer et Veneri, non armatus sed togatus et pileatus*. According to Giosuè Carducci, *Rime di Francesco Petrarca sopra argomenti storici, morali e diversi* (Livorno: Vigo, 1876), 157, the Latin quotation is from the letter *Sine Titulo [Nomine]* 18, which is number 16 in the Basel edition of 1581. See *Opera omnia*, 3 vols. (Basel: Sebastian Henricpetri, 1581), 731. See *Sine Nomine* 7 in Paul Piur, *Petrarcas "Buch ohne Namen" und die päpstliche Kurie* (Halle: M. Niemeyer, 1925), 191-93. For the English translations see Norman P. Zacour, trans. and ed., *Petrarch's Book Without a Name* (Toronto: Pontifical Institute of Mediaeval Studies, 1973). For Petrarch's life at Avignon from 1342/43 and 1345/47 see Paul Amargier, "Pétrarque et ses amis au temps de la verte feuillée," in Marie-Humbert Vicaire, ed., *La papauté d'Avignon et en Languedoc 1316-1342*,

Cahiers de Fanjeaux 26 (Toulouse: Privat, 1991), 127-40; Macek, "Pétrarch et Cola"; Wilkins, *Life*, pp. 32-38, 53-62. On Petrarch and Cola see pp. 63-73. On the *Sine Nomine* see Ernest Hatch Wilkins, *Studies in the Life and Works of Petrarch* (Cambridge, MA: Medieval Academy of America, 1955), 179-81. For an analysis of this letter see Arnaldo Foresti, "Sognando la riforma del governo di Roma," in *Aneddoti della vita di Francesco Petrarca*, of *Studi sul Petrarca* 1 (Padua: Antenore, 1977), 263-67.

6. If Petrarch considered Cola's words divinely inspired, his own words must certainly have made the same impression on the fiery imagination of the scholarly Cola di Rienzo, even more so considering that Petrarch was preoccupied with his *Africa,* which he had just completed. Probably Cola was the first person to whom Petrarch, carried away by the enthusiasm of the moment, recited in abundance pertinent verses from his epic, verses that were so eagerly sought by the learned but that Petrarch so constantly and so jealously refused to make known. The poet's relation to his younger contemporary, therefore, and his never-failing words of advice give good ground for comparing him to the nymph Egeria. See Giuseppe Brizzolara, "Il Petrarca e Cola di Rienzo," *Studi storici* 14: 96, in the note carried over from p. 95; and M. Joubert, "Rienzi and Petrarch," *The Contemporary Review* 166 (July-December 1944): 34-42.

7. Ps. 43 (44): 23-24.

8. Fracassetti continues to print these words in italics, as if they were still a quotation from the Bible. See *Epistolae de rebus familiaribus et variae*, Giuseppe Fracassetti, ed., 3 vols. (Florence: Le Monnier, 1859-63).

9. Petrarch's words (Fracassetti 3: 55): *Quid agis in te sperantium salus,* are reminiscent of Ps. 16 (17): 7: *qui salvos facis sperantes in te.*

10. Compare this with the statement made in the following letter: "beggarly thieves judge themselves unpardonably offended if they are not addressed as gods."

11. Again a loose quotation of Ps. 69: 2 (70: 1).

12. It is reasonable to assume that this impassioned language reproduces the tone of the conversations between Petrarch and Cola di Rienzo. Indeed, the many arguments of the poet may be readily understood as reflecting those of the young patriot and ambassador from Rome.

CHAPTER 2

AVIGNON, JUNE 24-27, 1347

Cola di Rienzo returned to Rome after Easter of 1344. Clement VI, realizing how valuable an aid Cola might prove to be, had gladly complied with his request and on April 13, 1344 had appointed him notary of the civic camera.

We will not give Cola's history here. We will merely mention the growing power of the pope's protegé; his antagonism to the barons who scoffed at his rhetoric, which they despised as the ravings of a madman; and the allegorical paintings and the fanciful interpretations with which he tried to reawaken in the Roman people a sense of their ancient and inalienable rights. By these means Cola sought to attach everyone to his cause; and when, in May 1347, the Roman soldiers under Stefano Colonna were absent from the city, Cola decided to take advantage of the opportunity. After hearing mass in the church of Sant' Angelo in Pescheria on the morning of Sunday, May 20, 1347, he proceeded to the Campidoglio, addressed the people with that eloquence that had always proved irresistible, and was proclaimed master of the City of the Apostles.

The news of Cola's peaceful elevation was carried to Provence immediately. It startled not only the Curia, but even more the person we might consider Cola's arch co-conspirator. During the years from 1344 to 1347 – tedious years of waiting and hoping – Petrarch and Cola must have exchanged countless letters on the subject that lay nearest their hearts. Whatever Petrarch's previous solution for Rome's difficulties may have been, the enthusiasm caused by the arrival of this news in June 1347 swept it aside like a flood. He had prayed much and earnestly, and now he gave himself up utterly to the great, alluring figure that had suddenly appeared above the Roman horizon.

It is doubtful whether in June 1347 Petrarch had an exact and precise knowledge of Cola's aims and purposes. Indeed it is doubtful whether these were clear to Cola himself. Nevertheless, with the characteristic abandon of impulsive natures, Petrarch gave free rein to his overflowing joy and immediately wrote Cola a letter that should actually be called a panegyric. Indeed Baldelli does not hesitate to pronounce the following letter the most virile and eloquent philippic of modern times. It is a psalm that declares the supremacy of Rome. It is a hymn to liberty.[1]

PETRARCH TO COLA DI RIENZO & THE ROMAN PEOPLE
(VARIAE 48, HORTATORIA)

I am somewhat undecided, noble soul, whether I should first congratulate you on the achievement of such great glory, or the citizens of your rescued city for your services on their behalf and for the most happy recovery of their liberty. I congratulate you both equally. I shall address you both together, nor shall my words distinguish those whom I see linked so inseparably by fate itself. But what terms shall I use in the midst of such sudden and unhoped-for joy? With what vows can I fitly describe the emotions of my exultant soul? Hackneyed words have become utterly unfit; I dare not attempt new ones. I shall steal myself away from my occupations for a short time; and though I should most properly robe my thoughts in Homeric dress, lack of leisure obliges me to present them in a more irregular and more disordered fashion.

Liberty stands in your midst. There is nothing dearer, nothing more earnestly to be desired; and never are these facts more clearly understood than when liberty is lost.[2] Enjoy this great blessing, this realization of your dreams of many years. Rejoice in it, but do so with moderation, with discretion, and with calm. Give thanks to God, the dispenser of such gifts, who has not yet forgotten his most holy city and could no longer behold her, in whom he had placed the empire of the world, enchained in slavery. Therefore, brave people and descendants of brave people, if sane thinking has reasserted itself together with liberty, let each one of you prefer death itself to the loss of liberty. Without liberty life is mockery. Keep your past servitude constantly before your eyes. In this way, unless I err, your present liberty will be somewhat dearer to you than life itself. In this way, if at any time it should become necessary to part with one or the other, there will be no one who will not prefer to die a freeman rather than to live a slave, provided a drop of Roman blood still flows in his veins. The fish that has once slipped from the hook lives in constant fear of whatever stirs in the waters. The lamb that has been snatched from the jaws of the wolves trembles at the sight of gray dogs, even from a distance. The winged creature that has freed itself from the bird lime dreads even the harmless boughs.[3] You too, believe me, have been baited with the blandishments of vain hopes; you too have been rendered helpless by the tenacious power of pernicious habits; you too have been encircled by bands of famished wolves.

Consider all things with alert minds. Make sure that whatever you plan, whatever you do, savors of liberty. Let all your cares and vigils be directed to this one end; let all your deeds tend to it. Whatever is achieved for another purpose, consider an irreparable loss of time – a delusion and a snare. Drive from your hearts the ill-deserved love you may have conceived for your tyrants through long subjection. Expel all memory of this unworthy affection. Even the slave bends the neck to his haughty master for the time being, and the caged bird makes sweet music for its jailer. But the former will throw off his shackles when the occasion offers; and if escape is possible, the latter will take wing with eager flight.

O most illustrious citizens, you have been living as slaves – you whom all the nations once served. Though kings used to kneel at your feet, you have lain passive beneath the tyranny of a few. But what makes the cup of grief and shame overflow is the thought that you have had as tyrants strangers and lords of foreign birth. Enumerate the ravishers of your honor, the plunderers of your fortunes, the destroyers of your liberty. Think of their separate origins. The valley of Spoleto claims this one; the Rhine, or the Rhone, or some obscure corner of the world has sent us the next.[4] That one, who only recently was led in the triumph with hands fastened behind his back, has from a captive suddenly become a citizen; no, not merely a citizen but a tyrant. Small wonder, then, that the city of Rome, its glory and its liberty, yes, the very blood that flows in your veins, should be a source of hatred to such people when they meditate on their former country, on the disgrace of their former slavery, and on the fields drenched with their life blood.

I marvel much more at where, armed Romans though you were, you drew your long patience from, or on what they based their insufferable pride. What superior qualities do they possess that they should be so highly complacent? What air do they breathe? What virtues do they possess? No group of men ever existed who were more sadly lacking in these. Is their pride based on their overabundant wealth, which can never appease their hunger except with thoughts of theft and plunder? Is it based on their great power, which will end the moment you assert yourselves as men? Is it possible that they can glory in the splendor of their name and origin, or in their stolen and, perhaps, transient stay in this city? What grounds have they for boasting of their Roman stock? And yet they do make this boast most impudently. They have falsely declared themselves Romans for so long a time that, as if falsehood legalized their claims, they now consider themselves real Romans. Indeed, the name of Roman citizens has become low and base in their eyes. They no longer style themselves Roman citizens but Princes of the Romans! I scarcely know whether such pretensions are to be received with laughter or with tears. But I am less indignant at this when I behold that they have lost sight of even their human origin. They have lately reached that stage of insanity that they wish themselves considered gods and not men.

Oh, unutterable shame! In that very city in which Caesar Augustus, the ruler of the world and the lawgiver of the nations, by special edict forbade that he be called a god,[5] in that same city, today, beggarly thieves judge themselves unpardonably offended if they are not addressed as gods. Oh wretched wheel of fortune! Oh unheard-of change of times! Let us dispel the darkness, let us remove all errors, let us attain the truth. Let those who desire to establish hair-splitting definitions of terms decide whether these lords, who are entirely devoid of reason, are worthy of the name of men. Whether they are to be your masters, since it is your interests that are at stake, I leave you to decide yourselves, Romans, provided that you keep clearly in mind that they cannot be lords and you free men at the same time and in the same city. The one fact, however, that I can decide is that they surely are not Romans. All these, as you remember, were so fastidious about their empty titles of nobility, no matter where they came from, no matter what ill wind blew them here, or what barbarian country turned them loose, even though they roamed about in your Forum, though they ascended the Capitol attended by hordes of armed retainers, and though they trod haughtily on the ashes of illustrious Romans. I say there was not one of them who was not an alien. As the satirist says,[6] there was not one but

with whiten'd feet
Was hawk'd for sale so lately through the street.

And the words of another poet[7] are still true:

Our war no interfering kings demands,
Nor shall be trusted to barbarian hands:
Among ourselves our bonds we will deplore
And Rome shall serve the rebel son she bore.

If only you too had had this consolation in your misery, that you were slaves to only one man, whether fellow-citizen or king, and were not subject to many foreign robbers at once!

What Hannibal, formerly the most renowned enemy of the Roman people, is reported to have said[8] is all too true: "It is easier to censure past events than to correct them."

I do not desire to goad you further, nor to reproach you with bygones. I wish, rather, to offer you a way to hide your embarrassment. Even your ancestors were ruled by kings – and by kings who were not always of Roman origin but also, at one time, of Sabine, at another of Corinthian, and – if we are to believe tradition – of servile origin.[9] But evil fortune must come to an end as well as good fortune. The restorer of the early Romans' liberty and the restorer of your liberty were both unexpected. Each age produced its Brutus. There are now three named Brutus celebrated in history. The first exiled the proud Tarquin; the second slew Julius Caesar; the third has brought exile and death to the tyrants of our own age. Our third Brutus, then, equals both the others because in his own person he has united the causes of the double glory that the other two divided between them. He is, however, more like the earlier Brutus in disguising his nature and in concealing his purpose. Like him he is young[10] but of a far different temperment; and if he assumed the false exterior of that other Brutus, it was so that, biding his time beneath this false veil, he might at last reveal himself in his true character – the liberator of the Roman people.[11]

Livy, prince of historians, bears testimony to the valor of that ancient Brutus; your own experience bears testimony to the valor of the present Brutus. The former Brutus was scorned by kings; the present by tyrants to whom he afterward became a source of fear. You have read about the former; with your own eyes you have seen the latter disdained by his fellow men, men who deemed it basest slavery to live under the same laws with their fellow citizens, men who esteemed nothing noble unless it were unjust and arrogant. They spurned, they trampled on the lowliness of this man, beneath which, however, a great soul lay concealed. I hereby testify on his behalf that he has always had the end that he has finally attained close to his heart.[12] But he was awaiting a favorable opportunity. The instant this presented itself he was quick to take advantage of it. In restoring your liberty he has presented you with as great a blessing as the elder Brutus presented his fellow citizens when he held high the dagger that he had drawn from the heart of Lucretia. There is this difference, however: the patience of the early Romans was taxed by one shameful crime, whereas yours has yielded only after countless deeds of shame and countless intolerable wrongs.

These barons in whose defense you have so often shed your blood, whom you have nourished with your own substance, whom you have raised to affluence to the detriment of the state revenues, these barons have judged you unworthy of liberty. They have gathered the mangled remnants of the state in the caverns and abominable retreats of bandits. They have felt no shame that their crimes were known abroad. They have been restrained neither by pity for their unhappy country, nor by love for it. They have irreverently pillaged the temples of the Lord; they have seized the strongholds, the public revenues, and the regions of the city. They have forcibly divided the different magistracies among themselves – the one cause in which they have united in an amazing and ferocious league of crime, though at all other times they have been restless men full of civil discord, disagreeing entirely in their plans and conduct of life. Lately neither commiseration nor pity for their unhappy city has prevented them from venting their rage on the bridges[13] and the walls of the city and on the undeserving stones.

Ultimately, after the palaces of ancient Rome had sunk into ruin, either through age or the hand of man, palaces that were once the homes of noble Romans; after the triumphal arches had been dismantled, arches that may have commemorated the conquest of these barbarians' ancestors; these haughty barons have not been ashamed to seek filthy lucre in the base sale of the fragments that had survived the passing of time and the barons' own ungodliness.[14] Oh my present grief! Oh unpardonable sin! Indolent Naples is being adorned[15] with your marble columns, Romans, with the porticos of your churches, to which only recently the most devout believers hastened from all quarters of the globe, with the statues pilfered from your sepulchres, in which the sacred ashes of your fathers rested. Gradually the ruins themselves will cease to exist – those eloquent memorials to the ancients' greatness. And you, so many thousand brave men, you have not uttered a syllable of protest in the face of a few freebooters rioting about as if in a captured city. You have not even been like slaves but like sheep. You kept your peace while your common mother was being torn apart. Small wonder, then, that they drew lots for the distribution of plunder!

We marvel and are indignant that disasters such as these should have befallen peaceful Athens; that she should have been stripped of her marks of honor, bereft of her illustrious children, and subjected to the rule of the Thirty Tyrants. But that this could have happened in the city of Rome, the conqueror of cities and the mistress of the world, even now exalted and ennobled as the seat of the Empire and the home of the Holy See; that Rome could remain subject to the lusts and caprices of tyrants only slightly more numerous, or perhaps even fewer, than those who held sway at Athens – that such things could happen, no one until now had considered sufficient cause for righteous indignation and displeasure. Who of your tyrant lords, pray, has ever been content with mere servile obedience on your part? Who of them has not insisted, rather, on despicable and vile submission? Slaves of superior ability, even the beasts of the field, are spared by their owners, not out of consideration for them, but because of the loss that might be incurred through harsh treatment. Have you ever been spared? What baron has not torn each and every one of you from the arms of your beloved wives and has not sent you abroad in the cold and darkness of a winter's night, when the rain fell in torrents and the lightening threatened, exposing you to the perils of death? What one of them has not led you in his train over snow-covered peaks and through slimy marshes, as if you had been purchased slaves?

You seem to have awakened at last from your heavy sleep. If you feel any shame, any grief for your past savage condition of life, sharpen your intellects and be ready for every emergency. Do not allow any of the rapacious wolves whom you have driven from the fold to rush again into your midst. Even now they are prowling restlessly around, endeavoring through fraud and deceit, through false howlings and alluring promises, to regain an entrance to that city from which they were so violently expelled. May the winds sweep away the omen, which is so dire that my soul trembles at the mere thought. How much more dire its possible realization! But unless you take care, do not suppose that they will return to the city as famished as they left it. Their hunger will be far more ravenous and will have become more and more furious with time. They now thirst equally for the blood of both the flock and the shepherd. They consider your liberty and the glory of your deliverer their dishonor and disgrace. Have faith in yourselves. Rise against your enemies. They will be only a contemptible handful if you stand united.

I love much, hence I fear much; for the same reason I dare much, for love makes the weak bold. I know full well, alas, that at the time of the early republic, which I mentioned above, there were some who favored the tyranny of the few against the freedom of all. This treason was committed, moreover, not by men of obscure birth but by most illustrious youths, indeed by the sons of the liberator himself, youths who had been rendered forgetful of their better selves by the bonds of intermarriage, by custom and common ties. All were punished with death by the father who, though perhaps wretched in his bereavement, was most fortunate in possessing a courageous heart. He considered it his more sacred duty to grieve over the loss of his children than over the loss of his country's liberty.[16] I fear the recurrence of this treason today even more since the hearts of men are now more easily manipulated and more changeable. I fear there will be many, very many, who, through intermarriage with the tyrants or through their long and wretched period of servitude, are persuaded that the cup of the slave is sweeter than the abstinence of the freeman. There will be many who believe that they have attained a great and noble end if they are greeted on the streets or are summoned hastily by their lords and plagued by lewd commands. There will be many famished and filthy parasites who seat themselves at their tyrants' wicked table and greedily gulp down whatever escapes their lords' gullets. This and nothing else is the compensation of these unfortunates; this is the only reward for their hazards and toils.

But you, most brave man, you who have buttressed the immense weight of the tottering state with your patriotic shoulders, gird yourself and watch with equal vigilance against such citizens as against the most bitter enemy. You, younger Brutus, always keep the example of the first Brutus before you. He was Consul, you are Tribune. If we compared the two offices we would find that the consuls performed many acts hostile to the welfare of the Roman plebs; indeed – and I will speak out bravely – they often treated it harshly and cruelly. But the tribunes were always and constantly the defenders of the people. If then that consul slew his own sons because of his love of liberty, realize what is expected in all circumstances from you as a tribune. If you won't spurn a loyal friend's advice, do not heed considerations of either birth or affection. Remember that the man you have felt to be an enemy of freedom cannot possibly be a stauncher friend to you than to himself. Such a man endeavors to deprive both you and liberty of what is dearest.

Sallust was speaking of the city of Rome when he said: "In so large a state many and various are the inclinations of men."[17] How numerous, indeed, are those who today, in that same city, would sell themselves and the entire state for a small sum and would prove traitor to all law, both human and divine! Divine providence has already shown distinct marks of favor in our behalf since the greater portion of the people is of one mind and has shaken off the lethargy that was crushing it. Even in its affliction the name of the Roman people inspires respect and awe. Great are its resources, great its riches, if both are managed wisely. The Roman people have great power, provided they desire to be united. Indeed, a beginning has been made; the desire now exists. All who feel otherwise should not be reckoned in the number of citizens but of enemies. The state must be relieved of these as a body would be freed of its poisonous excretions. Thus the state, though diminished in numbers, will be stronger and healthier. Be prudent, be brave, and strength will not fail you either in protecting the liberties of the city or in reestablishing its ancient sway.

What inspiration, truly, cannot be derived from the memory of the past and from the grandeur of a name once revered throughout the world? Who does not wish Rome the best of fortune in her efforts to attain her rightful empire? Both God and humanity champion such a just cause. Italy, which only recently lay listless and enfeebled, with head bowed to the ground, has now risen to her knees. If you Romans show perseverance in your undertaking, if the happy news of your doings continues to prevail, joyful hopes will soon spring in human hearts. All who can will rush to your assistance. Those who are prevented by circumstances will at least second your aims with their vows and prayers. On the other hand, the betrayers of their country will be punished by the avenger's sword in this world. In the lower world they will suffer the tortures they have deserved, tortures with which they are threatened not merely by the learned men of today, but also by those of antiquity. These are the traitors whom Maro has placed in the circle of most dire punishments[18]:

> This to a tyrant master sold
> His native land for cursed gold,
> Made laws for lucre and unmade.

With men such as these, or rather – to really say what I feel – with such wild beasts, all sternness is benevolence, all pity is inhuman.

You, extraordinary man, have opened the path to immortality for yourself. You must persevere if you desire to reach your goal. Otherwise, remember that the more illustrious the beginning, the more ignoble the end. Many dangers beset him who travels this road, many intricate and troublesome questions will present themselves. But courage delights in obstacles, patience in adversity. We are born for the accomplishment of a glorious task. Why should we sigh then for indolent inactivity? Consider too that many tasks that seem difficult when first attempted become very easy after further application. And yet, why should I discourse on the nature of things, when we owe much to our friends, still more to our parents, but everything to our country? You will have to clash with the hostile lances of civil enemies. Rush fearlessly to the combat, inspired by the example of Brutus himself, who met the son of the proud king in battle and slew him, though he himself fell covered with wounds. He thus pursued him whom he had driven from the city[19] right into the regions of Tartarus. You, however, will be victorious and will survive their death uninjured. But if you must fall, if you must sacrifice your life for your country, while the ghosts of your enemies hasten to the regions of darkness, you will gain heaven to which your courage and your goodness have prepared the way for you, leaving behind on earth the monuments of an enduring fame.[20]

Can we hope for anything better? Romulus founded the city; this Brutus, whom I so frequently mention, gave it liberty; Camillus restored both. What difference then, most illustrious man, exists between these and you? Romulus surrounded a small city with weak ramparts; aren't you encircling with mighty walls the very greatest of the cities that are or have been? Brutus rescued liberty from the clutches of a single man; aren't you reclaiming a freedom usurped by many tyrants? Camillus restored the city from a devastation of recent occurrence, from ashes that were still smoking; aren't you restoring old ruins that had long been despaired of?[21] Hail then our Camillus, our Brutus, our Romulus! Or – if you prefer to be addressed by some other name – hail author of Roman liberty, of Roman peace, of Roman tranquility. The present age owes you the fact that it will die in liberty; posterity will owe you the fact that it is conceived in liberty.

I had resolved, illustrious man, to beg you for two favors, briefly and easily asked, but far-reaching and most beneficial in their effect. You have of your own accord anticipated me in one of these; it will suffice then to have asked you for the other. I hear the following reports about you: every day since your accession to the rule of the republic, at dawn and before attending to any transactions of either public or private nature, it is customary for you to receive the sacrament of Our Lord's body with sincerest devotion and after a most searching examination of conscience. This is doubtless as it should be for the wise man who regards the frailty of the flesh and the brevity of life and who beholds the manifold dangers that threaten on all sides. That most illustrious of Rome's generals would have followed the same course, I believe, had he lived in these days. For he was as duly observant of his sacred duties as his age permitted, an age shrouded in darkness and deprived of the knowledge of heaven.[22]

It remains for me to ask therefore that you should not deprive your mind of its nourishment, neither when reclining, nor lying sleepless on your couch, nor when administering to the needs of the flesh, nor when enjoying a moment of relaxation from your labors. Read whenever you have any spare moments; if you can't do so conveniently, have others read to you. In so doing you will be imitating that most worthy Augustus, of whom it is written that:

> after retiring to bed, he never slept more than seven hours of unbroken sleep; for, within that period, he would awaken three or four times, and if unable to regain uninterrupted slumbers, would summon to his assistance his readers or storytellers.

Of the same Augustus it is said that he was so economical a steward of his time that he either read or wrote even while eating and drinking.[23] For one in your present circumstances, what could be read or heard to greater advantage than the deeds of your ancestors, of whom no city has had a greater number? You have native examples of all the virtues. And surely in the work of that famous and venerable Cato the Censor we read that the Romans used to sing the praises of their heros to the sound of the trumpet.[24] On this I do not insist; but even this, as occasion warrants, will cause the eye to flash and stir the heart to emulation. I will be content if the annals and history of Rome are frequently read in your presence. And with this I have said enough about you.

But you, citizens, now for the first time truly deserving the name of citizens, be fully convinced that this man has been sent to you from heaven.[25] Cherish him as one of the rare gifts of God. Hazard your lives in his defense. For he too could have lived his life in slavery together with the rest.[26] He too could have submitted to the yoke that so great a people was enduring without a murmur. If such an existence had seemed too burdensome to him, he could have fled far from the sight of the unhappy city and could have escaped the shower of abuse and insults by voluntary exile, as we know was the case with certain prominent citizens. It was only love of country that kept him back. He considered it sacrilege to abandon it in such condition. In this city he resolved to live; for this city to die. He took pity on your misfortunes.[27] You see to what dangerous heights he has risen. Now give him your support lest he fall. Recollect, I beg you, how frequently you have exposed yourselves to the perils of death on behalf of most haughty and ungrateful tyrants. Recollect how often you drew the swords in defense, not of your property, but of theirs. Finally, recollect how often you fought to decide which of them should be the most powerful and who should display the greater licentiousness in plundering, pillaging, butchering, killing, and slaying. You have dared so much for unworthy lords and in the pursuit of shameful servitude. It is only fitting that you should now nobly dare on your own behalf and in the defense of liberty, liberty for which men have rid Rome of its kings and have deprived the Caesars of their lives. Tell me, Romans, if you did not endure the unbounded license of the Roman kings and emperors, will you so patiently tolerate the sanguinary rage and the insatiable greed of foreign-born robbers? I do not think that God is so deaf to the prayers of the devout. To live with these tyrants is far sadder than to die without them. Dare to do something for your children, for your wives, for the hoary heads of your fathers and mothers, for the graves of your ancestors.

There is nothing that should not be risked on behalf of the republic. It was patriotism that compelled the Decii to offer their devoted lives to their country; that urged Marcus Curtius to leap full-armed and mounted into that yawning chasm in the earth; that urged Horatius Cocles to oppose his own body, firm as a wall, to the Etruscan legions, to wait until the bridge had been destroyed and then, though heavily laden with arms, to plunge headlong into the Tiber's tide. It was love of country that made Gaius Mutius Scaevola inflict on his erring right hand a penalty that struck admiration and fear in his enemies. Love of country drove Attilius Regulus back to the tortures of his angered executioners, though he could have remained safe at home. The same noble cause made the two Scipios die in Spain and block the path of the Carthaginians with their dead bodies when no other course remained.

The son of one of these two Scipios preferred to die in poverty and obscurity rather than to impair the liberty of the people in the slightest degree. The son of the other, though a private citizen, crushed the turbulent measures of Tiberius Gracchus with death. Patriotism induced many other Romans to employ the same redress against unruly citizens. As a last example, I shall recall Marcus Cato the Younger, who received a surname from the city of his death and who committed suicide rather than behold the face of his tyrant, remarkable and unique man though he was, or witness the enslaving of his country.[28]

It is interesting to recall the names of these men, and particularly so in the presence of those citizens from whose blood have sprung not merely individuals, but entire families of the same firm and united resolve. Of this let the Cremera bear witness, the scene of the memorable though pitiful end of three hundred and six Fabii.[29] Not only families, but legions and entire armies have considered it dear to rush to their death in defense of their country. I desire, moreover, that these deeds be read on that very Capitol from whose summit I assume bold Manlius was hurled headlong, Manlius who but recently had been guardian of that hill and suffered death for this one reason: that he was suspected of plotting against the liberty that he had previously defended and of desiring an outcome not in accord with his excellent beginning. One and the same rock bore witness to his great glory and to his death and served as an everlasting warning to all who should attempt similar treason.[30]

No one should falsely suppose that those who watch vigilantly over their liberties and who have, until now, championed the cause of the abandoned republic are performing a duty that rightfully belongs to others. It is their cause they are defending. Let each man be convinced that only in this way will his interests be safe. This is the only way that the merchant gains peace, the soldier glory, the farmer plenty, the devout their religious services, the scholar leisure, the old rest, the child rudiments of learning, the young women weddings, and the matrons honor. Only in this way, finally, will all find happiness.

O citizens of Rome, strain every nerve, bring every public and private resource to bear on the advancement of the public and the private welfare. Let all other cares give way to this. If you neglect this care, all your other deeds will be of no avail. If, on the contrary, you devote all your energies to it, even though you may seem to accomplish nothing, you will still perform fully your duties as citizens and as individuals. Erase every vestige of civil fury from your midst, I beseech you. Let the flames that had been fanned among us by the breath of tyrants be extinguished by the warnings and the guarded kindness of your deliverer.[31] Take this friendly rivalry upon yourselves: not who is to be the more powerful, but who is to be the better and more patient citizen, who is to reveal the deeper love of country, the greater humility toward his neighbors and the more implacable hatred for the tyrants. Enter this contest with your tribune: as to whether he will show greater foresight in the honest administration of government than you readiness in obeying. And if, perhaps, love – than which there is nothing stronger – proves insufficient to bring your hearts into harmony, then may considerations of common interest persuade you. At least be united by this bond. Cling to each other tenaciously, peaceably. Wield the arms handed down to you by your fathers only against the enemies of the commonwealth. Offer the exile, the destitution, and the punishment of the barons as most pleasing sacrifice to the ashes of your dead. The dead will rejoice in such deeds; and had they foreseen the future, they would surely have breathed their last with greater resignation and peace of mind.

But I fear that my words have detained you longer than is fitting, especially at a time when there is far greater need of action. Neither my calling, alas, nor my lot permit me to assist you in action. Therefore, I send you words, the only means of assistance at my disposal. I confess that at first I was roused by the glorious reports to envy your great honor. I heaped countless reproaches on my lot that had deprived me of taking active part in so joyous a consummation. But I was not entirely excluded. Over lands and seas there came to me my due share of happiness. Hastily I seized my pen that, in the midst of such great and such remarkable harmony of a delivered people, my voice might also be heard, though from a distance, that I too might perform my duty as a Roman citizen.[32] Moreover, this subject that I have now treated in loose prose, I may attempt in the near future in different meters, provided that you will not deceive my hopes and wishes and will not deny me perseverance in your glorious undertaking. Crowned with Apollo's wreath, I shall ascend lofty and inspiring Helicon. There, at the brim of the Castalian font, I shall recall the Muses from their exile and sing resounding words in abiding memory of your glory, words that will ring throughout the ages.[33] Farewell, bravest of men! Farewell, best of citizens! Farewell most glorious City of the Seven Hills!

NOTES

1. Bardelli, p. 81. This letter is also edited in Burdach and Piur, Letter 23, 2.3: 63-81. On the background to the letter and a brief analysis see Wilkins, *Life*, pp. 63-65; and more recently Natalia Costa-Zalessow, "The Personification of Italy from Dante through the Trecento," *Italica* 68.4 (1991): 316-31, esp. 321-28; and Musumarra. Generally good background is also found in Ernest Hatch Wilkins, *Petrarch's Correspondence* (Padua: Antenore, 1960).

2. Compare the similar sentiment of the following lines:

> Libertà, dolce e desiato bene,
> Mal conosciuto a chi talor no'l perde.

These lines are from the canzone *Quel c'ha nostra natura in sè più degno,* celebrating the capture of Parma by Azzo da Correggio. For detailed study of this poem and of its authenticity, see Francesco Berlan, "Parma liberata dal giogo di Mastino della Scala, addì 21 Maggio 1341," *Scelta di curiosità letterarie,* 109; and Giosuè Carducci, *Rime di Francesco Petrarca sopra argomenti storici, morali e diversi* (Livorno: Vigo, 1876), 79-96.

3. See Eccl. 9: 12.

4. These are references to the two preeminent families of the Roman nobility, the Orsini and the Colonna. In medieval fables, which were widely believed, the Colonna were represented as coming to Rome from the banks of the Rhine (Gregorovius 4: 320, n. 2); but their ancestry has been traced, with greater probability, back to the tenth century, to Alberic, count of Tusculum (Felix Papencordt, *Cola di Rienzo und seine Zeit,* [Hamburg and Gotha: A. Perthes, 1841], 15). According to Gregorovius, even this would stamp the Colonna, by far the most renowned nobles of medieval Rome, as being of German descent. See Gregorovius 6.1: 263, n. 1, which lists the names of thirty-three families of the Roman nobility who are stated as being of undoubted German origin.

At any rate, the first member of this family to make his appearance in history is a certain Petrus de Columpna, a relation of the count of Tusculum, who in 1101 appears as the strenuous opponent of Pope Paschal II. The Colonna soon made themselves lords of Palestrina, which became and remained, with short interruptions, the stronghold around which the power of the Colonna always rallied. From the very beginning this family was the main support of the Holy Roman Emperors, and was, consequently, of strong Ghibelline tendencies. See Papencordt, pp. 15-16; Gregorovius 4: 319-20.

The origin of the Orsini is even more obscure. The family records, which are said to be devoid of critical value, trace their origin to the valley of the Tiber near Spoleto; but these statements are not reliable. Some authorities, though evidently in the minority, would also trace the Orsini ancestry back to the Rhine. See Gregorovius 5: 39 and 6.1: 263, n. 1; the commentary to Petrarch's Eclogue 5 in Florence, Biblioteca Medicea-Laurenziana, Cod. 33, Plut. 52, Laur., and that by Francesco Piendibeni da Montepulciano in Antonio Avena, *Il Bucolicum Carmen e i suoi comenti inediti* (Padova: Società Cooperativa Tipografica, 1906), 215 and 271. Unlike the Colonna, the Orsini were, as a rule, partisans of the Guelph cause; and this may account in great part for their hereditary and unceasing warfare with the Colonna. For recent work on the Colonna, Orsini, and other major Roman families, see Brentano, pp. 173-89; and Carocci. On the Italian nobility in general see Larner, pp. 93-105. On the barons' use of the ancient monuments of the city see Krautheimer, pp. 271-310; and Carocci, especially 168-73.

5. Suetonius, *Divus Augustus* 53: *Domini appellationem ut maledictum et obprobrium semper exhorruit.*

6. Juvenal 1.3, in Gifford translation 1: 25.

7. Lucan 7.354-56, in the Rowe translation.

8. Livy 8.30, 7. Petrarch had had this same passage in mind when he wrote the *Africa*, in which Hannibal says to Scipio (7.245-46; ll. 316-18 in Bergin and Wilson, p. 150): *Culpari transacta tamen licet usque loquendo; Mutari vetitum est.*

9. The three kings meant are, respectively, Ancus Martius, Tarquinius Priscus, and Servius Tullius. The Sabine origin of Ancus Martius is not actually mentioned but is clearly implied in two other passages. The first of these is *De remediis* 1, *Dialogus* 58, *De nepotibus,* in which Petrarch says (p. 225): "Ancus Martius, the grandson of Numa on his mother's side, with great glory held the royal power at Rome that his grandfather had held before him." The second passage is a precisely similar one from the shorter life of Ancus Martius in Petrarch's *De viris illustribus* 1.48. *Numae nepos ex filia.*

Tarquinius Priscus was the son of Demaratus of Corinth, who belonged to the family of the Bacchiadae. The story as told by Cicero in the *De republica* 2.34 (a work not known to Petrarch) is as follows: "They say that there was a certain Demaratus of Corinth, who, because of his integrity, influence, and wealth, was easily the foremost citizen of his state. When Demaratus could no longer endure the rule of Cypselus, tyrant of the Corinthians, he is said to have fled with vast sums of money and to have gone to Tarquinii, the most flourishing city of Etruria." Fracassetti (*Epistolae* 3: 426) does not seem to have understood the expression "Corinthian origin," for he erroneously prints a "sic" after the word *Corinthiae.*

The obscure origin of Servius Tullius is mentioned – together with that of Tarquinius Priscus – in another dialogue of the *De remediis* (2.5, *De originis obscuritate*, p. 364): "Tarquinius Priscus was the son of a trader and a foreigner; indeed, he was not even of Italian stock. Servius Tullius, who was born of a slave or, as some would have it, of a woman of noble birth held in captivity, gained the throne of Rome by his merits." The example of the latter king is again cited in *De remediis* 2.9, *De damno passo*, p. 384: "And the sixth king, though of lowly origin or, as others have thought, of servile origin, rose to the very heights of power." The classical sources for all the statements made here by Petrarch are Livy 1.32, 34, 39, 40, 47; Eutropius 1.5-7; Florus 1.4, 5, 6; and Seneca, *Epistolae* 108, 30.

10. Cola was born toward the middle of 1313, which would make him thirty-three years old at the time of his rise to power on May 20, 1347.

11. Petrarch expresses the same ideas with reference to L. Junius Brutus in *De viris illustribus* 1.52. After narrating Lucretia's suicide, Petrarch continues that, while all the rest of Rome was undecided, Brutus revealed his true character and spirit, long concealed through fear of the tyrant who had slain his brother, and emerged as the leader in the vengeance demanded by the state. Compare Petrarch's *Africa* 3.684-772, Bergin and Wilson, pp. 63-68, ll. 811-1023.

The indirect sources are Valerius Maximus 7.3, 2: *obtunsi se cordis esse simulavit eaque fallacia maximas virtutes suas texit*; and *Auctor de viris illustribus*, x: *stultitiam finxit; unde Brutus dictus*. The primary source is, of course, Livy 1.56, 7-8, of which this passage of Petrarch's is a paraphrase.

The words of a contemporary biographer quaintly describe how Cola was made the butt of the barons' mirth during this period of his career. The anonymous *Vita di Cola di Rienzo* 1.4, Wright, p. 37, says:

> In these days he [Cola] used to dine with the nobles of Rome at the house of Giovanni Colonna, and the Roman barons would derive great amusement from his speech. They used to make him rise to his feet and urge him to speak. In the course of his address he would say: "I shall prosecute all the barons present here: this one I shall hang, that one decapitate." He would pass judgment on all of them, and the barons would die of laughter at it.

There are several editions of this *Vita*. See Zefirino Re, *La Vita di Cola di Rienzo, Tribuno del popolo romano* (Forlì: Bordandini, 1828); A.M. Ghisalberti, *La vita di Cola di Rienzo* (Rome, 1928); F. Cusin, ed., *Vita di Cola di Rienzo* (Florence: G.C. Sansoni, 1943); Arsenio Frugoni, ed., *Vita di Cola di Rienzo* (Florence: Le Monnier, 1957); as well as the editions cited in the Introduction, pp. xx, n. 10. For studies see Lucio Felici, "'La Vita di Cola di Rienzo' nella tradizione cronachistica romana," *Studi romani* 25: 3 (1977): 325-43; and citations to linguistic studies in the Introduction, p. xx, n. 11 above. Page references herein include those to Wright's English translation.

12. Petrarch refers here to the beginning of his acquaintance with Rienzo in 1343. See Letter 1 above.

13. The Colonna and the Orsini had, in the very nature of things, come to divide the city into sections within which they were the absolute masters. Whenever war broke out between them, it became all important to have control of the bridges that spanned the Tiber; and it is for this reason that a place of importance is assigned to the articles dealing with the bridges of Rome in the treaties and the papal briefs referring to these wars.

These princely houses had once again begun open warfare on May 6, 1333. After this struggle had continued for two years, Pope Benedict XII exhorted the Romans in a letter of July 21, 1335 to lay down their arms and to cease their fratricidal strife. See Augustin Theiner, *Codex diplomaticus dominii temporalis S. Sedis. Receuil de documents pour servir à l'histoire du gouvernement temporel des États du Saint-Siège. Extraits des Archives du Vatican*, 3 vols. (Rome: Vatican Press, 1861-62), 2, no. 11. The barons paid no attention, and on September 3, 1335 the Orsini destroyed Ponte Molle [Milvian Bridge]. On January 13, 1336 the nobles agreed to a truce, which was confirmed by Benedict XII two months later in a brief issued March 18, 1336 (Theiner 2, no. 20; compare Gregorovius 6.1: 187-95). After a lengthy preamble common in such documents this brief first settles the question of the bridges. The paragraph runs as follows (Theiner 2, p. 10, col, 1):

> And in the first place, indeed, concerning the tutelage and repair of certain bridges of the said city and of its surrounding district, of which bridges four are held by the said Stefano Colonna, a fifth by the said Jacopo Savelli, and several others by the said Orsini.
>
> After having taken due cognizance of the arguments submitted by both parties, and believing that the said bridges are known to belong not to the holders of the same but to the above-mentioned Roman people, we hereby wish, order, and decree that the said four bridges held by Stefano, and the fifth held by Jacopo, and the other bridges held by the said Orsini, be freely surrendered and placed in the power of the said archbishop and syndic, who shall see to it that throughout the continuation of this truce the said bridges, and especially the Ponte Molle, be diligently and faithfully guarded in such a way that they cannot fall into the hands of either party; [the said archbishop, moreover, shall see to it that] the said Ponte Molle and the other bridges that have been destroyed be repaired for the public welfare and at the expense of those who have destroyed the same, that no fortresses may be erected thereon – the construction of which we strongly forbid – but that provision may be made for the necessary and convenient passage over the said bridges of citizens, pilgrims, and other travelers.

It is hardly necessary to add that, with the French popes residing in the Babylon of the West, the above injunctions were not obeyed. See the letter of

April 13, 1338 in Theiner 2, no. 56. See also Mollat, *Popes*, pp. 146-60 for papal relations with the city during this period.

It was just one year after the above-mentioned truce had been agreed to that Petrarch visited Rome for the first time. The countryside had not had time to recover from the dread and anxiety caused by the reprisals of the barons; and Petrarch, who had reached the Colonna stronghold of Capranica toward the beginning of January 1337, was astonished first at the beauty of the country, and then at the unsettled and distressed condition of the wretched inhabitants. For a description of the Roman Campagna at this time read Petrarch's letter to Cardinal Giovanni Colonna. *Familiari* 2.12, in *Letters on Familiar Matters. Rerum familiarum libri*, Aldo S. Bernardo, trans. and ed., vol. 1 (I-VIII) (Albany: State University of New York Press, 1975), vol. 2 (IX-XVI) (Baltimore: Johns Hopkins University Press, 1982), vol. 3 (XVII-XXIV) (Baltimore and London: Johns Hopkins University Press, 1985), 1: 109-111. It is abridged in Morris Bishop, trans. and ed., *Letters from Petrarch* (Bloomington, IN and London: Indiana University Press, 1966), 34-36. See also Wilkins, *Life*, pp. 13-14.

14. Laments on the squalid appearance of widowed Rome, as Petrarch always considered the city, are found scattered everywhere in his works, especially in those letters that he addressed to the popes and emperors in defense of the cause of Rome and of the majesty of the Roman people. In a letter to Clement VI (*Epistolae poeticae* 2.5, written in 1342), Petrarch represents Rome as saying (*Opera omnia*, 3: 92, col. 2): "My wounds are as numerous as my churches and fortified places; the walls, thickly strewn with ruins, reveal only the remnants of a stately and lamentable city, and move all spectators to tears."

Perhaps the most specific lines on the disappearance of the monuments of ancient Rome caused by the intramural strife of ages are those that Petrarch penned in the Dialogue 118 of the *De remediis*, which discusses the futility of hoping for glory derived from the erection of monumental buildings. Compare this to *Familiari* 2.14; Bernardo 1: 113; Bishop, *Letters*, p. 36. For the image of Rome in Petrarch's thought see also Pierre Blanc, "La construction d'une utopie néo-urbaine: Rome dans la pensée, l'action et l'oeuvre de Pétrarque de 1333 à 1342," in Daniel Poirion, ed., *Jérusalem, Rome, Constantinople: L'Image et le mythe de la ville au Moyen Age*, Culture et civilisation medievale 5 (Paris: Presses de l'Université de Paris, 1986), 149-68; Miglio, "Et rerum facta est"; and Musumarra.

15. Alas, poor Naples! The corrupt government of Parthenope had driven the fond memories of six years before from Petrarch's mind. In 1341 he had visited Naples on his way to Rome to receive the laurel crown, had been enthusiastically welcomed by that King Robert whom Petrarch considered the only worthy judge of his fitness for the laurel, and had been dismissed on April 4 with gifts of regal robes and with a noble escort. Petrarch's cup of gratitude was overflowing. He never thereafter omitted the slightest opportunity to praise King Robert to the skies, the prince whom he always proclaimed the wisest, kindest, and most scholarly of monarchs.

CHAPTER 2, AVIGNON, JUNE 24-27, 1347

The death of King Robert on January 19, 1343 was a blow from which Petrarch never recovered and from which the Neapolitan kingdom recovered only after many decades. Robert's son Charles, duke of Calabria, had died in 1328, so that the throne fell to Robert's granddaughters, Giovanna and her young sister Maria. Both Giovanna and her consort, Prince Andrew, were minors, and a regency was established according to plans made by King Robert himself. This arrangement thoroughly displeased the pope who, in virtue of the high authority wielded by the church in those states and because of the terms of the investiture, claimed that the rule of Naples had reverted to him. Before pressing his claim, however, he resolved to send an envoy to gather more accurate information concerning the state of the kingdom.

Clement VI consequently looked for someone who would worthily represent his cause at the court of Naples. The choice inevitably fell on Petrarch, who on his former visit had made the acquaintance of prominent Neapolitans, such as Giovanni Barili, Paolo di Perugia, and Barbato di Sulmona. The torchbearer of the humanists, the poet laureate and the Roman citizen who only recently had received the priorate of San Nicola di Migliarino (near Pisa) at the hands of Clement VI, accepted the commission to represent the head of the Christian world at the Guelph court of Naples, which was the most powerful state of Italy at that time. He reached Naples on October 12, 1343.

Petrarch's dear and intimate friend, Philippe de Cabassole, bishop of Cavaillon, occupied the chief position on the board of regents. The poet therefore entertained bright hopes of successfully executing both the charge of Clement VI and the one entrusted to him by Cardinal Giovanni Colonna. Unfortunately, Philippe's control was only nominal, while the real power had been usurped by one of Queen Giovanna's female dependents (who was called the Catanese), by the queen-mother Sancia, King Robert's second wife, and by a certain Robert, a Hungarian monk of the Franciscan order. It is needless to add that Petrarch's mission was unsuccessful; and the disappointment at his failure, together with his horror at the degraded condition of the court, which so strongly contrasted with that of his earlier visit, inspired not only the present discourteous reference to Naples, but also the acrid description found in a letter written on November 29, 1343 and addressed to Cardinal Giovanni Colonna (*Familiari* 5.3; Bernardo 1: 232-37). See also *Familiari* 24.11 in Cosenza, *Petrarch's Letters to Classical Authors*, p. 138.

On Petrarch's trips to Naples see Wilkins, *Life*, pp. 26-27, 39-44. For his reactions to the "Hungarian" monk Robert, actually Robert of Mileto, see Vincenzo Forcellini, "*L'horrendum tripes animal* della lettera 3 del libro V delle familiari di Petrarca," in *Studi di storia napoletana in onore di Michelangelo Schipa* (Naples, 1926), 167-99. On Queen Sancia and her influence at Naples see Ronald G. Musto, "Queen Sancia of Naples (1286-1345) and the Spiritual Franciscans," in *Women of the Medieval World*, Julius Kirshner and Suzanne F. Wemple, eds. (Oxford: Basil Blackwell, 1985), 179-214.

16. Petrarch tells the same story in *De viris illustribus* 1.52, borrowed from Livy 2.5, 5-8; *Auctor de viris illustribus* 10. Petrarch's closing sentence (Fracassetti, *Epistolae* 3: 430), *sanctius aestimans sibi filios eripi quam patriae libertatem*, seems, however, to have been more directly inspired by Valerius Maximus 5.8.1: *Exuit patrem, ut consulem ageret, orbusque vivere quam publicae vindictae deesse maluit.*

17. Sallust, *Catilina* 51.35.

18. Virgil, *Aeneid* 6.621-22 (Covington trans.).

19. Petrarch was very fond of this story. He tells it briefly in *De remediis* 1, Dialogue 102, *De spe vincendi*, p. 283. One of the interlocutors is so hopeful of victory that he is warned that both leaders of the hostile forces may perish in the strife, as often happened abroad and also at Rome, "in the first battle that was fought after the expulsion of the kings, when the consul Brutus pursued the son of the proud king even into the regions of the dead."

But Petrarch naturally enlarges on these brief statements in his life of Brutus, *De viris illustribus* 1, p. 54:

> When the exiled king realized by this action [Brutus' killing of his own children; see above n. 16] that a return to Rome by fraudulent means was impossible, he resorted to open violence and sought the aid of the Etruscans. Relying on these, he entered Roman territory at the head of a large army. When Aruns, the king's son, saw Brutus adorned with the consular ornaments and advancing against him, maddened with poignant grief and goaded by the thought of his lost kingdom, he spurred on his horse and rushed on the consul. Seeing this, Brutus hurled himself against the enemy with equal fury. They clashed together with such violence, with such utter disregard for themselves, urged on by the single thought of wounding the opponent, that both were laid low at the same time, each pierced by the other's spear. Mortally wounded, Brutus breathed his last (to quote the word used by Florus) over the body of Aruns, whom he had killed with his own hand, as if to drive the adulterer (as Florus calls him), or, to speak more exactly, as if to drive the brother of the adulterer from this world, just as he had already driven him from the city, and thus pursue him even into the regions of Tartarus.

The reference is to Florus 1.10.8. The whole passage is based on Livy 2.6, 7-9; Valerius Maximus 5.6, 1; *Auctor de viris illustribus* 10.

Both the passages from Petrarch cited above are later than 1347, the date of this letter. The *De viris illustribus* was begun in 1350 and the *De remediis* in 1358. An earlier instance of our author's use of this story is *Familiari* 6.2, written in 1343, where Petrarch says: *ad inferos sequens consul* (the consul pursuing to hell itself). See Fracassetti, *Epistolae* 1: 312; Bernardo 1: 292. This differs only slightly from this passage in *Epistolae Variae* 48 (Fracassetti, *Epistolae* 3: 432): *in tartarum usque persecutus est*. Even earlier than this is the passage in the *Africa* written between 1339 and 1341/2 (3: 786-802, especially lines 795-96; Bergin and Wilson,

p. 68, ll. 1013-15): *Ferus ultor ad umbras, Perfide, Tartareas ferro sequar, inquit, acuto.*
20. For this entire paragraph compare stanza 7 of the canzone *Spirto gentil,* printed fully below in n. 33.
21. See the preceding note and compare especially verses 12-14.
22. *Vita* 1.20, col. 795: "And then he built a very beautiful chapel on the Capitol, enclosing it inside an iron railing overlaid with silver. There he had high mass sung by many priests and with great illumination." See Wright, p. 63.

To Petrarch's mind the most illustrious of Rome's generals was, of course, Scipio Africanus, the hero of his epic, the *Africa.* A few references to Scipio taken at random from our author's works are: *Roma caput rerum, Scipio dux summus in illa est* (*Africa* 3: 281; Bergin and Wilson, p. 51, ll. 351-52.); *oh summe virorum Scipio* (*Familiari* 23 1); *maximum ducem* (*De viris illustribus* 1 456). The story of Scipio's being as duly observant of his sacred duties as his age permitted is told in the *Africa* 4: 115-22; Bergin and Wilson, p. 73, ll. 155-64. After speaking of Scipio's divine origin, Laelius continues:

> ...for it is his wont
> at earliest sunrise, all alone, to seek
> the shrine of Jove, whose holiest citadel
> crowns the Tarpeian Hill where the god's priests
> in reverence perform their sacred rites
> and offer praises. There, with portals closed
> and locked behind him, drawing near the altar,
> long he will stand as in communion rapt;
> thence swiftly come away, and you might mark
> his mien display his loftiness of soul,
> his glance infused with a celestial power.

Petrarch repeats the story in *Rerum memorandum libri,* G. Billanovich, ed. (Florence: Edizione nazionale delle opere di Francesco Petrarca, 1943), 3, 1, chap. 6, p. 431; and in his *De vita solitaria* 2, sec. 9.5; Jacob Zeitlin, trans., *The Life of Solitude by Francis Petrarch* (Urbana, IL: University of Illinois Press, 1924; rpt. ed.,Westport, CT: Hyperion, 1978), 287-90. The whole passage is based on Livy 26.19; and Valerius Maximus 1.2, 2, with such minor sources as Gellius and the *Auctor de viris illustribus.*
23. Suetonius, *Divus Augustus* 78, 79.
24. Cicero, *Tusculanae disputationes* 1.3.
25. Compare, in n. 33 below, the canzone *Spirto gentil,* stanza 2, vss. 4-6.
26. In a letter dated July 15, 1347 Cola di Rienzo says of himself: "Cola di Rienzo used to live a far more tranquil life than the Tribune" (*multo vivebat quietius Cola Laurentii quam tribunus*). See Annibale Gabrielli, *Epistolario di Cola di Rienzo* (Rome: Forzani, 1890), in Istituto Storico Italiano, *Fonti per la Storia d'Italia, Epistolari, Secolo XIV,* Letter 12, p. 31, l. 39; and Burdach and Piur, Letter 18, 2.3: 54.

27. Compare, in n. 33 below, the canzone *Spirto gentil,* last stanza, vs. 3: *pensoso più d'altrui che di sè stesso,* to which we may add the statement of the *Vita* 2.23, col. 975: "There never was another such man. He alone bore all the weighty thoughts of the Romans." See Wright, *Life,* 4.12, p. 146.

28. This rapid survey is typical of Petrarch whenever he tries to instruct his readers. It is just such passages that have brought the charges of pedant and preacher on our author. Unfortunately, those who make the charge seem to forget that in the first half of the fourteenth century Petrarch was perhaps the only scholar who could correctly cite the Roman classics; that he was the only one who intelligently interpreted both the letter and the spirit of the classical authors. They forget that his correspondents and his friends looked forward to a letter from the poet laureate as though it were a letter from an ancient Roman, and that they preserved all such letters to refer to them later and to draw information from them as if from an ancient text or from a dictionary and encyclopedia of classical antiquities.

Examples of a similar historical survey can easily be found in Petrarch's works. To refer to only one, consult his epic, the *Africa* 3: 527-772; Bergin and Wilson, pp. 57-62, ll. 575-788, for references to Regulus, the Scipios, Curtius, and the Decii.

29. For a complete analysis of the story of the Fabii, see Pais, pp. 168-84.

30. Compare Livy 6.20, 12. For an analysis of the legends connected with the "Rock" see Pais, pp. 96-127.

31. Compare the canzone *Spirto gentil,* stanza 5, vss. 10-14 (11-14 in English translation in n. 33 below).

32. Remember that Petrarch had been officially admitted to Roman citizenship at the time of his coronation on Easter Sunday, April 8, 1341. See Wilkins, *Life,* pp. 24-29.

33. The promise made in these words has caused endless discussion among scholars. Those who have written lives of Cola di Rienzo, including Papencordt and Zefirino Re, are unanimous in maintaining that the poem here promised must be identified with the famous canzone *Spirto gentil,* which, they further argue, was addressed to the Roman tribune. See Francesco Torraca, "Cola di Rienzo e la canzone *Spirto gentil* di Francesco Petrarca," in *Discussioni e ricerche letterarie* (Livorno: Vigo, 1888), 1-87, especially p. 41.

In his note to this letter Fracassetti (*Lettere* 5: 414) argues that the canzone *Spirto gentil* was, in fact, addressed to Rienzo (compare *Lettere* 2: 190, 198) and that it represents Petrarch's preliminary keeping of his promise. He asserts that Petrarch wrote the Italian canzone first, intending to follow it up with a more worthy effort that was to have been composed in what Petrarch considered the more dignified and majestic Latin. Fracassetti further maintains that the concluding words of his *Hortatoria* refer to the Latin poem that never materialized. To strengthen his position, he cites a parallel from Petrarch's earlier compositions, namely that Petrarch wrote the sonnet *Vinse Annibal* (see

Gregorovius 6.1: 187, n. 1) to celebrate Stefanuccio Colonna's victory over the Orsini at Castel Cesario on May 22, 1333 (compare *Familiari* 3.3; Bernardo 1: 122-24), and that he followed it up with a Latin poem on the same subject (compare *Familiari* 3.4; Bernardo 1: 125).

Torraca, p. 41, does not think it necessary to suppose a second poem that was to have been written in Latin, pointing out that Petrarch wrote the canzone to the princes of Italy and the one celebrating the victory of the Da Correggio both in Italian. Torraca, however, does not identify the canzone *Spirto gentil* with the poem promised in the closing words of the *Hortatoria* on the grounds that the poem was promised only "provided you [the Romans] will not deceive my hopes and wishes, and will not deny me perseverance in your glorious undertaking," whereas the canzone alludes only to a glorious beginning and bears every trace of having been composed in haste (Torraca, p. 42). He concludes that the canzone *Spirto gentil* is a pendant to the *Hortatoria*, the latter celebrating the fact that liberty had been won, the former pointing out for what ends that liberty should be employed.

There seems to be only a very slight difference between the positions held by Torraca and Fracassetti. They agree that the canzone and the *Hortatoria* treat the same subject matter; that one is a pendant to the other (Torraca, p. 41); that the canzone was written hurriedly and, therefore, may have been meant to accompany the *Hortatoria* (Torraca, p. 42); and finally, that both the canzone and the *Hortatoria* are addressed to Cola di Rienzo. The one difference of opinion lies in their attitude toward the question whether or not the canzone *Spirto gentil* represents the conditional promise made in the *Hortatoria* in any way. Fracassetti answers the question in the affirmative, Torraca (p. 41) in the negative. Benjamin Crémieux, "Sur la destinataire de la canzone 'Spirto gentil,' un témoinage du xve siècle en faveur de Cola di Rienzo," in *Mélanges de philologie, d'histoire e de litterature offerts à Henri Hauvette* (Paris, 1934), 99-105, agrees that *Spirto gentil* was written for Cola di Rienzo.

Kenelm Foster, *Petrarch: Poet and Humanist. Writers of Italy*, vol. 9 (Edinburgh: University of Edinburgh Press, 1984), 57, notes that the scholarly opinion now holds that the canzone was written in 1337/8, after Petrarch' first visit to Rome. Nevertheless, the contents of the canzone *Spirto gentil* are so close to the spirit of the *Hortatoria*, and the poem itself is so stirring and so full of Petrarch's strong patriotism, that we present the entire text here from Petrarch, *Sonnets and Songs*, trans. Anna Maria Armi, introduction by Theodor E. Mommsen (New York: Grosset & Dunlop, 1968), 84-89 with facing Italian and English translation:

SPIRTO GENTIL

O gentle spirit who those members rule
Inside which like a pilgrim dwelt and trod
A gallant lord, as discerning as wise,

Since you have reached the honourable rod
By which you chastise Rome and every fool,
And remind her of her historic ties,
I speak to you because there does not rise
Elsewhere a ray of valour, which is gone,
And men are not ashamed of being knaves.
What Italy waits for, or what she craves
I do not know, she feels less than a stone;
Old and idle and prone,
Will she forever sleep and none will care?
Could I entwist my hands within her hair!

I do not hope that from her lazy sleep
She will turn round, however loud one calls,
So heavy is her burden, of such weight.
But not by chance the task to your arms falls,
That can shake her and raise out of the deep;
Our head, Rome, is entrusted you by fate.
Lay your hand on that venerable plait
Firmly, and in the braids loosened and lewd,
So that the slothful from the mud emerge.
I who repeat and day and night her dirge,
Have put in you all my solicitude,
For if Mars' people should
Ever look at their honour with their eyes,
I think that to your days belongs the prize.

The ancient walls that the world fears and loves
Still, and trembles, recalling to its mind
The time that was, turning to give a glance,
And the stones where were closed in and confined
The limbs of some of whom honour approves,
Unless the universe fall to mischance,
And all the things on which ruins advance
Through you hope to reform each vice and lust.
O you great Scipios, loyal Brutus, how
Happy you are, if the rumour by now
Has come below, of the well-given trust!
How Fabricius must
Rejoice when the good news catches his ears!
He says: – My Rome still beautiful appears. –

And if the sky cares for some earthly things,
The souls that have received a high estate
And let their bodies languish in the soil,

Beg you to stop this endless civil hate
Which does not soothe the people's sufferings
And closes against them their homes of toil;
These were once so devout, now they recoil
Like dark caverns of thieves that a war breeds,
So that only the good cannot find rest,
And among altars and statues undressed
Every cruel plot seems to sow seeds.
Ah, what different deeds!
Nor without trumpets does a charging shove,
Which to give thanks to God were placed above.

The weeping women and the unarmed crowd
Of children, and the old who cannot fight,
Who loathe themselves and life's wearisome pass,
And the black little monks, the grey, the white,
With all the ailing masses cry aloud,
Saying: – O kindly lord, help us, help us! –
And the poor folk bewildered, tired, alas,
Open to you their more than thousand sores
That would move others and Hannibal too.
And if you look at the house of the true
God, that now blazes, who few sparks abhors
To peacefulness restores
The wills that such a glowing flame have raised,
Whence your works up in heaven will be praised.

The bears, the wolves, the lions, eagles, snakes,
To a column of marble often are
Just a nuisance and to themselves a wrong.
For them weeps the good woman, from afar
Begging you to uproot and tear with rakes
The evil plants that for blooms do not long.
The thousandth year has passed since she was strong,
Since those beautiful souls went to another
Place, who had raised her where she was seen then.
Ah, new-made people measurelessly vain,
Who feel no reverence for such a mother!
You husband and you father,
All comforts are expected from your hands;
For the great Father fills other demands.

It seldom happens that a noble feat
Is not contrasted by insulting Chance
Who ill agrees with the spirited deed:

Now since she clears the step whence you advance,
I must forgive her, though she likes to cheat,
For this time with herself she disagreed;
Because, after the world had known our seed,
To a mortal the way was never free
To acquire as you will eternal fame,
Being able to raise, the truth I claim,
To great estate the noblest monarchy.
What glory will it be
To say: – The others helped her young and bold;
This one saved her from death when she was old! –

On the Tarpeian height, song, you will see
A knight whom all Italy admires,
To whom our good beyond his own is dear.
Tell him: – One who has not yet seen you near,
Except as by hearsay we feel love's fires,
Says that Rome who suspires
Every hour, with tears that grief distils,
Begs for your mercy from her seven hills.–

CHAPTER 3

ROME, JULY 28, 1347

The preceding letter was written about June 24-27, 1347. It must have reached Rome, accordingly, about July 12-15. At this time Cola and the Prefect Giovanni di Vico were at war. Peace negotiations were begun July 16; and the Roman army returned to the city on July 22.[1] In the midst of such pressing occupations, Cola could not find time to answer Petrarch's letter of exhortation. On July 27, however, he began to draw up a report for the pope, but the lack of messengers delayed its sending. Finally, on July 28 he wrote the following letter acknowledging the receipt of Petrarch's *Hortatoria*.

COLA DI RIENZO TO FRANCESCO PETRARCH
(EPISTOLARIO 15)

Nicholas, the severe and clement, by the grace of our most merciful Lord Jesus Christ tribune[2] of liberty, of peace, and of justice, and illustrious deliverer of the Holy Roman Republic, sends greetings and wishes for abundant joys and honors to Messer Francesco Petrarch of illustrious fame, poet laureate most worthy, and his well-beloved fellow citizen.[3]

Your numerous and most charming letters, so eloquently written and so thickly crowded with truthful and inspiring arguments, have filled the eyes of the reader and the ears of the hearer with pleasure. When their contents had been more deeply and maturely considered, the intellect feasted on them with greater pleasure. In your very gratifying letter of exhortation, you have summoned the praiseworthy examples of the heros of old to spur us on to emulate their virtuous deeds, whereby our spirits are and have been thoroughly revived.

We clearly discern from your letters the fullness of your love for the city and your anxiety for its welfare. The most positive proofs, indeed, of the sincerity and the depth of the affection that you cherish for us and for the city are your human kindness and sagacity, with which I became personally acquainted.[4] We and all the Romans feel warmly attached to you, and the more sincerely do we pledge ourselves to serve your glory and advantage. If only you were present at Rome in person! For, just as a most precious stone adorns a golden ring, so your illustrious presence would adorn and embellish the nourishing city.

Liberty is now the very life and breath of the Romans. Its sweetness is tasted anew after the lapse of ages. After suffering the error of servitude for so long, every Roman would now sooner permit life itself to be torn from his heart than to be reduced once again to most bitter slavery. For all things easily revert to their natural state, and the city stands out once again as the very head and fountain of liberty, the city that – to our mortification – has experienced the irreverent lot of a handmaid for so long. Therefore the Romans, pulled from the noose that was about to strangle them, make a joyful song to the Lord and shun no death, no dangers in defense of their reestablished liberty. We ourselves, moreover, are most eager to do everything that pertains to your advantage and to your glory.

Given on the Campidoglio, where we live a righteous life under the reign of justice, on the twenty-eighth day of the month of July, in the fifteenth indiction, and in the first year of the city's freedom.

NOTES

1. On Cola and the events mentioned here, see *Vita* 1.15-16, Wright, pp. 54-57; Gregorovius 6.1: 265-67; and Wilkins, *Life*, pp. 65-66.
2. For the text of this letter see Gabrielli, pp. 37-38; Burdach and Piur, Letter 25, 2.3: 85-86.
3. See Chapter 2, p. 32, n. 32.
4. This is evidently a reference to the friendship established between the poet and tribune at Avignon in 1343. See above Chapter 1, pp. 1-8.

CHAPTER 4

AVIGNON, JULY 24-26, 1347

Before the age of global mail and telecommunications, and with the insecurity of the highways during the fourteenth century, maintaining anything like an accurate correspondence between two cities so widely separated as Rome and Avignon was extremely difficult.[1] A further difficulty for the modern student lies in the fact that many of Petrarch's letters are undated. We have, however, dated the following letter July 24-26, 1347 for reasons that will be advanced in the notes. The letter itself does not contain references to current events at Rome, because Cola's report to the pope on Vico's submission was not dispatched from Rome earlier than August 5. During this interval Petrarch wrote frequent letters, seizing on the slightest pretext, communicating to the tribune his every thought and describing to him scenes and occurrences in the pope's household.

PETRARCH TO COLA DI RIENZO
TRIBUNE OF THE ROMAN PEOPLE
(*VARIAE 38*)

I shall not stop writing to you daily, so that your may be the first to know all my anxious thoughts about you, and that I may disclose to you all my uneasiness about your welfare.[2] I do not, however, expect any answers from you. Considering your important and overwhelming duties, I confess that I desire an answer rather than expect one. I realize this serious fact: that you have elevated yourself to a very high pinnacle where you are subject to the gaze, the criticism, and the judgment not merely of the Italians, but of all mankind, and not merely of those who live, but of all generations yet unborn. I am conscious that you have assumed a heavy burden, but at the same time a noble and an honorable one. You have set yourself an extraordinary and glorious task. In my opinion, never will the present age, never will posterity cease to speak of you. The opinions of other men are vain and discordant, changing with the whims of each and every individual. But your resolution stands as firm as that very rock of the Capitol on which you dwell.[3] It too remains unshaken by the blowing winds.

I do not know whether you are aware of, or suspect, or are entirely ignorant of, a certain fact. Do not suppose for a moment that the letters that you write from Rome remain long in the possession of those to whom they are addressed. On the contrary, everyone rushes to make a copy of them with as much earnestness, and circulates them around the pontiff's court with as much zeal, as if they were sent not by a man of our own race but by an inhabitant of another world or of the antipodes. All press round to interpret your epistles; and never was an oracle of the Delphic Apollo turned and twisted into so many different meanings. I therefore praise the caution that you have displayed up to now. Until now you have exerted great care in moderating your tone and have succeeded beyond reproach. I urge you and beg you to display greater and greater care in the future. Your words reveal the great soul of the writer and the majesty of the Roman people, but neither the reverence nor respect due to the Roman pontiff is obscured and forgotten. It is fitting that your eloquence and wisdom can blend harmoniously two concepts that seem to be mutually exclusive but are not so in reality.[4] In your letters each concept maintains its own proper dignity. I have witnessed several persons struck with amazement as they read, when they saw your self-assurance struggling with your modesty so as to leave only a doubtful victory; astonished when they saw that neither debasing fear nor swelling pride found admittance to that contest.[5] I have seen others perplexed as to whether they should more deeply admire your deeds or your words and unhesitatingly call you Brutus[6] for your gift of liberty, and for your eloquence Cicero, whom Catullus of Verona[7] addressed as "most eloquent."

Persevere, therefore, as you have begun. Always write as if everyone were to read, and not merely read, but as if they were about to set out from every shore and bear your message to every land.[8] You have laid the strongest of foundations: truth, peace, justice, and liberty. Build on these. Whatever structure you erect will remain firm; and whoever hurls himself against it will be dashed to pieces. He who wars against truth

40

will declare himself a liar; against peace, a restless spirit; against justice, a dishonest man; and if against liberty, an arrogant and shameless wretch.

I also praise the fact that, no matter what corner of the earth you write to,[9] you keep copies of your letters,[10] so that what you are about to say may be in harmony with what you have already said and so that, if the occasion makes it necessary, you may compare your letters with their replies. I discovered this custom of yours from the dating of your letters. When you sign them so gloriously "in the first year of the City's freedom," it smacks of a purpose to reform the annals of the state. The expression pleases me and gives me delightful comfort.[11] And since you are occupied in performing noble deeds, until you find a genius capable of recounting your deeds in worthy language, I promise you the service of my feeble intellect and of my pen – if God permits me to live. In this way I shall – to borrow Livy's words – perform my part in enhancing the memory of the most noble people in the world.[12] Nor will my Africanus mind yielding to you for a short while.[13] Farewell, most illustrious man.

NOTES

1. Even in the sixteenth century, under the best conditions, it took couriers on fast horses four days to travel the distance from Venice to Rome. To cross the Alps from Avignon to Rome took about two weeks. On time, distance, and communications in late medieval and early modern Europe see Fernand Braudel, *The Mediterranean and the Mediterranean World in the Age of Philip II*, Sean Reynolds, trans., 2 vols. (New York: Harper & Row, 1972), 1: 206-24, 276-95, 355-76; and J.R. Hale, *Renaissance Europe, 1480-1520* (London: Collins, 1973), 31-41.

2. This letter is also edited in Burdach and Piur, Letter 24, 2.3: 62-63. There are eight letters in all addressed directly to Cola. Petrarch's last letter to him is *Familiari* 7.7, dated Genoa, November 29, 1347, when the poet's faith in the tribune began to waver. See Bernardo 1: 349-52. In that letter Petrarch reproaches Cola for his wayward actions and closes with the following stinging rebuke: "Consider all this, and you will realize that you are not the master of the republic, but its servant." If Petrarch did write to Cola daily, or as frequently as a reasonable interpretation of that word would warrant, it is a thousand pities that the letters have been lost. Let us hope that they are still buried in the libraries of Europe, and that they are patiently awaiting scholarly research.

3. Compare the dating of Cola's letter to Petrarch. For a brief review of the letter see Wilkins, *Life*, p. 66.

4. Francesco Filippini, "Cola di Rienzo e la Curia Avignonese," *Studi storici* 10 (1901): 241-87; 11 (1902): 3-35, especially 11: 8. Filippini considers Cola's ability to blend seemingly irreconcilable ideas as one of the surest indications that he had deliberately adopted a policy of duplicity toward the Avignon Curia. His thesis is that Cola wished to strip the papacy of its temporal power. He maintains that Cola constantly wrote to the pontiff in one tone and to the cities and princes in a far different one. For an analysis of the secularist trends in Cola's political thought see Pier Giorgio Ricci, "Il commento di Cola di Rienzo alla *Monarchia* di Dante," *Studi medievali,* ser. 3, 6 (1965): 665-708.

5. It may be reasonable to deduce from this statement that when this letter was written Cola's actions had not yet irritated the pope and that relations between Rome and Avignon had not yet reached the straining point.

6. Rienzo is compared with Brutus here not for having freed Rome from the tyranny of a monarchy, but for having rescued the Romans from the yoke of the foreign barons. The distinction correctly represents the attitude of the Curia at this time. It accepted and furthered Cola's prosecution of the barons, whose lawless conduct the Curia had not been, and was not now, strong enough to curb. At the same time it claimed that Cola's deeds were all performed in the name of the church, whose head was, of course, the legitimate monarch of Rome.

7. Catullus, *Carmina* 49.

8. Giuseppe Brizzolara, "Il Petrarca e Cola di Rienzo," *Studi storici* 8 (1899): 239-51, 423-63; p. 433, regards this as a veiled warning to Cola of the Curia's increasing suspicions and hostility.

9. In the few months following his revolution Cola di Rienzo reached out to the leadership of Europe and beyond. His addressees included Clement VI, the princes of Italy, the cities of Viterbo, Lucca, Florence, Mantua, Todi and others; Charles of Bohemia, Louis of Hungary, the kings of England and France, and even the Byzantine Emperor and the Sultan of Egypt. See the calendars of letters in Gabrielli and in Burdach and Piur, as well as the *Vita* 1.10, Wright, pp. 47-48; 1.12, pp. 50-51; 1.22-23, pp. 64-68; and 1.26, pp. 72-73. For Cola's relations with the cities of Italy, see Mariani; and Massimo Miglio, "Il progetto politico di Cola di Rienzo ed i comuni dell'Italia centrale," *Bollettino dell' Istituto Storico Artistico Orvietano* 39 (1983, act. 1988): 55-64.

10. Petrarch himself used to keep copies of his letters for the same reason that he now commends in Cola. See Cosenza, *Letters to Classical Authors,* p. 10; and Fracassetti, *Epistolae* 1: 245.

11. Compare the dating of Cola's answer to Petrarch. The first letter among those now extant in which Cola employed the phrase, *liberate reipublice anno primo,* is one addressed to Pope Clement VI and dated July 8, 1347. See Gabrielli, *Epistolario* 8, p. 27, ll. 193-94; Burdach and Piur, Letter 15, 2.3: 41-49, especially p. 49, ll. 199-200. Gabrielli, p. 20, n. 4, points out, however, that there must have been earlier letters to the pope, of which no traces can be discovered. Surely

CHAPTER 4, AVIGNON, JULY 24–26, 1347

Cola must have notified the pope of his elevation by the beginning of June, for we find him recognizing both Cola and Raymond as his rectors at Rome in a letter of June 27, 1347 (Theiner 2, no. 174, p. 178). Petrarch, who as of the end of July or beginning of August was still *persona non grata* at the papal court, may either have seen, or have heard of, these earlier letters. From these he may have become acquainted with Cola's use of the expression. It is therefore not necessary to assume from Petrarch's comment on this phrase that *Variae* 38 was written only after the receipt of Cola's letter dated July 28.

The phrase *Datum in Capitolio* must also have pleased Petrarch; for it must have reminded him of the same phrase employed in dating the coronation diploma given to him on the Campidoglio six years before. (See *Opera omnia* 3: 6: *Privilegii laureae receptae a Francisco Petrarcha exemplar*; for the date see p. 7.)

12. Livy, *Praefatio* 3.

13. This is a reference to Petrarch's own epic, the *Africa*, whose hero is Scipio, surnamed Africanus. Though the poem was nearing completion about the time Petrarch met Cola at Avignon in 1343, it is clear from the closing statement of this letter that Petrarch was still at work on it, giving it the polishing touches. In fact, the Africa was not published until after the poet's death. See Adolf Gaspary, *Geschichte der Italienischen Literatur*, 2 vols. (Berlin: Robert Oppenheim, 1885-88), see especially 1: 426. See also Bergin and Wilson, pp. ix-xiv; Bernardo, *Scipio and the Africa*; Foster, *Petrarch*, pp. 143-49, 177-78, and 180-82; and Mann, *Petrarch*, pp. 21-22, 48-51 and 105-8.

We can only explain Petrarch's laying aside a work on which he had expended such great labor with the supposition that, for the time being at least, he considered his new undertaking even more important. Perhaps we are justified in assuming that by July 1347 Petrarch meant to devote himself to the Latin poem in honor of Rienzo promised in the closing words of *Variae* 48 (June 1347): "I shall recall the muses from their exile and sing resounding words in abiding memory of your glory – words that will ring throughout the ages." See Chapter 2, *Hortatoria*, pp. 10-24, and p. 32, n. 33.

CHAPTER 5

We can readily picture Petrarch's uneasy life during the months of July and August 1347. The Curia had rejoiced at the first report of Cola's elevation to the tribunate – for in Cola the church saw merely a dutiful son who had broken the lifted horns of the unruly barons. In fact, the pope had granted him only the title of Rector, never recognizing Cola's own title of Tribune. The intention was quite plain: Cola should continue to rule Rome in the name of the pope and should submit all his proposed actions to the pontiff's more mature judgment.

The tribune soon began to act in such a way as to arouse the suspicions of the church. In the midst of the gathering storm, Petrarch constantly championed his idol's cause; and his unrestrained speech estranged many of his former friends. He was gradually losing the general affection that he was so proud of. It is plausible that the members of the Curia began to shun his presence; or, if this were impossible, they may have regarded him as an enemy, may have refused the warm handshake, the welcoming glance, and may have passed on in silence. Such conduct would have cut deeply into Petrarch's sensitive soul. Nevertheless, we do know that he continued to defend the justice of Cola's tribunate and the sincerity of his aims. We would assign the following letter to the period between August 21 and 25 and the beginning of open hostilities. It relates some thoughts that occurred to Petrarch one evening, or perhaps it was a vision, for he himself scarcely knew whether he was fully awake or half asleep.

PETRARCH TO COLA DI RIENZO
TRIBUNE OF THE ROMAN PEOPLE
(VARIAE 40)

You can easily imagine, best of men, my great concern and suspense over the outcome of your fortunes. I call God to witness that I seem somehow to partake in your dangers, your labors, and your glory. And to tell the truth, I neither wish to, nor can, conceal it. As often as Fortune brings me among those who are discussing your affairs with stubborn insolence, I take up arms in your defense. This is a well-known fact, and the people can testify to the great partiality and the eagerness with which I have argued against those who were decrying the justice of your tribunate and the sincerity of your aims. I have paid absolutely no regard either to the past or to the future; nor have I cared whom I might sting or offend with my words. Thanks to my unrestrained speech, I have estranged many whose favor I had gained through long intimacy.[1] But I am not surprised at this. For I have long recognized this verse of Terence[2] to be most true: "Homage begets friends; truth, enemies." Provided my conscience absolves me, however, I do not care who accuses me.

I wanted to tell you this by way of preface, so that you will not wonder at the frequent letters I write to you nor consider my zeal inopportune. For I do not regard your affairs from afar as if I were absent. On the contrary, I feel as if I were in the very center of the battle line, as if I were destined to conquer in the great struggle or be conquered by it. Consequently my days are disturbed by harassing cares and my nights by dreams. I toil both asleep and awake; and I never find a moment of rest. Under such conditions my pen is my one consolation. When I write I seem to be with you, and I hurriedly jot down, not what is more pleasing to hear, but whatever first occurs to my mind. I do not so much strive to write in a brilliant style as, without regard to style, to pour into your ears the cares of my soul and so lighten my heavily laden heart. Therefore receive my letters with the expectation of finding in them the conversation of a friend rather than the elegant exposition of your deeds. Tormented by my cares, I think of your fortunes day and night; and since the memory is fleeting and forgetful, lest my thoughts should escape, I confine them to the unyielding fabric of letters. On returning home I record the thoughts that accompanied me during the day; on rising in the morning I record those of the night. Indeed, if I should yield to my inner promptings, no day would pass without a letter from me.[3]

Now I shall tell you some thoughts that came to me last night – or perhaps it was a vision, for I scarcely know whether I was fully awake or half asleep. I seemed to see you in the center of the world on a very high place, such as the topmost ridge of a precipitous mountain. You were so high that you seemed to touch the very skies. In comparison to that height all the mountains that I have seen in our own land and all that I have heard or read of in foreign lands would be only low plains. Olympus itself, sung by the poets of both Greece and Rome, would be a very insignificant hill. Clouds floated far below at its feet, and the sun gleamed not far above its summit. Countless multitudes of brave folk crowded around you. You were seated in their midst on a shining throne and were elevated above the rest. You were more majestic and resplendent than all humanity, so much so that you seemed to have stirred Phoebus himself to envy. I moved around in the surrounding multitude, and behold! my eyes fell on endless masses that I could never even have imagined. I almost fainted with wonder. In my utter amazement I asked the person standing nearest me the meaning of the marvel I beheld or, perhaps, of the delusion that I labored under. For never, I believe, had even one-twentieth of that multitude inhabited the earth.

"You were not mistaken," answered the person I had addressed. "You should know that there are assembled here not only everyone who is now living, but also all future generations, summoned here at the command of Him in whose palm the universe, and all humanity, and centuries untold rest."

"And what are they doing here? I have never seen people so attentive."

"They wait to see what fortune attends that man," he answered, raising his eyes to you, "because of whom, as you see, not merely the earth, but the very sky and stars have lost their peace." And to this he added: "Don't you hear the heavens rumbling?" I listened, and behold! the deep thunder of a distant cloud – like the warning of an approaching storm.[4] "Mars," he said, "threatens with his thunderbolt, but Jove remains calm."

"And what is your opinion?" I asked. "What do you suppose will be the end of such great expectations?"

"God alone knows," he answered, "but whatever the end, it will neither remain unnoticed nor be passed over in silence. All this great throng will always remember it and speak of it. So far as mortal wisdom can see into the future, the glory of this man will be vigorous and eternal, provided only that he does not bend before the gales. And he will not. Truly, what has that man to fear whose firm resolve is to die for the right, if need be? I only fear one thing – the wavering loyalty of some of these who stand close around him on the very summit of the mount and who look with distrust on the success of others. I fear the faltering loyalty of those who aspire to rise to preeminence by unworthy means and who hope that on that man's destruction they will gain his throne. But they deceive themselves. If he is wary of these, he will continue in safe possession of his power."

"Alas!" I cried, "is there anyone so savage, so inhuman as to plot the fall of the very man under whose guidance he has scaled such glorious heights? What madness, gracious God, what folly not to desire the welfare of one's preserver as much as one's own! But what will they accomplish," I asked, "if – and may the Omnipotent avert the omen – this man fall? Under what leader will they find security?"

"I shall answer in a word," he said. "They will rush headlong after him, down into the same abyss in which we have been living a life of misery. For," he added, "envy brought death into the world, and envy is blind. When spurred by chagrin, it pays no heed to the suffering it brings on itself provided it inflicts injury on another. I trust, however, that he will be more successful in evading all the pitfalls of fortune, for God is with him." And here he left me.

I was thirsty, however, for further information, and I seized him by the hand and said, "Where are you rushing?" "Night speeds on," he said, "and I must be off." And I: "Tell me this at least: what toil has raised this man to such high station, what devotion, what chance?" And he very appropriately replied, quoting those most charming lines of Virgil[5]:

"He is one of the few
whom heaven has marked for love,
Or glowing worth has throned above."

Having said this he disappeared, just as the sky became tinged with the rosy dawn. And I, I either recollected my scattered thoughts, or else I awoke. Farewell, remarkable defender of liberty!

Postscript: I can testify on behalf of your envoy Messer Giovanni,[6] and with me the Curia and truth itself can testify that he has conducted himself in your interests and in those of the republic with such integrity as to merit the praise, esteem and, in my opinion, even the gratitude of his chief. I am sure that you would have known this even had I made no reference to it; but I did not think it should be passed over in silence.

NOTES

1. At first, of course, Cola's prosecution of the barons pleased the pope, as we have already pointed out (Chapter 4, p. 40, nn. 5-6 and p. 42 above). But as the news of Rienzo's further doings reached the Western Babylon, the Colonna's resentment and anger must have become greater and greater. These were the most prominent of the Roman barons and the leaders of the opposition to the tribune. There were also many other high dignitaries and prelates at the Avignon court who shared their feelings. The difficulties of Petrarch's position with the Colonna at this period were surely not enviable. As he himself acknowledges (*Familiari* 7.13), he owed them everything. For a review of Petrarch's situation at Avignon and his growing uneasiness, see Wilkins, *Life*, pp. 68-70.

2. Terence, *Andria* 1.1.41, vs. 68.

3. This statement clearly proves that when Petrarch said, "I shall not stop writing to you daily," he was not to be taken too literally. See the opening sentence of the letter in Chapter 4, p. 39, and n. 2.

4. It is scarcely necessary to suppose that Petrarch meant to warn Cola of the growing enmity of the papal court (see Brizzolara, "Petrarca," *Studi storici* 8: 435, n. 1). It is quite evident that this entire letter is one of warning and advice, the result of Petrarch's "concern and suspense over the outcome" of Cola's fortunes. Wilkins quotes this vision in full. See *Life*, p. 69.

5. Virgil, *Aeneid* 6.129-30.

6. This is a postscript that like so many of its kind, either carries more information or causes greater difficulty than the letter itself. The question naturally arises, "who is this Messer Giovanni?"

Jacques F.P.A. De Sade, *Mémoires pour la vie de François Pétrarque, tirés de ses oeuvres et des auteurs contemporains* (Amsterdam: Arskée et Mercus, 1764-67), 2: 354, n. a; and Fracassetti (note to *Variae* 40) identify Messer Giovanni with the messenger mentioned in the *Vita* 1.10. The *Vita* runs as follows (col. 757; Wright, pp. 47-48):

> Then the tribune held a general council, and wrote excellent letters to the various cities.... In these letters he set forth his name in the lofty title shown in the following formula: "Nicholas, the severe and clement, tribune of liberty, of peace, and of justice, and illustrious

deliverer of the Holy Roman Republic...." The couriers who bore his letters carried in their hands wooden wands plated with silver. They carried no arms. His couriers increased to such an extent that there were a great number of them. They were welcomed courteously and every one paid them great honor. They were handsomely rewarded. One of his couriers, a Florentine, was sent to Avignon to the pope and to Cardinal Janni (Giovanni) de la Colonna. He brought back a casket of wood inlaid with very fine silver that represented the arms of the Roman people, the pope and the tribune. Its value was thirty florins. On his return the courier said: "This wand I have carried publicly through forests and over highways. Thousands have knelt before it and kissed it with tears, because of their joy that the highways have been rendered safe and free from robbers."

This chapter's mention of the couriers occurs in connection with the statement that the tribune had held a general council and had written most excellent letters to the various cities. It is natural to assume that the courier mentioned was the bearer of one of these letters, and that therefore he was the first messenger dispatched to the pope by Cola after his elevation to the tribuneship. See Filippini, *Studi storici* 10: 268, n. 2.

The date of Cola's letter to the city of Viterbo (May 24; see Gabrielli, *Epistolario* 2; Burdach and Piur, Letter 7, 2.3: 17-27) seems too early for the description given in Chapter 10 of the *Vita*. But such a description seems to point to the circular letter addressed by the tribune to the cities of Perugia, Florence, and Lucca, all of which bear the date June 7 (Gabrielli, *Epistolario* 3, 4, and 5; Burdach and Piur, Letter 8, also 2.3: 17-27; compare Torraca, p. 52). See also Miglio, "Progetto." The contents of these letters must have become known at Avignon in the latter part of June, when the pope must have received a direct notification from Cola as well; for we find Clement VI recognizing both Cola and Raymond as his rectors at Rome in a letter of June 27, 1347. See Theiner 2, no. 174, p. 178; and Eugene Déprez, ed., *Clément VI, Lettres closes, patentes et curiales intéressant les payes autres que la France publiées ou analysées d'après les registres du Vatican* (Paris: A. Fontemoing, 1901-60).

But with this dating of the events and the messenger mentioned in *Vita* 1.10, which we judge to be correct, there would be insufficient time either for the natural development of the enmity described by Petrarch in the opening sentences of the present letter or for Petrarch's repeated defense of Cola's tribuneship and the sincerity of his aim. For up to the latter part of June the Curia could not have become incensed at Cola. The latter's backslidings were still a thing of the future. Our first conclusion, therefore, is that both De Sade and Fracassetti are in error. The messenger of *Vita* 1.10 must be identified with the bearer of Cola's first message to the pope in June; hence, he cannot be identified with the Messer Giovanni of Petrarch's letter, which must be dated in the second half of August.

Let us now examine Filippini's view. He points out (*Studi storici* 10: 268 and n. 2) that Cola sent an envoy to Pope Clement VI by his letter of August 5, 1347. This is Letter 16 of the *Epistolario*, and it consists of two parts. The first part is dated July 27 and contains the statement (Gabrielli, *Epistolario* 16: 44, l. 157; Burdach and Piur, Letter 28, 2: 3: 106-12): *ambassiator ad pedes vestre Clementie trasmittetur.* In other words, the first half of the letter clearly promised that an ambassador would be sent. The second part of the letter is dated August 5 and contains the statement (Gabrielli, *Epistolario* 16: 45, l. 189; Burdach and Piur, pp. 112-16) that the ambassador *dirigitur,* is being sent. Filippini gives the former reference instead of the latter.

Filippini continues (*Studi storici* 10: 268 and 11: 13, n. 2) that the envoy thus sent on or about August 5 is mentioned as being on the way in Cola's letter to Rinaldo Orsini dated September 17, 1347 (Gabrielli, *Epistolario* 23; Burdach and Piur, Letter 40, 2.3: 144-51). Filippini refers the reader to *Epistolario*, p. 66, l. 130, but he should have given ll. 131-32. (See the English translation in Chapter 7, pp. 72-73 below.) Even so, there we find Cola's statement that he is not writing to the pope nor to the other cardinals, because he believes that a worthy envoy representing both himself and the Roman people is about to be dispatched to the Curia: *quia ad Curiam credimus quod ambassiata Romani populi et nostra honorabilis dirigetur.* The form employed here, *dirigetur,* is in the future tense, and therefore the sentence must mean that Cola intended to dispatch still another envoy, one quite distinct from the envoy sent on or about August 5. As a matter of fact, we have not been able to discover any further reference in Cola's correspondence to the envoy of August 5, unless such a reference is to be inferred from Cola's remark in the same letter to Rinaldo Orsini to the effect that he was being undeservedly accused in Avignon (Gabrielli, *Epistolario*, p. 66, l. 135; Burdach and Piur, p. 149, l. 126-p. 150, l. 135).

Filippini concludes that the envoy sent on August 5 is the Giovanni of Petrarch's postscript. His conclusion is correct, but in our opinion he has not provided proper proofs. The fault lies in the following misstatements:

a. *Epistolario*, p. 66, ll. 131-32, does not say that any envoy is on the way; the form found there is the future *dirigetur* and not the present *dirigitur.*

b. Even granting that the reading of l. 132 is, or should be, *dirigitur,* it is unlikely that a special envoy from Rome to Avignon bearing a message direct to Clement VI should have been traveling from August 5 to September 17, a period of forty-four days, and still not have reached his destination at that time of year. See Chapter 4, p. 39, n. 1.

We think, however, that we can prove the identity of Messer Giovanni with the messenger dispatched by Cola on or about August 5. Any envoy sent on that date would accompany, or would follow, reports of Cola's doings in the latter part of July and in the beginning of August. We have positive proof that the pope at Avignon was kept accurately informed by Raymond, bishop of Orvieto and his vicar at Rome. On August 1 Raymond dispatched a letter to his lord and master Clement VI (Papencordt, Document 8). On August 2 Cochetus de Chotitis sent a similar letter to his patron in Avignon, Rinaldo Orsini, archdeacon of Lüttich and a papal notary. This letter was written in greater detail than Raymond's; in fact, it is quite a catalog of events, beginning with the attack of Cola's army on Vetralla, then going over the same ground as the letter of the bishop, and finally including the events of August 2 as well (Papencordt, Document 9).

Both these letters, dispatched respectively four and three days before Cola's letter of August 5, must have reached their destination a similar number of days before Cola's letter. Raymond's letter was directly to Clement VI; and we are safe in assuming that Rinaldo Orsini duly notified the pope of the contents of the letter from Cochetus de Chotitis. Hence, on the arrival of Cola's messenger, the pope must already have known the following astonishing events: the tribune's edict decreeing the existence of the Italian Nation and annulling all genuine and spurious privileges assumed by the popes; the famous festival, in the course of which Cola assumed the dignity of knighthood and bathed in the sacred baptismal basin of Emperor Constantine; the proclamation of Rome as the capital of the world; the summons sent to Emperor Lewis of Bavaria and to King Charles of Bohemia; and, finally, the distribution of the standards to the Italian cities during the memorable festival of the Unity of Italy. See the letter of Clement VI to Bertrand, cardinal-legate of the kingdom of Sicily, dated August 21, 1347; Theiner 2, no. 175, pp. 179-80, beginning with *Post hoc autem.* Compare Oderico Rinaldi, ed., *Annales ecclesiastici,* vols. 25-26 (Rome: Vitale Mascardi, 1643), 25: 443-44.

In the middle of the fourteenth century the papal court might truly have considered this news from another world. No envoy, either bearing such news or reaching Avignon together with such news, could have escaped the resentment of the self-exiled Vicars of the Lord. We see a clear indication of this resentment and of the chilly atmosphere then reigning in the papal palace in Petrarch's postscript when he feels obliged to commend Messer Giovanni for the integrity and the ability with which he conducted himself under such difficult circumstances.

Chapter 1.21 of the anonymous *Vita* provides an independent verification of this identification of Messer Giovanni. Chapter 16 had given an account of the submission of the Prefect Giovanni di Vico; chapters 17 to 19 constitute the author's excursus on the subject of dreams; chapter 20 gives an account of Cola's nepotism. Chapter 21 then resumes the thread of the political history where it had been broken off at chapter 16. Here the *Vita* tells how Cola finally dismissed his colleague Raymond and how he sent an embassy to the pope (*Vita,* cols. 797 and 799; see Wright, pp. 63-64):

> At a time of such great prosperity Cola, wishing to be the sole ruler, dismissed the pope's vicar, his colleague, who was a foreigner born

beyond the Alps [*uno tramontano*], a man deeply learned in the Decretals, and bishop of Viterbo [sic]. This man he dismissed in spite of the fact that he received many letters and many embassies from prominent ecclesiastics in Avignon. Then Cola sent an ambassador to the pope, acquainting him with these conditions. This ambassador, upon his return, said that the pope and all the cardinals entertained the gravest doubts.

From other sources we know that the Roman army marched out against Giovanni di Vico in the second half of June; that negotiations for peace were on foot on July 16; that the Roman army reentered the city on July 22. See Torraca, p. 46 and the references given there. On July 27 Cola began to write a report to the pope giving the account of Vico's submission (Gabrielli, *Epistolario* 16; Burdach and Piur, Letter 28, 2.3: 106-16). This letter's dispatch was postponed because of the lack of messengers (Gabrielli, *Epistolario,* p. 44, ll. 161-62; Burdach and Piur, p. 112, ll. 161-62). On July 28 Cola found a few spare moments to write his long-delayed answer to Petrarch's *Hortatoria* (Gabrielli, *Epistolario* 15; Burdach and Piur, Letter 25, 2.3: 85-86; see Chapter 3, pp. 37-38 above.). On August 5 Cola again takes up his letter to the pope begun on July 27, taking the opportunity of adding the news of the further developments of August 1 and 2. The pope, however, had become acquainted with these facts even before the receipt of Cola's letter. See above, pp. 48-51. We cannot help identifying the messenger dispatched with the one in *Vita* 1.21. Thus we can assert that the messenger bearing Cola's letter of August 5, the messenger of *Vita* 1.21, and the Messer Giovanni of the present letter are one and the same person.

Cola's doings were taking on an alarming and unprecedented nature. The relations between Rome and Avignon were becoming more and more strained, though they had not reached the breaking point. By this time, therefore, the household of the pope, the cardinals, and other dignitaries of the church had sufficient cause for their stubborn intransigence and for their doubts about the justice and sincerity of their rector in Rome. The doubts of the Curia described by Petrarch seem to correspond precisely to the gravest doubts entertained by the pope and by all his cardinals as described in *Vita* 1.21. Finally the identification of Messer Giovanni would date the present letter toward August 21, a date that would satisfy all those but Filippini (*Studi storici* 11: 14-15) who have considered this subject.

CHAPTER 6

VAUCLUSE, AUGUST 22-31, 1347

The pope in Avignon was in constant communication with his vicar in Rome, Raymond, bishop of Orvieto. On August 1 Bishop Raymond sent a letter to Clement VI in which he reported Cola's investiture as a knight, the citation of the emperor and the princes of the empire, and his own protest against Cola's fantastic proceedings. On the following day, August 2, Cochetus de Chotitis dispatched similar news to his patron in Avignon, Rinaldo Orsini, papal notary. This letter also contained information on the festival of United Italy celebrated on August 2, 1347. It was followed by the official report sent by Cola on August 5, 1347.[1]

From the ecclesiastical standpoint, the rector's deeds were now becoming alarming. The pope, the cardinals, and others in high office now had good grounds for their stubborn opposition. Petrarch's position among the Avignon prelates was therefore becoming more intolerable by the day. The increasing suspicions of the Colonna, the Orsini, and other families of the Roman nobility in the pope's household; the exaggerated fears of the general clergy for the maintenance of their positions and privileges in Italy; the strain of having to defend the tribune from the accusations showered on him from every side; and the feeling that his pleasant relations with all those around him were being slowly and steadily undermined – all this must have filled Petrarch's heart with sadness.

To give up Cola was impossible. He loved his friends deeply and sincerely, but even more deeply did he love Rome and Italy and the cherished dream of years. The relations between Cola and the Curia were strained; still, open hostilities had not yet been declared. The enmity developed thus far existed only between individuals; the church as an institution had not yet broken with Cola. Under the circumstances Petrarch, wearied by his constant troubles in the "Hell of the Living," fled eagerly to the quiet, peaceful solitude of Vaucluse, the "Enclosed Valley." The surroundings gave him relief from the distracting whirl of the city but could not banish thoughts of Rome. Consequently, he composed an eclogue on the subject uppermost in his mind and sent it to

Cola di Rienzo, accompanying it with a letter of explanation.[2] Fortunately both eclogue and letter are extant.

PETRARCH TO COLA DI RIENZO
TRIBUNE OF THE ROMAN PEOPLE
(VARIAE 42)

I have been sailing the stormy seas of this Curia that calls itself Roman for a long and difficult time. I have grown rather old in the service but am still an awkward and inexperienced sailor. Consequently I recently fled from the troubled waters of Avignon and sought the haven that, as ever, offers me the quiet of solitude – that Enclosed Valley that receives its name from its very nature. This retreat is fifteen miles distant from that most boisterous of cities and from the left bank of the Rhone. Though the intervening distance is so short, still the two places are so utterly different that, whenever I leave for that city, I seem to have encircled the globe from the farthest west to the extreme east. The two places have nothing in common except the sky: the people have a different nature, the waters possess a different quality, the land produces a different vegetation.[3]

Here I have the Fountain of the Sorgue, a stream that must be numbered among the fairest and coolest, remarkable for its crystal waters and its emerald channel. No other stream is like it; no other is so noted for its varying moods, now raging like a torrent, now quiet as a pool. I am astonished, therefore, that Pliny should have placed this fountain among the wonders of the province of Narbonne; for as a matter of fact it is situated in the province of Arles.[4] This is the country seat where, beyond the confines of Italy, I am detained by the inexorable claims of necessity. And yet the spot is most suitable for my studies. The hills cast a grateful shadow in the morning and evening hours; and at noon many a nook and corner of the vale gleams in the sunlight. Round about, the woods lie still and tranquil, woods in which the tracks of wild animals are far more numerous than human ones. Everywhere a deep and unbroken stillness, except for the babbling of running waters, or the lowing of the oxen browsing lazily along the banks, or the singing of birds. I should speak of this more at length, were it not that the rare beauties of this secluded dale have already become familiar far and wide through my verses.[5]

Here then, as I was saying, I fled with great longing both to give my mind and my ears rest from the distracting whirl of the city and also to put the finishing touches to some work I had in hand, the thought of which, in its unfinished condition, weighed heavily on me. The very look of the forest urged me to compose a poem dealing with the wild woodlands. To that pastoral poem that I composed the preceding summer in that same valley I, therefore, now added a chapter.[6] Or rather, since we should always use poetical terms in matters of poetry, I should say that I now added an eclogue. The laws of this species of poetry forbade me to choose for a background any other than a sylvan scene. I therefore wrote a pastoral in which the interlocutors are two shepherds, two brothers, and forwarded this poem to you, who are so devoted a scholar, intending that it should serve as a relief from your numerous cares.

The nature of these compositions is such that, unless the author himself provides the key, their meaning might not be divined.[7] In fact, they are likely to remain quite unintelligible. I will not oblige you, who are straining every nerve in solving most serious questions of state, to waste any energy over the words of even one of these fictional shepherds. And so that your divine intellect may not be engaged even for one instant in unraveling my trifles, I shall briefly disclose to you the substance of what I have written.

The two shepherds represent two classes of citizens living in the same city but entertaining widely divergent sentiments concerning that same republic. One of them is named Martius, that is to say, warlike and restless, or perhaps he is named after Mars, whom tradition makes the father of him who founded our people. This Martius is affectionate toward his mother and has compassion for her. His mother, indeed, is Rome. The second shepherd is his brother Apicius, a name once borne by the master connoisseur of the art of cooking. Apicius, as you see, must therefore typify that class of citizens totally given over to idleness and the pursuit of pleasure. The scene represents the two shepherds in heated conversation on the love due their aged mother and especially on the question of restoring her ancient homestead, which, of course, is the Capitolium, and the bridge by which she used to visit her farms, which, again, is the Milvian. The bridge spans a stream descending from the lofty summits of the Apennines, the Tiber. This river, whose course is outlined there,[8] leads to the ancient orchards and the home of Saturn, in other words, to the ancient city of Orte and to Sutri. It also leads to the shaded valleys of Tempe, by which is meant Umbria, in which are Narni and Todi and many other cities; and farther south it enters Etruria, whose people, as you well know, are descended from the Lydian race.[9]

The shepherd who is mentioned in the following passage – he who caught the thieves on the bridge and slew them – is Marcus Tullius Cicero, who, as you know, seized the Catilinarian conspirators on the Milvian Bridge.[10] He is rightly portrayed as a shepherd, because he was consul; he is rightly portrayed as sharp and keen because of his supremacy in the field of eloquence. The woods that the ruined bridge menaces and the diminished flock that dwells there both symbolize the Roman people. The women and children for whom Apicius has abandoned his mother and whom alone he cherishes, are the lands and their rural dwellers. The caverns are the fortified palaces of these lords on which they rely to scoff at the sufferings of the citizens. Apicius does not wish the Capitolium to be strengthened; on the contrary, he proposes that it be split in two, so that this faction and that may alternately reign supreme. His brother tries to bring about union. In referring to their mother's riches for restoring the Capitolium, he means to emphasize that Rome is still a power, if only her children were of one mind. For, he says, Rome nourishes both sheep and bullocks, naturally representing the impoverished majority and the wealthy few. Among the remnants of their former fortune Martius also mentions a quantity of hidden salt, by which we may simply understand the revenues from the tax on salt, which I hear are quite considerable. However, understand it to mean the practical wisdom of the Romans that has lain dormant too long out of fear of the tyrants.

While the brothers are debating all this, a winged messenger arrives. This is Rumor, than whom, to quote Virgil,[11]

...never plague that runs
Its way more swiftly wins.

This courier declares their cares vain and their altercations useless, announcing that they have both been disowned by their mother and that with their mother's consent, their younger brother rebuilds the old homestead and rules the forests. He announces, furthermore, that their brother thereby imposes silence on them while he himself sings sweetly to the flocks and the herds, that is to say, while he himself promulgates just laws and abolishes the unjust. In these verses I have veiled the names, the natural dispositions, or the armorial bearings of several of the tyrants under the figures of wild animals. So far you have proven yourself to be the youngest of the three brothers. Everything else is clear. Farewell, illustrious man, and keep me in your thoughts.

ECLOGUE 5, VAUCLUSE, AUGUST 22-31, 1347

THE SHEPHERDS' AFFECTION

MARTIUS[12]: Why is our revered mother so afflicted, brother? What can have happened to her to cause such groans? Why is she so full of sadness, and why does she constantly shed fresh tears, when our own eyes are not even moistened?

APICIUS: The fleeting years devour everything. Time, itself unconquerable, conquers all things. Our mother's fortune has vanished, and her beauty; and vigorous youth turns its back on withered old age.

MARTIUS: But look around and see how many aged women are still hale and hearty in spite of the pressing years.[13] The source of her sorrow is different. These sighs spring from her bleeding heart for other reasons. Our love urges us to discover these causes and, when discovered, to combat her destiny. Our filial duty commands us, and our mother's excellence demands it in return for the labors of childbirth and for her constant and tender care for us.

APICIUS: Nature will brook no interference. Though all the powers unite against her, though mankind summons every art and struggles in the vain contest, Nature will proudly raise her unconquered head and will scorn all fetters.

MARTIUS: But this very Nature of whom you speak, Apicius, wills that our parents be almost equal to the gods.

APICIUS: Yes, and this same Nature forbids us to divert the course of life; forbids us to derange the established order of things. Our mother cannot regain the vigor of her youth. But there is another duty that claims our attention. Let each of us think of his spouse and consider how best to aid his infant children.[14]

MARTIUS: And are we to do nothing for our mother? As for myself, my concern for our widowed mother is greater. I can conceive no dearer duty.[15]

APICIUS (*aside*): What prevents my pretending affection? Gentle words are only a light burden.[16] (*To Martius*): She alone has given us these shoulders, these hands, these arms. Then let her alone reap the benefits of her gifts. I surely shall not refuse to attend her at whatever hour she calls or to be a staff to her feeble old age.

MARTIUS: The gods in the serene sky have given you wisdom. Now filial affection takes up its arms and asserts its sway. Now you are a son. Brother, do you want us to relieve our mother's need?

APICIUS: Why do you check your words? Speak out. Every delay is torture to one who loves.

MARTIUS: Mother dwells in a home surrounded by shady groves and built on a hill.[17] For many years her sons – who until recently demonstrated a noble spirit – adorned their home with loyal care. The fame of their mother was great in the land. She stirred abundant envy throughout the woodland pastures. She was blessed in her children and renowned for her rustic treasures. She ruled as queen of the forests when envious death snatched her children from that disconsolate mother. The clay perished, but their fame lives on. We, on the contrary, are put off with promises in our youthful years and live a life of mockery. The seeds of fame are still among us, but they are buried deep in darkness. In our times our home has suffered change. Our fortunes, which had remained unimpaired over the years, sank unable to resist our own mad fury. We must now rebuild this ruined home for our mother. Nothing could give her greater pleasure than to see ancient times return and see her children, whom the fates weigh down, spring again from the shattered graves.

APICIUS: Men are numbered by the thousands; their cares by the millions. Each man considers himself a sage. But where do these dreams of yours come from, brother? In this world just to ward off poverty is a heavy task that shows no hope of ending. As for us, our fortune is so spiteful that, toil as we may, we can barely squeeze out a living from the forest. I shall mention facts well known to you, brother. In the present condition of the countryside, we do not draw a comfortable life from theft and plunder combined. As matters stand we cannot drive home our booty even from sheepfolds that are well provided. In spite of all this, would you begin building a new home for our mother, who is so soon to descend into the grave?

MARTIUS: Not a new home, no! I only wish to repair the shameful ruins of our former home. Come, dear brother! Give me your hand and courageously assume your share of the burden. Let your filial duty remain unconquered and let it overcome all obstacles. Let us dry our mother's tears and soothe her sorrowing heart at the same time, lest she grieve that she has given birth to such sons.

APICIUS: Useless cares distract your mind. Your hopes are vain for a progeny like the one that once peopled the plains far and wide – a hardy band not content with its own walls or small holdings. We are now reduced to a mere handful. The wilderness will nourish us with wild berries from now on. Our spacious grotto with its double roof will shelter us from the threatening skies and ward off the winds and rains. Our mother will live with us alternately, attending festivals of both houses and will thus enjoy a double homage.[18]

MARTIUS: True, Apicius, but she will be despised and abused by our haughty wives and will have to bow her head to her domineering daughters-in-law.[19] No, abandon your plan and listen to a better one. Let us both protect our mother's home and with due reverence worship the threshold that her sacred feet have touched.[20] I make no harsh demand. It is sweet for you to aid an aged mother. I will not feel shame at being seen early in the morning standing at the entrance, anxious for her every command.[21] Why should we not toil over our own flocks and reconstruct the customary home of our household gods? From this our children's children will inherit their power. Let there be only one house; let there be no divided authority and no division of honors among brothers. Our neighbors will live in fear of us if we stand united, and true worth will win greater respect than the sword. Let us gird ourselves for the task before us. Some things become easier for those who try. Mother herself will lend her assistance if she only perceives our friendly disposition; for she rears a flock of sheep and a herd of bullocks,[22] the foundation of our entire wealth and substance.

To deceive a mother's expectations is only for children. Long years ago, mother buried remnants of our former fortunes and a large quantity of salt[23] that she had secretly and lovingly prepared for her sheep. They were so fond of it, and by sprinkling it around she made their grazing more flavorful. In addition, an impetuous stream, descending from the high mountain range, flows down to our ancient orchards, to the shaded valleys of Tempe, to the abodes of Saturn and to all the lands that we once possessed beyond its northern bank, but which our cruel Lydian guest now holds.[24]

With its raging waters this stream checks the further progress of our feeble mother when she desires to revisit her pastures. A bridge once spanned it, a bridge that had been built by the hands of our revered ancestors and stood firm until this day. On this bridge one night a keen shepherd seized those stealthy robbers who had plotted death for the flock and destruction for the forest. That shepherd punished the robbers with death, as they deserved. But it was your right hand, Apicius, as you well know, that hurled this bridge into the swollen waters. In your haste to harm me you inflicted an injury on our mother, on yourself, on our flocks, and on our entire forest home.[25] But I avoid recriminations. The bridge now demands our earnest attention and, though innocent of all blame myself, I shall not refuse to shoulder my share of the burden.

APICIUS: It was your continued arrogance, brother, that drove me to commit the deed. But we possess a small skiff in which anyone who wants to cross may do so easily. Only a small parcel of land remains on the farther side of the stream.[26] Fortune has circumscribed our extensive possessions and has marked out for us the same boundaries that it originally set for the two brothers whose relations were as friendly as ours. Scanty were the lands of our earliest ancestors; scanty are those of their last descendants. Between the two periods our fathers extended their territory, but daring wins only happy results, not permanent ones. Look, all things have returned to their primitive state. Base Fortune amuses herself with her incessant whirl. What if we do remain without a bridge? Isn't it safer on the bank for that very reason? As for the rest, it is somewhat too late to erect a new home when our mother's feet are already on the brink of the grave.

FESTINUS: Why do you both waste the passing hours in useless wrangling? Your younger brother – whom you used to keep under foot – is now lord of the forests. He has already laid the foundations of new palaces on the ancestral estate. Your mother has entrusted her lands and flocks to him. She now rests securely on her son's breast. All classes swear allegiance to him; and though a youth, he is burdened with the cares of an aged statesman and stands alert with drawn sword. Beneath the trees of the forest snares have been spread to catch the feet of birds and the necks of thieves.[27] Strong bolts guard the well-fed and tender sheep against thirsting wolves. The ill-humored bear no longer growls; the blood-thirsty boar has stopped his raging, the serpent his hiss. The swift lions no longer drive their prey away, nor do the eagles fasten their hooked talons on the lamb.[28]

High on a lofty eminence the guardian shepherd sits, singing sweetly to his flock. The pasture lands rest quietly in the lap of security. And now both shores listen to his song.[29] The far-off Calabrian hears it, and the remote waters of the Ligurians, and those who dwell on the curving shores of cleft and wave-breaking Pelorus. If he were only to raise his voice, he would arouse the Moors and the shepherds of India,[30] the snows of the North and the parching sands of the South. He bids you hold your tongues. Go home and shear the helpless sheep. Your dear mother protests that you are not the fruit of her womb and vows that you were fraudulently substituted in place of her true children. You, Apicius, were sent against us by the neighboring valley where the wild herds and the flocks of Spoleto go out to reap the lush meadows of the Apennine forest. The pasture lands and the distant region of the Rhine gave you birth, Martius.[31]

MARTIUS: Now I remember; I had heard some old herdsmen say so.

NOTES

1. On Cola's coronation and the events surrounding it, see Gabrielli, *Epistolario*, 16, pp. 39-48; Burdach and Piur, Letter 28, 2.3: 106-16; Mollat, *Popes*, 150-51; Mollat and Wolff, pp. 101-2; and Wilkins, *Life*, p. 67-68. For background see Duprè Theseider, "L'attesa escatologica."

2. See also Burdach and Piur, Letter 26, 2.3: 94-99; and Wilkins, *Life*, p. 67. For the excerpted text of this letter see also Ernest Hatch Wilkins, trans. and ed., *Petrarch at Vaucluse* (Chicago: University of Chicago Press, 1958), 69-71. Thomas G. Bergin, trans. and ed., *Petrarch's Bucolicum carmen* (New Haven: Yale University Press, 1974), 225-26, quotes extensively from the translation of Petrarch's commentary in E.H.R. Tatham, *Francesco Petrarca, The First Modern Man of Letters*, 2 vols. (London: Sheldon Press, 1925-26), 2: 407-8.

3. In *Familiares* 13.8 (Bernardo 2: 204-6; Wilkins, *Vaucluse*, pp. 119-23; Bishop, *Letters*, pp. 122-25) addressed to Francesco Nelli, prior of Santi Apostoli at Florence, and dated to the summer of 1352, Petrarch describes his simple life at Vaucluse, closing with some pertinent remarks on the contrast between his retreat by the Fountain of the Sorgue and nearby Avignon. He speaks as follows (Fracassetti, *Epistolae* 2: 252, and *Lettere* 3: 262, n. 1; Bernardo 2: 206):

> What would you have me do? I could, perhaps, pass my life here were Italy not so far away, or Avignon so near. To tell the truth, why should I try to conceal my soul's two weaknesses? My love for the former soothes and torments me; my hatred of the latter enrages and exasperates me. Its most horrid stench brings a plague on the entire world. What wonder, then, if it has polluted the clear, pure atmosphere of a modest country seat that is all too near? This stench will drive me out of here – I have a premonition of it.
>
> You are now informed of my present way of life. There is nothing that I desire except you and the few friends who still survive. There is nothing that I dread except a return to the cities. Farewell.

CHAPTER 6, VAUCLUSE, AUGUST 22-31, 1347

4. Pliny, *Naturalis historia* 18.22 (51), 190: *Est in Narbonensi provincia nobilis fons Orge nomine.*

5. Vaucluse and its beauties are spoken among others in *Epistolae poeticae* 1.4 (Wilkins, *Vaucluse,* pp. 15-18), which invites Dionigi Roberti di Borgo San Sepolcro to visit Vaucluse; and in 1.6, which extends a similar invitation to his very dear friend Philippe de Cabassole, bishop of Cavaillon. The dates assigned to these compositions are 1339 and 1346, respectively, hence they are both earlier than the present letter to Cola.

6. The *Eclogues* were begun in the summer of 1346 (Gaspary, *Geschichte* 1: 431; Wilkins, *Life,* p. 57). Since the eclogue that Petrarch now added, *"Pietas pastoralis,"* is the fifth "chapter" in the series, it is clear from this passage that at least Eclogues 1 to 4 were composed during the preceding summer. Wilkins (*Life,* p. 61) dates these to the summer or early autumn of 1347.

7. In *Familiares* 10.4, addressed to his brother Gerardo and dated Padua, December 2, 1348, Petrarch gives a lengthy exposition of the meaning of Eclogue 1, entitled *Parthenias.* See Bernardo 2: 69-73.

8. This passage has confused earlier translators. The phrase that has caused the misunderstanding consists of the two words, *Iter illud* (Fracassetti, *Epistolae* 3: 411). *Iter* has regularly been taken in the sense of road or highway (Fracassetti, *Lettere* 5: 370; Victor Develay, *Pétrarque: Lettres à Rienzi* (Paris: Librairie des Bibliophiles, 1885), 1: 79, 2: 121 and note). Victor Develay has repeated his version in *Pétrarque: Églogues,* 2 vols. (Paris: Librairie des Bibliophiles, 1891), 1: 90, note. Compare Giuseppe Adorni's translation of Eclogue 5 in Domenico Rossetti, *Poesie Minori del Petrarca, sul testo latino ora corretto, volgarizzate da poeti viventi o da poco defunti,* vol. 1 (Milan: Società Tipografica de' Classici Italiani, 1829), 69-87 and notes on pp. 265-70. See especially pp. 80-82.

Using this meaning for *Iter illud,* translators have been compelled to give a forced and untrue reading of the passage in *Variae* 42 (Fracassetti, *Epistolae* 3: 411, *Iter illud....non ignoras*), and also the corresponding passage in Eclogue 5 (Avena, p. 117, vss. 88-92; Bergin, *Bucolicum carmen,* p. 66). In fact, in Eclogue 5 there is no mention whatsoever of *la strada* of Fracassetti or of *la route* of Develay. Eclogue 5 and Letter 6 were sent to Cola at the same time and must have been composed within a brief interval. In writing the letter Petrarch could not have so forgotten the substance of the eclogue as to refer to a road in Eclogue 5 that he had not mentioned there. The only meaning that can be correctly given to *Iter illud,* then, is "that course," meaning the river whose course is outlined there. Only with this interpretation do the cities and districts mentioned by Petrarch remain in their proper geographical position, being named in order according to the southward flow of the Tiber from its source to its mouth and not according to the northward direction of any road leading out from Rome. Furthermore such a reading gives the solution of the *ulterius* of Letter 6, which had been an insurmountable obstacle to commentators.

It should be noted in passing that Petrarch indulges here in a play on words, if he is not actually dabbling in philosophy. He connects *Hortanum* with *hortus*, *Sutrium* with *Saturnus*, *Umbria* with *umbrosus*. In commenting on the corresponding passage of Eclogue 5, Piendibeni says (Avena, p. 269):

> to the ancient orchards: the city of Orte, which is an ancient city; the shaded valleys of Tempe: the delightful valley of Spoleto; the abodes of Saturn: that is, Sutrium, so called from Saturn. Defeated by his son Jupiter, he (Saturn) hid in these parts, whence Latium, so called from his hiding (*a latendo*).

For more recent work see Bergin, *Bucolicum carmen*, p. 227, ll. 88-90, who agrees with Cosenza.

9. Pliny, *Naturalis historia* 3.5 (8), 50: *Umbros inde exegere antiquitus Pelasgi, hos Lydi, a quorum rege Tyrrheni, mox a sacrifico ritu lingua Graecorum Thusci sunt cognominati.*

10. Cicero, *In Catilinam* 3.2, 5-6 and 3.3, 6.

11. *Aeneid* 4.174.

12. The Latin text also appears in Burdach and Piur, Letter 26, 2.3: 87-93. See also Bergin, *Bucolicum carmen*, pp. 58-73 and notes pp. 225-27. Biblioteca Medicea-Laurenziana Codex 33, Plut. 52 contains a commentary on the *Eclogues* that Rosetti and Hortis have ascribed to Petrarch's friend, Donato degli Albanzani. Avena (pp. 84 ff.), however, cannot agree with them and argues that for the present the commentary must be attributed to an anonymous author. We quote from this debated commentary (Avena, p. 207):

> The argument of the eclogue is as follows. When the Roman power had been reduced to its lowest state and had been divided between two factions (that of the Orsini and that of the Colonna, to which families all the other noble and prominent houses and the entire people gave their adherence), among other causes of strife between said Colonna and Orsini, the following became the chief cause.
>
> The Colonna wished that the Roman Senate and power should have their seat on the Campidoglio, as had been the ancient custom; the Orsini, on the other hand, stated their desire that that same Senate have its seat at their home, the Castello Sant' Angelo; or else, that it should be stationed there when the rule of the city lay in their hands, and, in turn, at the home of the Colonna, that is to say at San Marcello, when the rule of the city fell to these. For each house ruled supreme in alternate months. In this way the state was divided: the Orsini desired to drag the Senate off to a strange and private abode; the Colonna, on the contrary, to its neutral and customary abode. Therefore, the title of the eclogue is "The Shepherds' Affection" (*Pietas pastoralis*), because the shepherds speak of a queen as if of their mother, widowed, desolate, and abandoned.

CHAPTER 6, VAUCLUSE, AUGUST 22-31, 1347

The speakers are Martius – that is, the house of the Colonna, which has risen to the height of power by force of arms (for this has ever been a warlike house), and Apicius, that is, the house of the Orsini, for apitiosus means bald, without hair; and the bear itself is an animal without a tail, and so Apicius represents the house of the Orsini. Festinus is Rumor, in other words a messenger, so called because he travels swiftly. These two, Martius and Apicius, speak of Rome herself as if of their mother; for Rome had begotten them, hence she is their mother; and for this reason the eclogue is entitled "The Shepherds' Affection," because the conversation is as if it concerned their actual mother.

The early commentators reached some strange conclusions in trying to explain the symbolism of the three characters of this eclogue. Martius is, as a rule, correctly interpreted, being identified by Biblioteca Apostolica Vaticana, Cod. Vat. Lat. 1679 and by Avena's N commentator with Stefano Colonna himself (Avena, pp. 76, 266, 267). Codex N attributes Petrarch's calling Martius warlike to the fact that a member of the Colonna family caused the death of Pope Boniface VIII (Avena, p. 266).

Apicius has caused greater confusion. The author of argument D explains it in words reminiscent of Petrarch himself (Avena, p. 85): *Appitius domus Ursina ab appitio summo in arte epulandi magistro.* Cod. Vat. Lat. 1677 is also correct. Cr. gives Apicius as the proper name of one of the Orsini (Avena, p. 266). N gives a new variant, explaining in a wild and rambling manner that Apicius is derived "from a (privative), that is 'without,' and *pictos*, that is *pietas*: hence, without affection (*sine pietate*) or without a cap (*sine apice*), that is to say without the cap (*sine birrieto*) that he himself used to wear, and hence Apicius stands for Messer Rinaldo degli Orsini" (Avena, p. 266).

Festinus, finally, is explained by the author of argument D as the Roman people, so called for their fickleness (Avena, p. 73). This is repeated by Cr. and by C.B., the former adding the saving clause, "or it may be understood as Rumor" (Avena, p. 266). C.B. lastly offers the suggestion that Festinus may be Petrarch himself.

Enough has been said to demonstrate how far from the truth the early commentators strayed. It also shows that in Petrarch's words: "the nature of these compositions is such that, unless the author provide the key, their meaning might not be divined. In fact, they are likely to remain quite unintelligible."

13. Francesco Piendibeni da Montepulciano gives Padua as an example of a city that is even older than Rome and is still hale and hearty. See Avena, p, 267. See also Bergin, *Bucolicum carmen*, p. 227, l. 7.

14. Cod. 33, Plut. 52, Laur. (Avena, p. 208): "We must think of our cities, and castles, and farms, and of all the property that we possess in our own right; and let each one consider how best and legally to aid his infant children, that is, the peoples and all those subject to us, and the farmers who attend us or serve us

and obey our orders." The indiscriminate shifting between the singular and the plural is a faithful reproduction of the Renaissance original.

15. Piendibeni (Avena, p. 268): "And by this the author means to show that the Orsini always disregarded the welfare of the state, striving instead for their own private advantage."

16. We are indebted for the suggestion to make this verse (24) an aside remark in Cod. 33, Plut. 52, Laur. (Avena, p. 209): *et ideo, postquam intra se hoc dixerat, ad Martium dirigit sermonem.* Compare the rendering of Develay, *Lettres à Rienzi*, 2: 113: *Qui t'empêche de l'aimer? De douces paroles coûtent peu.* Compare also his translation of Eclogue 1.82-83, where the above reading has been repeated unchanged. See Bergin, *Bucolicum carmen*, p. 227, l. 24, which agrees with this reading.

17. Cod. 33, Plut. 52, Laur. (Avena, p. 209): "that is on the mountain itself (the Campidoglio) with its many palaces constituting a veritable forest (*more silvarum conditis*), and with its towers and very lofty halls."

18. Compare above n. 12; also Avena, pp. 211, 269, and note.

19. See Cod. 33, Plut. 52, Laur. (Avena, p. 211). These represent the barons and the princes "who are consorts of the cities adjoining and bordering on Rome: the Colonna, the Orsini, the Conti, the Savelli, and the others who rule all those cities. Therefore when he [Petrarch] says daughters-in-law, he means the cities betrothed by the ancestors of these same princes."

20. Cod. 33, Plut. 52, Laur. (Avena, p. 211) would render: "which sacred feet have touched," meaning those of the ancient Roman heros.

21. Piendibeni (Avena, p. 269): "This (i.e., the willingness of Martius to stand at the entrance) may be understood to signify that, when the Senate was convened in the home of the Orsini, the Colonna did not go there, and conversely."

22. Cod. 33, Plut. 52, Laur. (Avena, p. 212) explains the sheep as *ipsos populares homines qui labore et sudore vivunt*; the bullocks, as *cives bonos romanos*. Piendibeni explains the latter as *potentates et magnates alios* (Avena, p. 269).

23. See Gregorovius 6.1: 256. Bergin, *Bucolicum carmen*, p. 227, ll. 83-84, discusses the various translations of this and the previous lines.

24. The reference is to the prefect of the city, Giovanni di Vico, who had been tyrant of Roman Tuscany, that is, of the Patrimony of St. Peter in Tuscany. See Papencordt, pp. 23-24.

This verse is spoken before the arrival of Festinus; it occurs, therefore, in that portion of the eclogue that describes conditions in Rome before the elevation of Cola on May 20. Therefore it cannot be argued from this verse that the eclogue was composed before the news of Vico's submission reached Avignon, that is, before August 21. The date of this eclogue, however, can be inferred from other data. In Chapter 5, n. 6, we tried to prove that the letter was written on the arrival of a messenger from Rome bringing news of Vico's downfall. The consequent doubts arising in the papal court and the equivocal position in which Petrarch was placed were the causes, we think, of his leaving the troubled waters of Avignon and seeking the quiet haven of Vaucluse. Both *Variae* 42 and

Eclogue 5 should therefore be dated only a few days later than Letter 5 (*Variae* 40), that is somewhere between August 22 and 31, 1347.

From the point involved in the word "Lydian," see above, p. 64, n. 9. With the statement of Pliny given there compare the similar account given by the author of Cod. 33, Plut. 52, Laur. (Avena, p. 212) and the myth reported by Piendibeni (Avena, p. 269).

25. See Chapter 2, pp. 27-28, n. 13. Cod. 33, Plut. 52, Laur. (Avena, p. 213): "Recently, however, during the time of these Colonna and Orsini, and because the Colonna had part of their possessions across the bridge (i.e., the Ponte Molle), the Orsini destroyed that bridge, *which still remains in ruins.*" This codex dates from the end of the fourteenth, or the beginning of the fifteenth century. See Avena, p. 26. The clue given here by the commentator, if properly traced, would assist in establishing either the date when the Ponte Molle was finally restored, or the date of the composition of the commentary contained in this codex, or, finally, the identity of the commentator himself. Compare the account given by Piendibeni (Avena, pp. 269-70). See also Bergin, *Bucolicum carmen*, p. 227, l. 93.

26. Compare above, n. 24.

27. Piendibeni strangely explains (Avena, p. 271): "of birds: the less important men; of thieves: the powerful and mighty; feet: some were hung by the feet, others by the neck."

28. If only Petrarch had distinctly stated the identity of these wild animals. The families for which they stand are likely to remain veiled. The bear represents the Orsini, of course, and all the manuscripts have so identified it. From Gregorovius we derive the further information that the bear was to be found only on the coat of arms of the Monte Rotondo branch of that powerful family (5: 40, n. 1; compare Papencordt, p. 21).

The remaining animals have different claimants. The boar has been variously identified with the Colonna (Piendibeni in Avena, p. 271 and n. 2), with the Tebaldi (Cod. N, Avena, p. 271, n. 2), and with the Conti of Tusculum (Re, p. 372). The serpent has been identified with the Gaetani (Re, p. 372) and the Anibaldi (Cod. V, Avena, p. 271, n.2). The lions are almost certainly meant for the Savelli (Gregorovius 5: 643, n.1; Re, p. 372; compare Piendibeni in Avena, p. 271). The eagles seem to represent the prefect of the city, Giovanni di Vico (Papencordt, p. 23; Piendibeni in Avena, p. 271), though Re identifies them with another branch of the Conti of Tusculum (p. 372), and Codex M of Piendibeni's *Commentary* with the Conti of Rome (Avena, p. 271, n.2). See also Bergin, *Bucolicum carmen*, p. 227, ll. 124-27.

29. Cod. 33, Plut. 52, Laur. (Avena, p. 215): *adriaticum et occeanum*; Piendibeni (Avena, p. 271): *Italie et Affrice*; Codex N (Avena, p. 271, n. 2): *calabrie et lombardie*. Judging from Petrarch's verses immediately following, it is certain that, without reference to East or West, to North or South, he meant simply that all of the Italian peninsula had been awakened by the reports of Cola's deeds. Those beyond the confines of Italy, "the Moors and the shepherds of India," will be aroused if Cola were only to "raise his voice."

30. *Vita* 1.12, cols. 765, 767; Wright, pp. 50-51.

> The fame of so virtuous a man spread throughout the entire world. All Christendom was aroused, as if awakening from sleep. A certain citizen of Bologna, who had been a slave of the Sultan of Babylon, was the first who recovered his freedom. He made his way to Rome as directly as he could. He said that it had been reported to the great Rajah that a man of the people – a man of great justice – had risen to power in the city of Rome. At this, the Rajah, fearing for himself, answered and said: "May Mahomet and Saint Elimason help Jerusalem," that is to say, the country of the Saracens.

The credulity of the medieval chronicler, and the unconscious, bitter satire of the anecdote are both delightful.

31. Compare Chapter 2, pp. 24-25, n. 4.

CHAPTER 7

PROVENCE, AUGUST-SEPTEMBER 1347

After the first of August events at Rome developed very rapidly. In a letter to the pope written between August 15 and 31, Cola di Rienzo reported the astonishing details of his coronation on August 15, 1347.[1] Even before receiving this letter, on August 21, 1347 Clement VI had written to Cardinal Bertrand de Déaulx, informing him, among other things, of the coronation of the tribune that was to have taken place on August 15. He could draw this information from Cola's letter of August 5, which he may have received on the very morning of August 21, and from which, in fact, he quotes. We present the pertinent portion of the pope's letter here[2]:

> Afterward, however, and before the said letters of ours had reached them, the said bishop and Cola dispatched ambassadors and envoys to us[3] and humbly requested that we confirm them in the office of tribune or at any rate renew the grant of such office for them. While we deliberated with our brethren [in Consistory?] over what was to be done in the matter, we learned from the indirect and direct reports of many that Cola, not content with the title of Rector conferred on him by us, but still styling himself Tribune, had, together with several of his fellow-citizens, girded himself with the belt of knighthood on the first of August just passed. We learned, furthermore, that he had appointed the day of the Assumption of the Blessed Virgin Mary (which is likewise just passed but which was then still to come) for receiving the laurel wreath, with which, as he claims,[4] tribunes used to be crowned in ancient times. We learned also that he had invited to the coronation the syndics of all the cities and of all the famous places of Italy; that he had begun to strike a new currency and to make many other innovations. Among other innovations, he is said to have issued various orders to several individuals and to communes within the territory of the church and to have imposed on them unaccustomed tax burdens. From these facts it is palpably evident

69

that he is aiming at the occupation and the usurpation of the territory of that same church, to withdraw it from the dominion of said church, and to subject it to the sway of the Romans.

It is likely, we suppose, that these and other innovations instituted in that city have come to your notice; and unless an opportune remedy be quickly applied, perilous scandals and serious dangers may arise from these – as your discretion can readily understand. Therefore, desiring to prevent such scandals and such dangers and hoping that a timely and effectual remedy may be employed by the exercise of your foresight and by the grace of God, we, by this apostolic letter, bid your discretion that without delay you get ready to go at a moment's notice as far as the city or its neighborhood, provided this can be done without serious prejudice to the conduct of those affairs in the kingdom of Sicily [Naples] that have already been entrusted to you. We bid you to go there that you may provide against such innovations and for the safety of the city in accordance with the power conferred on you by your liege lord and that you may diligently strive to provide a remedy in due season, for every possible avenue must be closed to the dangers and the evils that can arise.

We shall unhesitatingly dispatch to you whatever letters seem necessary to you for this purpose, whatever letters, indeed, you yourself will ask for and dictate. For it seems to us and to our brethren that these affairs of the city absolutely require either your presence or that of some other of our brethren, [this is] on account of their great difficulty and the dangers that must be avoided – dangers that threaten a very probable loss unless proper measures for their remedy be taken in advance. If, however, the management of affairs in the kingdom of Sicily renders your presence so indispensable that you may not absent yourself without serious prejudice, then do not fail to inform us immediately through our beloved son...the bearer of these presents, both of the impossibility of your leaving and of whatever you judge that we can advantageously do with reference to these matters in the city.

In order, however, that you may be more fully informed regarding what has already been done in these matters, we enclose copies of letters that we have recently forwarded to the bishop, to Cola, and to the Roman people, and we also enclose copies of other letters. Finally, we have sent a full statement of our information concerning the above-mentioned matters to our venerable brother Matteo, bishop of Verona, and we have provided that he be assigned to the city and ultimately to you.

Given at Avignon, on August 21, and in the sixth year [of our pontificate].

We may safely assume that Cola was no more expeditious in sending the pope a report of what had occurred on August 15 than he had been in making a report of what had occurred on August 1 and 2. We saw that on that occasion his letter was dated August 5, representing a delay of three days, even assuming that Messer Giovanni started on his journey the very same day. A similar, or even a shorter, delay on the present occasion of the coronation would have afforded ample time for some papal agent, Bishop Raymond, for example, to draw up a scathing indictment of Cola's six-part coronation. On August 21, therefore, the pope was sufficiently alarmed to bid Cardinal Bertrand to keep a watchful eye on Rome and, if possible, to move to that city from his post at the Neapolitan court.

The reports of the deeds of August 15 must have been raining in on the pope from all sides during the last days of August. His displeasure with Cola must have been mounting higher and higher, for, instead of continuing to crush the barons, the tribune was now turning his attention to questions affecting the papal states in Italy and extending the rights of Roman citizenship to all Italians in imitation of ancient days. Whatever sentiments of mercy and forbearance the pope may have nourished must have been quite thoroughly stifled by the ultramontane cardinals who surrounded him. Therefore it is quite possible that by the time the unsuspecting messenger bearing Cola's coronation letter[5] reached the south of France, the pope and his household had already decided on an actual break with Rome and on open opposition to the tribune. The thorough beating administered to this innocent messenger was the first blow struck after this decision had been reached and the turbulent Durance had become a fourteenth-century Rubicon.

Whether the instructions for such a beating were issued by the pope himself or by one of the cardinals of his household is a matter that we cannot decide. The only statement that we have is that of Cola himself; and in this connection it must, of course, be taken with all due caution. In his letter of September 17, written to the papal notary, Rinaldo Orsini, he says[6]:

> We are not writing to our liege lord the pope nor to other cardinals because we believe that a worthy embassy representing both ourselves and the Roman people will be dispatched to the Curia. Nor do we intend to trouble ourselves about keeping many representatives at the papal court. God and the truth, to whom all hearts lie open, will judge between us and our detractors. We are fully aware, indeed, that as a reward for our good works we are assailed in Avignon undeservedly, yes even to displeasing God. We are fully aware that we are charged there with the sin of having taken care of our person on the Sabbath, and this, indeed, by men who regard our works madness and our life disgraceful. Our hope is in God, from whom we hope for everlasting rewards hereafter.
>
> Yesterday [September 16] I received news that as our messenger was approaching the Curia with dispatches, and just as he had advanced beyond the Durance, his letters were taken away from him and torn in pieces; the wand that he bore was broken over his head; the letter case that hung at his side was likewise snatched from him and shattered; and finally, he was told that instructions had been issued for a similar reception to each and every one of our couriers.[7] And so he has returned to us empty-handed and with his head covered with gore. The reverence due to our lord and master the pope subdues and checks the righteous indignation of my soul, great though it be. Otherwise, in defense of our courier, we should take legal action against the ruler, the governing body, and the people of the city of Avignon.
>
> With a struggle we yield to the reverence due to our lord and master the pope, hoping that such evils may be corrected by an edict of His Holiness so that they may not recur in the future. However, we reserve for the deliberation of our own parliament the question of taking said legal action.

Given on the Campidoglio, where we live a righteous life under the reign of justice, on the seventeenth day of the month of September, in the first indiction, and in this first year of the city's freedom.

Petrarch received the news of the beating of Cola's courier at the Fountain of the Sorgue during the first week of September. His indignation and his anger immediately urged him to write the following letter to Cola,[8] the most bitter and the most violent that he had yet penned against Avignon and the enemies of the Romans.[9]

PETRARCH TO THE PRINCE OF THE ROMANS

(SINE NOMINE 2)

Your Excellency's courier, who has recently experienced cruel treatment, will bear witness to you of the kindness and the mercy, yes, of the justice that you may expect in these quarters. A new species of barbarity that a youth, unescorted, unsuspecting, and entirely innocent of all blame, should have been set upon like an enemy! His ambassador's wand, which they should have respected and feared – if anything is considered sacred in their eyes – and likewise his letter case, which was filled with most important and grateful dispatches, were both plied about his innocent head until they broke to pieces. The letters themselves were torn and scattered to the winds, although they might have softened hearts of stone. This is hospitality! This is charity! Your messenger was seized at the River Druentia. There he was tortured and scourged and forbidden to enter the city. Now, his features covered with gore, he casts himself at your feet and delivers his message of threats and blows and lashes.[10] River, truly are you named the Durance in the common language, for you truly exhibit the hardened insensibility of the inhabitants.[11] In fact, some authors call you the Ruentia, naming you after your rushing current. You are a headlong and destructive stream, but the people dwelling along your banks are no more gentle than the waters rushing in your channels. They, too, are always ready to run with equal fury to commit the most revolting crimes.

O rivers so elated at your shameless deed! O irreverent and impious streams! O Fountain of the Sorgue that swallows waters that are not yours and surges so proudly against your master! O all-corroding Rhone! Is this the way you welcome the Tiber? Is this how you honor Rome, your queen? O Avignon, if we are to believe scholars, you were named from your vineyards that yield most bitter grapes and a vintage of blood. Is this your respect for Rome, your mistress? Is this the way you consider yourself and her position, your slavish condition and her supreme authority? Woe to you, unhappy city, the day she begins to waken from her sleep, yes, woe the day she lifts her head and sees the injuries and the wounds inflicted on her as she slumbered.[12] Even now she is roused. Believe me, she no longer sleeps but is silent, and in her silence she ponders dreams of the past and resolves what must be done when she arises.

Wait a while longer, Avignon, and you will witness mighty deeds performed on earth. You will marvel at the accomplishment of tasks previously judged impossible. Don't you realize who you are, nor where, nor to whom you are subordinate? Don't you know where the name "Provence" comes from? What frenzy is this, what madness? Has forgetfulness of past storms crept insensibly on you merely because the skies have been fair for a while? Is this how you worship her who ruled all the provinces? She was only stunned, and you thought her dead. You thought yourself restored to liberty by the death of your mistress but considered yourself still a slave unless you confirmed your liberty by committing licentious acts. You desired to be of some account in the world; you desired, at any rate, to give this impression to others. For some time and with due deliberation we have gratified your wishes.

But now it is time that you heed our advice and recover your senses. As you know, the power of many does not lie so much in their own strength as in the weakness of others. Such power, therefore, must vanish when the opponent regains his strength. Only then, Avignon, will you know your proper place, when you realize how powerful Rome still is – Rome, whose envoys you now trample into the dust, supposing that there is no one to avenge the wrong. You are deceived; you play the fool; you act like a madman. God will be the avenger in heaven; and on earth one of our fellow beings who truly worships the God you do not know will likewise avenge the deed. There are forces at play whose power you cannot even conceive. Ah, wretched city! I hope that you will shortly discover them by sad experience. The wrongs that you have heaped on us have restored our strength to us. The very moment we began to grieve over them we regained our full health and vigor by great leaps and bounds.[13]

But you, remarkable man, take pity on our condition. Give your hand to the state that struggles to rise to its feet and prove to these men of little faith the power that Rome still possesses.[14] As for the rest of Italy, who can doubt that it can again regain the power it once wielded? To accomplish this end I maintain that neither strength, nor resources, nor courage is missing. Harmony alone is missing. Give me this, and by the words of this very letter I predict the immediate ruin and destruction of those who deride the name of Italians.[15] And you, I say, you whom the fates have appointed the instrument of this great deliverance, persevere as you have begun. Do not fear; the rays of the sun will dispel the gloomy clouds in your sky. The nets spread by these puny foxes cannot resist the lion's paw. You have made a glorious beginning. Advance bravely and consistently to the very end. Make clear to these men that their pride is far beneath the humiliation of the poor; that avarice is far meaner than generosity; that intrigue coupled with wisdom is folly; and that their passions are scandalous when weighed in the balance against self-restraint and decorum. Finally, let the mask of hypocrisy admit it has no effect when exposed to the brilliant light of true virtue.

Come now, no further delay! Crush, trample, grind under foot this frog that counterfeits the ox's massive bulk with its ridiculous puffing. I do not speak to urge you on. You require no one to incite you, no one to hold you back. You are your own spur, your own rein. I have spoken because I could no longer bear my soul's anguish in silence. Dwelling on my grief has made it sharper and has multiplied my laments. Words have fueled my indignation and, in turn, my indignation my pen. Who, indeed, could see such sights and remain calm? The rights of nations have been outraged in the person of your envoy; the common bond of humanity has been cut apart. Oh, the wrath that made men ignore their honor! Even among the barbarian nations your messenger would have received a kinder reception than among those you considered Romans and to whose good will you were entitled.

Let them turn the pages of history – if, indeed, they have eyes for anything but the riches they regard so longingly. Let them look and answer. What barbarian nation has ever violated the sacred rights of ambassadors, except very rarely, and then only for the gravest reasons? The deceitful and faithless Carthaginian rabble once attempted to maltreat our ambassadors, but their armed hands were checked by the intervention of their magistrates.[16] In the present case who, pray, checked the violence of the people? Who suffered punishment for this shameful deed? But perhaps I demand too much. Who, then, raised his voice in censure or in denunciation? How much safer would it have been for your envoy to travel in the country of the Parthians, where the Roman legions of Crassus were cut off and vanquished! How much more securely would he have gone into Germany, in spite of the slaughtered Teutons and the triumphant Marius! How much more safely guarded in either case than in coming here to represent you, a devout and dutiful son of the Roman church! Surely, neither the insolence of a conqueror nor the rage of the oppressed would have presumed as much as the hatred of your false friends has. Your youthful envoy would have scaled the wooded heights of Pelion and the frozen mountains of Taurus, even in the depth of winter, more easily than he has crossed the valley of Orgon[17] in autumn.[18] He would have swum across the Ganges and the Don with greater freedom than across the Durance.

I wanted to tell you all this merely to give an outlet to my feelings. As for yourself, noble man, do not be swerved from your course by these evildoers nor by the appearances of false power. To be able to inflict injury on others is not true greatness, nor is it a sign of power. The smallest and meanest of insects can do as much. True greatness lies in being able to do good; even nobler is the desire to do good. Very wicked men have had it in their power to harm an innocent boy and to make him this shabby return for the joyful message he bore.[19] What greatness is there in this? In truth, what is it but a power whose value must be reckoned at less than zero? If every sin is to be considered of zero value, then the greater the sin the greater must be its negative value. In any case, then, the greatness of sin – if the term "greatness" may be used in this connection – is always zero. This is the kind of greatness these honorable men have gained by exercising their arts. It is the greatness that a scorpion or a spider might have achieved.

They have vented their wrath on one of your following, but the greater significance of this act of cruelty is that they wished to harm you. Nor do I mean you personally but as the defender of liberty and justice. This, and no other, is the cause of their hatred for you. Indeed, they hate liberty and justice in themselves, knowing full well that such concepts are diametrically opposed to the regime that is their pride. Consider the loftiness of your own soul and you will scorn and despise the arrogant and empty goal that they have set for themselves. The measures that they have adopted are violent and severe, but after all they are matters of small significance. Far greater questions are at stake. These petty outbursts of their wrath will pass away just as other things of this earth, and avenging your envoy is only part of the vengence that the state will exact. Farewell, and may you bring to completion the work that you have begun.

NOTES

1. See Gabrielli, *Epistolario* 22, pp. 58-60; Burdach and Piur, Letter 35, 2.3: 128-31; and Frederic Duncalf and August C. Krey, "The Coronation of Cola di Rienzo," in *Parallel Source Problems in Medieval History* (New York: Harper & Row, 1912), 177-237.

2. Theiner 2, no. 175, pp. 179-80, beginning with the words *Post hoc autem*. See also Burdach and Piur, Letter 15, 2.4: 38-41.

3. That is, Messer Giovanni, with the letter of August 5.

4. See Cola's letter of August 5 in Gabrielli, *Epistolario*, p. 43, l. 1; Burdach and Piur, Letter 28, 2.3: 106-16. On Cola as tribune see also Arsenio Frugoni, "Cola di Rienzo 'tribunus sompniator'," in *Incontri nel Rinascimento* (Brescia: La Scuola, 1954), 9-23.

5. See n. 1 above.

6. Gabrielli, *Epistolario* 23, ll. 130-51; Burdach and Piur, Letter 40, 2.3: 144-51. See also Chapter 5, pp. 48-52, n. 6, above.

7. See Wilkins, *Life*, p. 70.

8. Ibid.

9. See Piur, pp. 167-71. This letter is also translated in Wilkins, *Vaucluse*, pp. 72-78 and dated September 1347 by him; and in Coogan, *Babylon*, pp. 49-53.

10. We now return again to the complicated subject of postal messengers. We have already tried to prove: first, the identity of the messenger in *Vita* 1.10 as the first messenger sent by Cola to the pope in the early days of June, and

second, the identity of the Giovanni in *Variae* 40 as the messenger of the *Vita* 1.21 and as the bearer of Cola's letter of August 5. See Chapter 5, pp. 48-52, n. 6.

Our task in the case of this beaten courier is not quite so complex. We identify him as the bearer of Cola's third extant letter to the pope, Gabrielli, *Epistolario* 22; Burdach and Piur, Letter 35. In this letter Cola notified his liege lord of his own coronation on August 15, "the fantastic caricature in which ended the imperium of Charles the Great" (Gregorovius 6.1: 284). The letter, therefore, must be dated some time after the coronation date between August 15 and 31. The pope did not know of the actual coronation when he wrote the letter to Bertrand de Déaulx. See Theiner 2, no. 175, August 21, 1347. This letter has enabled us to calculate an interval of sixteen days as the minimum time required for a courier to travel from Rome to Avignon. Such a time period has provided a good working hypothesis. See also Chapter 4, p. 41, n. 1 on distances and speeds of communications.

A more accurate analysis of the incident of the beaten messenger reveals some interesting coincidences. According to Petrarch (Fracassetti, *Epistolae* 3: 532, *Ad Druentiam captus*), the messenger was attacked at the Durance. But Cola, who had received the verbal report of his messenger on September 16, wrote with greater precision on the following day to Rinaldo Orsini, stating that the attack had been made beyond the Durance (Gabrielli, *Epistolario,* p. 66, l. 141; Burdach and Piur, 2.3: 150, l. 137). We shall further remark that, since the letters that the messenger was bearing were torn to shreds and scattered to the winds, it is almost imperative to assume that the pope received the information contained in them from sources other than the tribune. Finally, in connection with the same fact, it is interesting to consider the note by Gabrielli (*Epistolario,* p. 60, n. 1) to the effect that the codex from which he drew *Epistolario* 22 comes to a sudden break, clearly indicating that the letter did not originally end as it does now. This fact may or may not be pertinent to the question of the messenger's torn letters. It has been impossible, however, to resist the temptation to point out these coincidences.

11. Petrarch goes from the classical form of this name, *Druentia,* to the form *Durentia* from which the modern French *Durance* is derived. He furthermore plays on the word, saying that the name *Durance* fitly expresses the *durities* (hardened insensibility) of the inhabitants. In the beginning of the next paragraph Petrarch continues in the same vein, employing adjectives that have the same ring as their nouns: *insurgens Sorga* and *Rhodanus rodens.* The same spirit may have suggested to him a similar play on words in the sentence immediately following, where he refers to the vineyards of Avignon – *O Avinio, cuius vinea* – thus giving a derivation for the name that we have not been able to discover anywhere else.

12. Compare the second stanza of the canzone *Spirto gentil* in Chapter 2, pp. 33-36, n. 33.

13. In case the reader supposes that he has sounded the depths of Petrarch's hatred for Avignon, before the present mild rumblings die away, listen to the deep thunder of the letter *Sine Titulo [Nomine]* 8, *Opera omnia* 7: 718; Piur, *Sine Nomine* 8, pp. 193-95: *Si quicquid animus meus fert.* See also Carducci, pp. 148-49; Coogan, *Babylon,* pp. 64-66; and Wilkins, *Life,* p. 113.

In reading this letter we should not lose sight of the fact that Petrarch's thorough hatred for Avignon was due to its being the home of the papacy. The glory, the power, and the prestige thus acquired by the French city rightfully belonged to Rome. With the Curia situated on the banks of the Tiber, Petrarch felt positive that the many evils distracting and tearing Italy apart, the wars of commune against commune, and the everlasting, widespread contests of Guelphs and Ghibellines, would largely end. Petrarch saw the restoration of the church back to the rock on which it was founded as the first step toward the realization of his most cherished dreams, creating a free and united Italy. In a word, Petrarch was the first Italian to stand out as a patriot along national lines and to voice the sentiments of Italy for the Italians, and the Italians sufficient in themselves. To such a man the continuance of the papal see at Avignon and the undoubtedly scandalous atmosphere reigning in the papal court and consequently throughout the city were more than sufficient cause for his prophetic thunderings.

Unfortunately the letter that we shall quote is among those grouped together as *Sine Titulo [Nomine]*, that is, among the letters in which Petrarch suppressed the names of addressees for fear of the possible consequences from the violent language they used. From internal evidence, however, it is clear that the letter was addressed to a bishop, perhaps to his intimate friend Philippe de Cabassole, bishop of Cavaillon. The text follows:

> I would be afraid, Reverend Father, if I wished to commit to writing all that my soul feels on the condition of affairs in this western Babylon, where I so frequently reside either through fate or, rather, to atone for my sins. My laments would increase my grief, and my inconvenient and useless complaints would interrupt your most holy cares and most honorable occupations. In short, rest assured that neither my pen nor even Cicero's could render the subject justice. Whatever you have read about the Assyrian Babylon or the Egyptian Babylon, whatever you have read about the four labyrinths, about the threshold of Avernus and the forests of Tartarus and its lakes of sulphur is merely a fable when compared to these infernal regions.
>
> Here in Avignon is Nimrod [Pope Clement VI, who was fond of hunting], at the same time builder of turrets and sower of dread; here is Semiramis [Viscountess Cecilia of Turenne, the pope's mistress], armed with the quiver; here is Minos, inexorably severe; here

is Rhadamanthus; here is Cerberus, the all-devouring; here is Pasiphae, yoked to the Bull; here, in Virgil's words [*Aeneid* 6.25-26] is the

Minotaur, of mingled race
Memorial of her foul disgrace.

Here, finally, you may see whatever chaos, whatever virulence, whatever horror that exists or can be conceived of anywhere.

You, who have always been happy in your good qualities, well may you be happy now for your absence from Avignon. Do you think that this city is the way you once saw it? It is far different and far unlike it. The Avignon of former days was, to be sure, the worst of cities and the most abominable of its day. But the Avignon of today can no longer even be considered a city. It is the home of spooks and goblins, of ghosts and specters. In a word, it is now the sink of all iniquities and disgrace; it is now that Hell of the Living sung by David [Ps. 54: 16 (55: 15)] so long before Avignon was founded and known.

Alas! How frequently your truly fatherly advice comes to mind, your wholesome admonitions, when you said as I was preparing for my departure: "Where are you going? What are you doing? What ambition drags you and makes you forget yourself? Don't you know what you are looking for and giving up? This is why I am asking, what are you starting off so eagerly for? Where are you rushing? If I know you well, I assure you that you will regret your course. You have experienced the snares and fetters of the Curia so frequently. Don't you know that once you have been trapped there, you will not be able to free yourself at will?"

When you had finished these and other persuasive arguments, I had no answer to make except that I was returning to well known afflictions because I was held fast by love for my friends. This is how I answered you, nor did I speak falsely. Up to this day I have not regretted that love, but I am uncertain whether I regret having lost my liberty for love of my friends. I assure you that I am grateful for your counsels, so ill received then and now welcomed at a late hour. Until now my ignoring your words of advice has not come without its punishments. But I shall obey you better from now on, if I ever escape from here. I will not despair of this if Christ stretches out his hand. To this end I bend all my energies.

It was a sense of shame, Father, that prevented my writing this to you sooner; since it is shameful and unbecoming for a man to wish what he soon no longer will wish.

14. *Familiari* 6.2; Fracassetti, *Epistolae* I: 314; Bernardo I: 290-95, p. 293: "For who can doubt that Rome would rise again instantly if she began to know herself?"

15. All that has already been said regarding Petrarch's intense patriotism applies equally well to this note. The letter that we print here, *Sine Titulo 9, Opera omnia*, p. 719; Piur, *Sine Nomine 9*, pp. 195-96: *Persecutionum duo sunt genera*, constitutes a more philosophical exposition of Petrarch's ideas on a united Italy:

> There are two kinds of oppression; to one we submit willingly, to the other unwillingly. Someone else may discover more categories; indeed there are innumerable oppressions, as anyone advanced in years is well aware. All of them, however, reduce themselves to an oppression that is either forcibly inflicted or willingly endured. Against our will we endure exile, poverty, theft, disease, imprisonment, slavery, dishonor, chains, torture, the gallows, murder, and death. On the contrary, with our full consent we are weighed down by the yoke of our vices. With our full consent we submit to the rule of the vilest men, either through degenerate fear, or disgraceful inactivity, or dishonoring passivity, or the hope of vile gain. I have given examples from which you may grasp my meaning. You may collect others like them. The former kind of oppression seems to many to be the more severe; but to me the latter is more intolerable, for there the situation is open to discussion, and the calamity receives no compassion.
>
> Contemporary Italy sighs like a slave under the sword of this second form of oppression. She will see the end of her woes only when she begins to wish unity. The conditions are hard, I grant, but they are by no means unattainable. I have said "when she wishes unity," and by this I mean that she will be united not by the victory of this or that party but by the abolition of party lines [*non studiis, sed studiorum termino*] and through an utter disgust for her unmerited slavery.
>
> Oh, gods! We were used to ruling the greatest and the best of the earth; and now how low have we fallen! We are the slaves of the lowest! Hard is the lot, unendurable the change! But, barbarian foreigners, always stupid in the past and now even mad – yes raving mad – you scoff at Italy, your queen. If only all the Italians were of the same mind as I, and that they possessed a firmer purpose but no lesser love than mine! Trumpery and nonsense would soon have been banished, and serious matters would have been set on foot. May the all-powerful God attend to this, if he does not yet hate us to the last; may fortune attend to it, if there be any fortune and if it has any control over human affairs. If, however, you wish me to penetrate beneath the surface and to disclose to you what I really think, I shall say that they scoff with their lips, but they groan in their hearts; that they display a smiling exterior, but they tremble inside. For they know

both us and themselves very well, pretending scorn in place of their hatred and their fear.

Where are my words leading, you ask? I am writing this not because it may be to your advantage to hear it, but because it is to my disadvantage to keep it inside me. My burden is heavy and grievous, and I could entrust it to no one with greater assurance than to you. I have written these words in great haste and indignation, an exile from Jerusalem, dwelling among, and on the banks of, the rivers of Babylon.

16. The facts are these (Livy 30.24, 25). Toward the close of the Second Punic War, in 203 B.C., a truce was established between the Carthaginians and the Romans under Scipio. During this truce, a fleet of two hundred transports set sail from Sicily under the escort of thirty war galleys. The entire expedition was commanded by Cn. Octavius. The wind remained favorable until the fleet was almost within sight of Africa, when a calm ensued. This was followed by adverse winds that dispersed the fleet and stranded the transports all along the African coast within sight of Carthage. Great excitement swept through the Carthaginians, who argued that such an opportunity for inflicting loss on the Romans ought not to be passed by. They compelled their officials to go out and capture the vessels, despite the truce that had been agreed to. Thereupon Scipio sent L. Baebius, L. Sergius, and L. Fabius to the city to register his protests. We shall quote the rest of the story from Petrarch's *Africa* 6, vss. 789-94; Bergin and Wilson, p. 137, ll. 1024-32:

> An angry crowd
> presses around them and a vicious hail
> of stones flies through the air. The ugly mob,
> intent on violence, cries out; had not
> the highest magistrate there intervened
> with his authority, the very laws
> that rule all mankind would have been that day
> defiled by foul and bestial slaughter.

17. Orgon is a small town of 13,660 population in the Department Bouches-du-Rhône. It is situated on the left bank of the Durance, 35 km east-northeast of Arles. It still boasts a church dating from the fourteenth century. See René Oizon, *Dictionnaire géographique de France* (Paris: Larousse, 1979), 580.

18. The expression used by Petrarch: *quam Orgonis planitiem autumnali tempore* (Fracassetti, *Epistolae* 3: 535), excludes any possibility of dating the incident of the beaten courier to the month of August. We do not think that August could be called autumn by any stretch of the imagination. The messenger must have been attacked on September 1 at the very earliest. Allowing a delay of a few days for Cola to send off his Letter 22, the messenger would have left Rome on

August 17 and would have arrived at the Durance in about fifteen days, or September 1. The news of the attack on him must have reached Avignon by September 2, and Petrarch may not of heard of it at Vaucluse until September 3. The dating arguments presented above in n. 10, the present calculation, and Petrarch's *autumnali tempore* therefore concur in dating this letter, *Sine Titulo* [*Nomine*] 2 to the first week of September 1347.

The likelihood that the messenger was beaten on September 1 is also borne out by the following calculation. We may safely assume that at that time of year the courier's return trip to Rome was made as rapidly as he had traveled north. We have fixed September 1 as the day of the attack on him. Adding fifteen days for the return trip, we have the messenger back in Rome on September 16, a date that is corroborated by the "yesterday" of Cola's Letter 23, which is dated September 17. See above, pp. 72-73.

19. It is doubtful whether Petrarch really knew the contents of the torn letter, *Epistolario* 22. His confidence in Cola was still very high, and in the light of this confidence he could very well feel positive that any message from Rome was a message of joy. He may, of course, have received a letter direct from Cola or from some other friend, informing him of the coronation on August 15. He may have heard of it even from Avignon. One thing is certain: this letter, *Sine Titulo* [*Nomine*] 2, the first one to be written after the unpleasant episode at the Durance, is likewise the first one in which Petrarch addresses Cola as Prince of the Romans. To Petrarch the coronation must have represented a divinely appointed consummation of his cherished dream. In Cola's elevation from tribune to Prince of the Romans Petrarch believed that he could look forward to the final settlement of the question of the Holy Roman Empire. He was certain that he could now see above the horizon the star of a united Italy under the benevolent guidance of a man of the Italians, elected by Italians, and working for the Italians.

CHAPTER 8

VAUCLUSE, SEPTEMBER 2-8, 1347

After venting his rage in the last letter, Petrarch returned to enjoy the undisturbed peace of Vaucluse. This quiet retreat, however, was all too near Avignon. He was bound to receive news of what was going on in the papal city; and among the various unpleasant reports that soon reached him one told of a gathering of certain prominent men who calmly debated the question, "Whether or not it would make for the happiness of the world at large that the city of Rome and Italy should be united and should enjoy peace and harmony." Petrarch considered merely suggesting such a topic childish and absurd; and naturally he could not rest easy until he had unburdened his soul by communicating with Cola.[1]

PETRARCH TO THE PRINCE OF THE ROMANS
(*SINE NOMINE 3*)

What now dampens my spirit is light; but it must come out, for if neglected it is sure to destroy my physical well-being. It has stirred up greater anger inside me than one would think possible. Though trifling in itself, it has spawned boundless disgust, for it gives off the stench of a secret, deep, and inveterate hatred. So it seemed to me, and so, I am sure, it will seem to you. I am certain that the incident will become known far and wide and that it will sow the seeds of righteous indignation in the heart of every Roman and every Italian. I am certain that the news will shake off the heavy torpor and again kindle the fire of that noble genius and original vigor to which the nations of the globe once rendered obedience either through choice or necessity. By now, shame! the lowest people scoff at the Romans! The general knowledge of what has occurred will, I hope, accrue greatly to the state's advantage. A small spark can kindle an immense fire, and a single word has marked the beginning of many great movements.

But now for the facts themselves. Their significance will be measured not so much by what I say as by the reader's displeasure. Recently there gathered together certain men who pass as wise in their own opinion but are not quite so in that of others. A doubt prevailed in their minds, which after some time shaped itself into the following inquiry: "Whether or not it would make for the happiness of the world at large that the city of Rome and Italy should be united and should enjoy peace and harmony." The mere suggestion of such a self-evident fact was sufficiently childish and absurd. Yet one might have excused the disputants on the plea that the question offered them an opportunity for displaying their skill as logicians and their powers of debate. After countless arguments had been exchanged, however, the one considered the wisest among them closed the discussion with this venemous statement: "That such an outcome would by no means be advantageous!" And this decision, to tell the truth, was received with great applause and with general approbation.[2]

The next time you address the Roman people, ruler, I beg you, who are endowed with such wonderful eloquence, to acquaint them with this event and to do so in my very words. Let them know what opinions these high and mighty nobles entertain about our safety. Such sentiments can do us no harm, of course; nevertheless their verbosity betrays their innermost feelings. The fate they wish for us, they long for so ardently that they cannot repress themselves. In their shameful blindness and poverty of intellect they greedily cast their hostile vows and prayers in the form of scholarly treatises. But they will perish in their error. We are in the hands of God and shall endure not the fate that they desire for us but what God himself has ordained.

I was not present at this delirious session. I should, perhaps, have saddened the joy of some of those gentlemen, for it would have been neither honorable nor possible for me to keep my peace in the midst of such irreverent prating. As soon as the news reached me, however, I grew enraged with indignation. With what little authority I possess, I rendered the opposite decision to my friends, as I now do to you, the defender of our liberty. I beg of you before all others, ruler, in the name of all the angelic hosts I humbly beseech you, and the Roman people, and all Italy that you confirm by deeds what I have simply asserted.

PETRARCH & COLA DI RIENZO

 ⎧May you live long and prosperously, and may you successfully govern
that republic whose freedom you have so bravely restored. ⎫

NOTES

1. See Piur, pp. 171-73; Wilkins, *Studies,* pp. 179-81.
2. Cola di Rienzo himself referred to this incident three years later. It was during the summer of 1350, when, after having lived in disguise on Monte Maiella
for many months, he had traveled to Prague, the capital city of the Bohemian
emperor-king Charles iv. That August proved to be very busy for Cola. His
letters, very lengthy and detailed, follow one another in rapid succession. The
series begins with a long biographical letter addressed to the emperor. The
next letter, also to the emperor, answers the objections raised by the king and
explains prophecies that call on the king to be the savior of Italy. Then follow
two letters to Johann von Neumark, chancellor of the empire; and finally the
letter from which we shall quote.

It is addressed to Arnest von Parbubitz, archbishop of Prague (Gabrielli,
Epistolario 24, pp. 144-79; Burdach and Piur, Letter 57, 2.3: 231-78) and is dated
Prague, August 1350. Papencordt, relying on an inferior manuscript, dates it
August 15, 1350 (Gabrielli, *Epistolario,* p. 144, n. 2; Papencordt, document on p.
xlii). In the course of a lengthy account of his tribunate, Cola defends his actions and position against those of the church. We cite this passage in its en-
tirety (Gabrielli, *Epistolario* 25, ll. 154-302; Burdach and Piur, p. 241, l. 258-p. 242,
l. 306):

> Therefore, keeping the crucifix of charity before your eyes, which
> of the following two will your paternity consider the defender of
> the church: him who, when the sheep are abandoned, yes afflicted,
> admits and fosters the wolves; or him who leads back and gathers
> together into one fold the sheep scattered by discord and who, in
> defense of those same sheep, gladly exposes himself to the wolves
> and to death? Who will be the real schismatic: he who plants the
> seeds of disunion in the church of God, or he who removes them?
>
> Did I not, with God's help, overthrow the error of the sinners? In
> spite of the rivalry among the Romans, whose deadly partisanship
> was found to have spread to the considerable number of eighteen
> hundred men, did I not cause them to end their bloodshed and to lay
> aside all thoughts of offenses and wrongs among them? Did I not,
> contrary to the expectation of mankind, lead them to a sincere peace?
> Did I not restore true peace among all the hostile cities? Did I not
> decree that all those citizens who were living in exile from their na-
> tive cities because of party strife, should be led back together to their
> poor wives and children? Had I not begun to stamp out completely
> the disuniting names of Ghibelline and Guelph parties, in whose

defense countless thousands of souls and bodies perished under the very eyes of their shepherds? Had I not begun to bring this to pass by welding the city of Rome and the whole of Italy into a single, harmonious, peaceful, holy, and indissoluble union? by collecting and consigning to the different cities the consecrated standards and banners? and, in token of our holy alliance and perfect union, by bestowing with due solemnity on the ambassadors of all the Italian cities gold rings that had been consecrated on the day of the Assumption of our most Blessed Lady?

This union, like all other matters, was accomplished in the presence and with all the approval of him who was then the pope's vicar. Yet our lord the supreme pontiff, owing to the insinuations of wicked men and to his own lack of charity, regarded this union with such great suspicion that the following theme was discussed in the Consistory itself: "Whether the union of Rome and of Italy would be advantageous to the Roman church!" Listen, Father, to the theme of the separatists, of Satan himself, a theme loathsome to both God and angels. To tell the truth, they brought into question whether the cutting off of sinners and the creation of a union had advantage to the believers in Christ, and whether the soundness of the flock benefited the shepherd!

Surely, as long as that union flourished, tyrants trembled, and the peoples gamboled in the pasture lands like lambs. Safety and peace reigned in every direction. The moment that this union was dissolved because of my absence, all things fell again beneath the tyrant's foot. Everywhere wars, attacks, invasions. With the destruction of souls and the butchering of bodies, disunion again raised its head. But in the Consistory there was no debating now on the question whether or not the renewal of such scandalous deeds brought detriment to the Roman church.

Indeed, it appears to them that the church, that is to say the wealth of the cardinals, is increased by the dissensions of cities. In truth, the cardinals consider their Consistory and the entire church as one and the same thing. For, if the cities are divided by discord and wars, each visits the supreme pontiff and the cardinals with gold in its hands, in order to curry favor. If, on the contrary, the cities repose peaceful and united, there is no necessity of their paying visits of this kind. Hence let there be discord everywhere, that the shepherds of the church may receive visitations. Let disease come, that easy access be had to the healer – may it indeed be to a healer and not to a leech! Let the wolves be called so that the sheep may have the shepherd they need and that they may fear him even more. Ah, charity, rejected, condemned, slain, yes, and buried too! Rise up a moment, for our Lord has arisen who was condemned and buried together with you!

CHAPTER 9

PROVENCE-GENOA, SEPTEMBER-NOVEMBER 1347

Events in Rome quickened after Cola's coronation. The struggle against the barons, particularly the Gaetani, continued as bitterly as before. At last, in a desperate attempt to stamp out all opposition, on September 14 Cola invited the barons to a sumptuous banquet on the Campidoglio, at the end of which he treacherously imprisoned them. On the following day, however, preaching on the text "Forgive us our trespasses," he pardoned them all, invested them with high offices, and two days later received communion with them at the church of Santa Maria in Aracoeli. On the very same day, September 17, Cola wrote to the papal notary Rinaldo Orsini, giving him a full account of these events and defending himself against the charges of having taken the bath of knighthood in the basin consecrated by Constantine's conversion; of having helped to desecrate the marble pontifical table in the course of the banquet at the Lateran on August 1, and finally of having acted in a generally childish manner.[1]

Cola's actions were, we grant, open to criticism. The difficulties that beset him made him more and more inconsistent and capricious every day. When he realized that he could not overcome each and every obstacle that presented itself with the same ease as in the early days of his power, he became increasingly irritable. In the months from May to September the close, compact body of the barons had ample time to form a well-organized opposition to the tribune; and the same flight of time made serious inroads into the number of the tribune's loyal friends. But what effect did Cola's actions have on his optimistic champion at Vaucluse?[2]

We shall see below that Petrarch considered Cola's release of the barons a very serious error. Examples of mass murderers – such as Ezzelino da Romano – were not lacking; and had Cola been endowed with the qualities of a real tyrant, he would have committed the deed that everyone expected him to commit under the circumstances in accordance with the standards of the age.[3] But by September 11 Petrarch had not yet heard of these events. There were other causes to disturb his high-strung nature. The affairs of Queen Giovanna's kingdom of Naples were in anything but a reassuring condition.[4] Rumors of the threatened invasion of Italy by Louis I the Great, King of Hungary, began to spread far and wide. Petrarch saw this calamity as punishment for the assassination of King Andrew of Naples. Still, he could not calmly witness the punishment of an innocent population and barbaric hosts treading on sacred Italian soil. In a letter addressed to Marco Barbato, whose native city of Sulmona was in the war-torn region, Petrarch affirms his sense of unease for the rest of Italy. He says[5]:

> But far be it from me to entertain fears for Italy. Her enemies, rather, will have cause to fear, provided the tribune's power recently restored to the city continues in a vigorous and flourishing condition, and provided Rome, our fountain-head, does not fall ill. Another portion of Italy makes me uneasy, however: Magna Graecia, including the modern Abruzzi, Calabria, Puglia, the Terrra di Lavoro, Capua once so powerful, and Parthenope [Naples], the present queen of cities.

Petrarch's thoughts of the army from the North sweeping down like a sullen cloud into the smiling skies of Italy, and particularly on Sulmona, cause a natural transition to an expression of anxiety for Barbato's personal safety[6]:

> I am racked by my great fears for you; but, as far as I am aware, I am helpless either to advise or assist. Still, since some men can now and then accomplish more that they hope to accomplish, exercise your rights as a friend if you can see any way in which I may be of service to you. I confess that I have no slight influence with the tribune, a man of lowly origin but of high mind and purpose; I likewise have influence with the Roman people. But it is due to no merits of mine. God's has compensated the wicked's hatred for me with love from the good, not because I have injured the former or have benefited the latter, or because I have ceased to err and am now an upright man, but simply because it has ever been my disposition to hate the wicked and to love the good. I have frequently desired to flee from the horde of the former to the handful of the

latter if the opportunity had only presented itself; and I still so desire, if the opportunity now presents itself. If at the present crisis, therefore, my intervention with the tribune and people can profit you, watch! Both my mind and my pen are at your service.

I also possess a home in Italy, in a region far distant [from the kingdom of Naples] and safe against the present disturbances.[7] It is a small home, to be sure, but no home is too small for two beings with a single heart. It is not inhabited by pernicious wealth, nor by poverty, nor by greed, but indeed by countless books. This home is now waiting for us: for me, who am about to return from the West, whose two-year absence she complains of; for you who are to come from the East, if the fates so compel you or if your pleasure so wills. I have nothing to offer you but this. You know where the home I invite you to is situated – in a healthful spot, free from terrors, full of joys, and suitable for quiet study. May God bring whatever you decide to a happy issue. I trust that in the meantime I may have been entertaining false fears, and that absence, according to its usual way, has increased the terrors of the lover. Indeed, my soul will not be at peace until I see you, or until I receive news by letter that you have survived the tempest safe and sound. Farewell.

This letter must have reached Barbato in the early days of October – if it reached him at all, owing to the unsettled condition of the country. Sulmona, in fact, was captured by Hungarian soldiers on October 20. The letter is important for our purpose, however, in that it contains the first hint of Petrarch's leaving France. The reason given is merely a desire to revisit his beloved Italy after an absence of two years. It is impossible to know what Petrarch did, or thought, during the weeks that followed September 11. There is a dearth of material for this interesting period. It is quite certain, however, that the contents of Cola's letter of October 11 must have become known to him by the beginning of November. An examination of this letter reveals some facts that will aid us in reconstructing their effect on Petrarch's feelings.

The letter in question is addressed to Clement VI.[8] It begins with Cola's protest that the pope had instituted proceedings against him.

Cola presents a defense based on three main arguments: first, that the pope should not rashly heed mere slanderous rumors that had been spread about him; second, that all his deeds had been performed on behalf of the Roman people. We cite the third part of his defense in full[9]:

> Third: seeing that I consider whatever is pleasing and agreeable to your holiness as sacred and just, whenever it please your Holiness that I be removed from this office, I am prepared to surrender my power, being resolved never to act contrary to your wishes. And to accomplish this end, it is not necessary to belabor the Curia and to make the whole world resound with the thunder of your accusations. Indeed, the least of your couriers would have sufficed and will still suffice whenever this pleases you. For God is greater than man, and you are greater than the kings and the princes of the earth.

We can imagine Petrarch's amazement on learning this. He may have considered it a rapprochement with the Curia. This calm surrender of Cola's power, which had cost so much toil to establish and from which Petrarch had hoped for the pacification and the regeneration of Italy, must have disturbed him greatly. He may now have begun to lose his confidence in Cola and to see his dreams begin to crumble. But there was still worse in that evil letter.

Cola informs the pope that he had received an embassy from the king of Hungary, who made three requests: first, that the murderers of his brother King Andrew be duly punished; second, that Cola and the Roman people should ally with the Hungarians; and third, that Cola permit the Hungarian king and his army to enter Rome.[10] Cola furthermore informs the pope categorically of his answers to these requests: that justice would surely never be denied to anyone seeking it; that he did not refuse the king's friendship, but that he neither wished, nor could, enter into an alliance without the pope's knowledge and consent and without consulting other friendly princes and states. To these, he adds, he sent a special embassy.[11]

Such news undoubtedly caused Petrarch greater uneasiness than the earlier portion of the letter. For here Cola is dealing with the foreigner, threatening to harbor the barbaric hosts within the city of Petrarch's dreams. Indeed, Cola adds to his answers the statement that the hostile attitude of the pope's rectors in Campania and in the Patrimony [Papal States] will very likely force him into an alliance with the king, though such action would be quite contrary to his own wishes. Here was the repetition of the error of centuries: the everlasting call to the outsider to decide petty internal dissensions. Here were new wounds about to be inflicted on the beautiful form of Italy, new incursions, new appeals to the stranger's sword, renewed drenching of Italian soil with the barbarian's blood, the desecration of the nest where Petrarch had been born, of the pious and benign mother that held the graves of his parents.

By the beginning of November, therefore, Petrarch had finally decided to go to Italy. Cola's wavering and the possible supremacy of the foreigner throughout Italy made it imperative for him to join Cola, to advise the tribune, the prince of the Romans, and so perform his duty as a Roman citizen and help steady the tempest-tossed bark.

This was undoubtedly the chief motive for Petrarch's departure. There were many minor incentives, of course. As we have seen in his letter to Barbato, Petrarch invites his friend to go and live with him at his small home in Parma. The choice of this house was not as haphazard as it might seem. There were two deciding factors: Petrarch wished to take actual possession of the canonry at Parma bestowed on him the previous October, and also he had received a hearty invitation from Azzo da Correggio, lord of Parma, to become a resident and an adornment of this court. Petrarch has left us a description of his departure from Cardinal Giovanni Colonna.[12] In answer to the cardinal's surprise that he was leaving just at this juncture, after so many years of intimate friendship, Petrarch answers that until now he had been held captive by destructive habit, by his love for the cardinal himself, which he declares will never abate, and by the presence of a charming and enticing young woman.[13] But wandering one day among the hills he met a shepherd named Gillias[14] who led him to the top ridge of the mountain and pointed out to him the smiling plains of Italy on the other side. But it is best to hear what followed in Petrarch's own words[15]:

> I step forward, and I see new valleys and fertile fields stretching far and wide. But turning my eyes back frequently to my usual fields,

the lands of this side of the mountain begin to seem despicable to me, the western sky misty and stormy, and the stars themselves melancholy. At once I recognize the strong love of country calling aloud inside me. On the farther side of the mountain the violets, moistened with dew, are a paler tint of yellow; the roses emit a sweeter scent from the thickets and grow to a deeper red; there a more limpid stream – the stream of my fathers – flows through the meadows; and the crops of Ausonia have now a sweeter taste for me.

The causes of Petrarch's leaving France, therefore, may be summarized here. First and foremost, he wanted to be with or near Cola in case of emergency. Second, he wanted to accept the invitation of Azzo da Correggio, who had become more and more insistent.[16] Third, he loved his native country, which, after all, is the feeling underlying and influencing all the other motives.

As is usual when one goes abroad, Petrarch's friends began to burden him with commissions.[17] A letter to Giovanni Coci, bishop of the Tricastrine,[18] a noted theologian and librarian of the Avignon library under Clement VI, gives us a clear picture of the still friendly relations between Petrarch and church authorities. The letter[19] bears no date but is clearly of this period, as is proved by the opening sentence.

I have forgotten neither your request nor my promise, and I am about to return to Italy – perhaps I had better say into Italy, if I do not wish to become involved in a grammatical discussion like the one Atticus carried on in his correspondence with Cicero. I well remember, I assure you, what you have asked of me so often in regard to collecting the various works of that same Cicero, arranging them in their proper order, and annotating them with my illuminating remarks, as you like to say. The Roman pontiff, aware of your great love for books, has generously entrusted to you an office worthy of your talents – the care of his library, thus following the example set by our emperors in the past. For it is common knowledge that Julius Caesar gave a similar appointment to Marcus Varro, and Augustus Caesar to Pompeius Macer, and the Egyptian king, Ptolemy Philadelphus, to Demetrius Phalereus. I repeat, I well remember how, to make your entreaty more irresistible than ever, you maneuvered so that the pope very discreetly made known to me on my departure his similar wishes in the matter. What was I to do? Though the poet be unknown, his words are familiar: "The requests of princes are like the scowling face of a commander; and those in power ask as if with drawn sword." And so I shall obey, if I can. For I must; and then, too, I delight to think that I can give you pleasure. Moreover, to spurn your entreaties would be unfeeling; whereas to disobey his commands would be sacrilegious.

The success of my undertaking hinges, however, in how far fortune will smile on me in discovering those carefully emended manuscripts that both of you are so eager to acquire. You are well acquainted with the crime of our age. You know, therefore, how great the scarcity of such manuscripts is, but with what care and toil, on the contrary, dangerous and destructive wealth is amassed even though it is of no use and though it already abounds. I shall exert tirelessly whatever power and energy I may possess. Moreover, I shall also employ the greatest care. And that you may not accuse me of having delayed, know that I have lingered in my retreat at the Fountain of the Sorgue awaiting the more temperate days of autumn in order to regain the health that my illness has impaired. I have hesitated to submit my weakened health to the ordeal of a long journey. Now that my strength has returned with the help of God, and the excessive heat has ended, I shall take the road. I wish that you could experience meanwhile the pleasure with which I roam through the hills and groves alone and free from care; how freely I breathe among springs and brooks in the company of my books and of the thoughts of the greatest men. Trying to forget the past and ignore the present, like the apostle I direct my mind to that life that still awaits me. Farewell.

Several facts emerge from this letter. The most important, as we have already pointed out, is the friendship with which Petrarch was held at the papal court, despite his clearly reiterated sympathy with the tribune. We attribute this friendship to his preeminent position in the world of letters. Unfortunately, Petrarch's political ideas were regarded as the wild, impractical dreams of a poet and scholar. They were good-naturedly tolerated whether at papal Avignon or at imperial Prague. For the same reason, his fiery outbursts at political conditions did not weaken his prestige as a scholar nor lessen the desires of potentates to attract him to their courts and to employ him on various diplomatic missions. Consequently, when Petrarch had announced his decision to depart for Italy, he felt duty-bound to take formal leave of the pope. We would date this visit in the first few days of November. From the letter just cited it is clear, furthermore, that the librarian Giovanni Coci had already requested Petrarch to do him the favor mentioned and had also enlisted the specific assistance of Clement VI. After this visit it would seem that Petrarch returned to Vaucluse to make final preparations for his journey. But he was obliged to postpone his departure because of ill health. Supposing that the librarian must have been impatient to hear of his actual departure, Petrarch, therefore, wrote him the above letter of explanation.

We assume that the librarian then informed the pope that Petrarch had not yet left Vaucluse. On his farewell visit and to answer some questions on his plans in Italy, Petrarch may well have communicated to the pope that he intended to visit Verona after arriving at Parma.[20] Remembering this, and taking advantage of the week's delay on Petrarch's part, Clement VI decided to enlist the poet in the capacity of ambassador and furnished him with the following letter to the ruler of Verona[21]:

> To our beloved Mastino della Scala, faithful and devoted son of the church of Rome.
>
> We render due thanks to your nobility for those acts that you have performed in the service, and to the advantage, of our very dear son in Christ, the illustrious Charles, king of the Romans. The affairs of the king are particularly close to our heart, and the Bavarian – that inveterate enemy of the evil days gone by – has now been removed from our midst. Since, therefore, we can now hope that, with the aid of God, the affairs of the king may be rendered fortunate and prosperous, we earnestly beg your nobility to be sure to continue industriously, loyally and zealously what you

have so worthily begun on behalf of the respect due to yourself, of the reverence due to the apostolic see, and of the maintenance of your own power.

Indeed, you must have heard that our very beloved son in Christ, the illustrious Louis, king of Hungary, desires to invade the kingdom of Sicily. So rumor has it. Since, however, this kingdom is within the jurisdiction and the possessions of the church of Rome; and since any hardships inflicted on it would, not without reason, be a source of disturbance to us also, we add to our former prayers the further request that you may manage to put obstacles in the way of all who are advancing to the invasion and occupation of that kingdom, and also that you may not grant to those thus inclined permission to cross through that territory that is under your control. With reference to these matters, kindly give credence to, and put into grateful and pleasing execution, what our beloved son, Maestro Francesco Petrarch, Florentine clergyman, will communicate to you on our behalf.

Given at Avignon on November 13, and in the sixth year [of our pontificate].

This letter is Petrarch's diplomatic portfolio to the court of the Scaligers. It recommended him as *persona grata* to Mastino della Scala, who also enjoyed the title of Papal Vicar. The letter, furthermore, is clear evidence of the opposition to the Hungarian invasion that was being organized by the pope and, incidentally, of the answer that Clement VI would have given to the ambassadors of the king of Hungary had they gone to Avignon instead of Rome. In opposition to the efforts of King Louis, the pope was certain of enlisting all Petrarch's eloquence. The mission entrusted to the poet may also have been a shrewd move of Avignon diplomacy to detach Petrarch from Cola's cause. At the same time the pope sent an envoy to many cities of northern Italy, but his efforts were in vain. Petrarch's mission, too, was doomed to failure. On December 5 the gates of Verona were thrown open to welcome the invading king.

On November 20, precisely one week after the date of the papal letter, Petrarch finally started for Italy – the fifth return to the land of his birth. On that very same day Cola was breaking the backbone of the

barons' opposition and was decimating the family of the Colonna outside the Porta San Lorenzo. Petrarch's departure was inevitably attended
with sad regrets. To be sure, he was leaving Avignon, which he so thoroughly detested, but he was also leaving his beloved Vaucluse. In spite
of all Petrarch's thundering, the western Babylon must also have enclosed the ten righteous men necessary to ward off heaven's fires. In
this number of the elect Petrarch surely placed Cardinal Giovanni
Colonna, whom he never saw again; and his dear friend Ludwig von
Kempen, Socrates, who was born in the cold North, but whom he always liked to think of as an Italian; and his equally beloved friend Lello di
Pietro dei Stefaneschi, Laelius, to whom he addressed numerous letters.

In fact, Petrarch received a farewell letter from Laelius on November
19 – the eve of his departure. On November 22 he halted his journey
long enough to write *Familiari* 7.5 in answer to it. He begins the letter
by telling Laelius that he has already spent three sleepless nights, ap-
parently caused by the contents of Laelius' letter. He then assures Laelius
that he will do what is asked of him, and at as early a date as possible.
After adding that he will finish the composition of certain verses already begun for Laelius, he concludes with the following sad remarks[22]:

> I have received the tribune's letter of which you enclosed a copy. I
> have read it, and I remain aghast. I do not know what to say in
> answer to you. I clearly perceive the ruin of my country; wherever
> I turn I discover causes and fuel for grief. For when Rome is thus
> mangled and mutilated, what will be the condition of Italy? And
> when Italy has been disfigured, what will my future life be? In this
> public and private calamity some will contribute their wealth, oth-
> ers their bodily strength, others their political power, and still oth-
> ers words of advice. As for me, I do not see what else I can offer
> but tears.
> Written on the road on November 22.

What was Cola's dreadful letter? What distressing news did it contain? We cannot answer these questions with certainty. The news may
have told of Cola's attack on the Orsini entrenched at Marino; or his
drowning of two hounds that he had previously, and in mockery,
baptized as Rinaldo and Giordano Orsini; or of Cola's childish visit to

Cardinal Bertrand de Déaulx. Stronger reasons were Cola's open alliance with King Louis of Hungary and the contribution by the latter of 300 horsemen for the war against the barons; the similar alliance with the Prefect Giovanni di Vico, the cruel Lydian guest of Petrarch's Eclogue 5[23]; and a repetition of the treacherous imprisonment of any nobles still within his reach. Enough cause has been given to make it perfectly clear that adverse circumstances had turned Cola into a haughty and arrogant ruler; that he was now surrounded by men of inferior character. In a word, that he was slowly but surely unfolding into a full-fledged tyrant. This was sufficient cause for Petrarch's tears. Those who accuse him of lack of courage and determination, of failing even words of advice in the hour of extreme necessity, forget that Petrarch could have nothing new to say. For six months he had done nothing but advise and exhort; he had defended Cola at every turn and had preached the gospel of Italian liberty as far as the power of his pen permitted. Such critics forget, in short, that these tears were absolutely normal and human. Petrarch saw yet another tyrant added to the endless list over whom Italy already wept and whom he always condemned. He saw new wounds, sorrows, woes. His idol was shattered. Instead of a united Italy under the paternal guidance of a native Italian; instead of a peaceful Italy constructed on national lines, he saw an addition to the hosts and legions of petty rulers and princes.

He reached Genoa on November 25.[24] For four continuous days he lay wrapped in gloom, receiving letters from his friends. Then, like a drowning man clutching at a straw, he began to hope against hope. He began to convince himself that the letter that he had received must have been dictated by envy and jealousy. He therefore came to the cheering conclusion that the unwelcome news was not, could not be, true. In these moments of relief and before the clouds of despondency again closed around him, Petrarch penned the following letter of mingled exhortation and rebuke to the man whom he once again addressed as Tribune of the Roman people.[25]

PETRARCH TO COLA DI RIENZO
TRIBUNE OF THE ROMAN PEOPLE
(FAMILIARI 7.7)

Your actions have been such that in these past months I have often re-peated with great delight the words that Cicero puts in the mouth of Africanus[26]: "What is this soft, sweet music that fills my ears?" What could I have said that would more fitly have answered the splendor of your name or the joyful news that poured in on us thick and fast? The lengthy letter of exhortation that I wrote to you full of encourage-ment and praise clearly indicates how fondly I repeated those words. I beg you, however, not to oblige me to change the refrain and ask: "What is this loud and deafening crash that wounds my ears?"

Beware, I beg you: do not let your own deeds dishonor your fair name. No man except you yourself can dislodge the cornerstone that you have laid. You alone can overturn the edifice that your hands have raised. As ever, the builder can best demolish his own works. You know by what difficult paths you have climbed to glory. Your footsteps are now turned in the opposite direction; you are descending from your glorious height, and nature herself makes the descent easier. Broad is the way; and the words of the poet, "Easy the descent to Avernus,"[27] are not true of the lower regions only. Our life in this world, however, differs from the hopeless misery of those who have descended to the abodes of darkness: so long as life remains we fall, to be sure, but we may rise again; we are always descending and ascending. But from the lower regions there is no return.

What greater folly than to fall when you might stand undaunted sim-ply because of your confidence to rise again? The higher the station, the more dangerous the fall. And what greater heights can be reached than those of virtue and glory, the very summits of which, though inaccessible to the rest of our generation, you scaled.[28] You fought your way to the summit with such energy and by such untrodden paths that I doubt whether anyone was ever exposed to a more frightful fall. You must advance with firm and deliberate steps and must take a resolute stand. Do not become the laughing stock of your foes or the despair of your friends. An illustrious name is not to be gained cheaply, nor is it kept cheaply. "Guarding a great name is itself a great task." Pardon me for quoting you a slight verse of my own, which pleased me so much that I was not ashamed to transfer it bodily from my daily letters to my epic *Africa*.[29] Please release me from this most bitter necessity: do not let the lyric verses that I began to compose in your praise and over which – as my pen can testify – I have spent much toil, end in satire.[30]

Do not suppose that I am writing like this merely by chance, or that I am complaining without just cause. Letters from my friends have followed me since I left the Curia.[31] In these letters reports of your doings have reached me that are far different from the earlier reports. I hear that you no longer, as formerly, love the whole people but only its worst element; that it is only these whom you humor, for whom you show any consideration, and whose support you seek. What can I say except what Brutus once wrote to Cicero[32]: "I am ashamed of such condition and such fortune"? Shall the world behold you, who have been the leader of patriots, become the accomplice of criminals? Has our star sunk so rapidly? Has Providence been angered so quickly? Where is your guardian angel now? To use a more familiar term, where is that Holy Ghost now? It was generally believed that you communed with that good counselor.[33] It was natural to suppose this, for it seemed impossible that your deeds could be accomplished by a mere mortal except through divine intercession.

But why grieve like this? All things must obey eternal laws. I cannot change conditions, but I can flee from them. You see, therefore, that you have relieved me of no little trouble. I was rushing eagerly, but now I have abandoned my plans. I am resolved not to see you other than as you were. And a long farewell to you, Rome, if these rumors are true. I shall visit the regions of Garamant and of India[34] instead.

But are they true? Oh, unexpected ending! Oh, my oversensitive ears! They had become used to noble reports; they cannot endure these. It is possible, however, that what I am saying is false. I wish it were so! Never shall I be more gladly proven wrong. The writer of that letter ranks high in my estimation; but I detect significant traces of an ill-will with which I have become familiar through many incidents. I scarcely know whether such envy is due to his noble birth or his eager courage.[35]

Therefore, though my grief urges me to write further, I shall check the impulse, a thing, I assure you, that would be impossible if I did not cheer my fallen spirits by refusing to believe the unwelcome news.

May the Lord look kindly on your actions, and may these have a more joyous result than is reported. I would much rather be offended by one friend's falsehood than by the other's disgraceful treason. After all, universal practice has made lying a daily and commonplace sin. On the other hand, no age, however dissolute, no social fabric, and no licentiousness has ever excused the traitor. Far better, therefore, that my correspondent causes me a few days of sadness by his false statements than you a whole life of gloom by deserting the cause of freedom. If he has sinned by word, by word he shall make amends. But if it is true that you have committed the heinous crime of treason — and I pray it is not true – with what sacrifices can you ever hope to atone for your sin?

Glory is immortal; immortal too is infamy.[36] Therefore, if by chance you have no regard for your own name, which I cannot believe, have some consideration for mine at least. You know how great a storm threatens me. You know how great a throng of slanderers will attack me the moment you give a sign of weakening. Therefore, to quote the words of the young man in Terence[37]: "While there is yet time, reflect again and again." Consider your every action most carefully, I beg you. Rouse yourself thoroughly. Examine your own conscience and do not be deceived about who you are and who you have been, where you came from and where you are going, and how far you can go without detriment to your country's liberty. Recollect the role you are playing in your city's history, the title you have assumed, the hopes you have aroused, and the promises you have made to the people. Consider all this, and you will realize that you are not the master of the republic, but its servant.

Written at Genoa, November 29.

NOTES
1. Gabrielli, *Epistolario* 23, pp. 61-67; Burdach and Piur, Letter 40, 2.3: 144-51. See *Vita* 1.25-29; Wright, pp. 69-77; Mollat, *Popes*, pp. 150-51.
2. See *Vita* 1.30; Wright, pp. 77-78.
3. For the social and political ethos of the Italian nobility see Larner, pp. 83-105. For Rome see Carocci.

4. See above Chapter 2, pp. 28-29, n. 15.

5. *Familiari* 7.1; Fracassetti, *Epistolae* 1: 355, l. 1; Bernardo 1: 331. See also Roberto Weiss, "Barbato da Sulmona, il Petrarca e la rivoluzione di Cola di Rienzo," *Studi Petrarcheschi,* Carlo Calcaterra, ed. (Bologna: Minerva, 1950), 13-22; and Wilkins, "The Correspondence of Petrarch and Barbato da Sulmona," *Studies,* pp. 213-53.

6. *Familiari* 7.1; Fracassetti, *Epistolae* 1: 356 to end; Bernardo 1: 332-33.

7. That is, his home at Parma.

8. Gabrielli, *Epistolario* 25, October 11, 1347, pp. 71-80; Burdach and Piur, Letter 43, 2.3: 158-72.

9. Gabrielli, *Epistolario* 25, p. 73, ll. 53-60; Burdach and Piur, p. 162, ll. 54-61.

10. Gabrielli, *Epistolario* 25, p. 76; Burdach and Piur, p. 167.

11. Gabrielli, *Epistolario* 25, p. 77; Burdach and Piur, pp. 167-68.

12. Eclogue 8. See Wilkins, *Life,* pp. 72-73 for his final days in Avignon.

13. See Avena, Eclogue 8, vss. 73-75.

14. Azzo da Correggio. Compare Avena, Eclogue 8, vs. 50.

15. Avena, Eclogue 8, vss. 52-60.

16. Compare Avena, Eclogue 8, vss. 106-7.

17. See references in Chapter 4, p. 41, n. 1.

18. Compare Mehus, p. ccxvi.

19. *Familiari* 7.4; Fracassetti, *Epistolae* 1: 366-67; Bernardo 1: 343-44; Wilkins, *Vaucluse,* pp. 61-62. Wilkins dates it to the summer of 1347.

20. To visit his ten-year-old son, Giovanni, whom he had left at Verona in 1345 under the tuition and care of the grammarian Rinaldo da Villafranca. See Wilkins, *Life,* pp. 51-52, 74-75.

21. See Cippola, *Giornale storico* 47: 256-57; Wilkins, *Life,* p. 74.

22. Fracassetti, *Epistolae* 1: 368-69; Bernardo 1: 345-46. Compare Wilkins' translation in *Life,* p. 72.

23. For these events see *Vita* 1.30-34; Wright, pp. 77-87.

24. Fracassetti, *Lettere* 1: 175, but compare *Lettere* 2: 197.

25. *Familiari* 7.7, Genoa, November 29, 1347; Bernardo 1: 349-52. Wilkins presents an abstract in *Life,* pp. 72-73.

26. *Somnium Scipionis* 5.1 (*De re publica* 6.18).

27. *Aeneid* 6.126.

28. Compare the canzone *Spirto gentil,* stanza 7, vss. 7-11; Chapter 2, p. 35-36, n. 33.

29. The original Latin of this verse is *Magnus enim labor est magnae custodia famae.* From what Petrarch says here, and from the occurrences of the verse elsewhere, we can readily reconstruct its history. It was first used in the lost letter to which the poet refers here. Between 1339 and 1341 he inserted it into his epic *Africa,* 7.292. In 1342 he again quotes it, this time as coming from the *Africa,* in his *Secretum,* or *De contemptu mundi,* Dialogue 3.363, (*Opera omnia,* ed. 1581), which was composed in that year. On November 29, 1347 he cites it to Cola in *Familiari*

7.7 (Fracassetti, *Epistolae* 1: 372). Finally he uses it once again in *Epistolae poeticae* 2.15, addressed to Cardinal Giovanni Colonna (*Opera omnia* 3: 100, col. 2). This must have been written either at Parma in December 1347 or at Verona in January 1348; for the *Epistolae poeticae* was prompted by the news of the slaughter of the Colonna at the gate of San Lorenzo on November 20, 1347, news of which Petrarch received only while he was staying at Parma. See Papencordt, p. 185.

30. Here we refer the reader to Chapter 2, pp. 32-36, n. 33. Continuing with the explanation offered there we are inclined to think that this poem on which Petrarch did so much work represents the Latin poem promised in honor of Cola at the end of the *Hortatoria,* to which he has already referred in the present letter, when he said *inscriptus tibi exhortationum mearum liber* (Fracassetti, *Epistolae* 1: 371).

31. If this is strictly accurate language, we must infer that Petrarch received other letters in addition to that of Laelius. Throughout the rest of this letter, however, he emphasizes only one letter and only one writer, Laelius.

32. Cicero, *Ad Marcum Brutum* 1.16.1: *quid scribam? pudet condicionis ac fortunae sed tamen scribendum est.*

33. In his citation of August 1 to the emperors (Gabrielli, *Epistolario* 17, pp. 48-51; Burdach and Piur, Letter 27, 2.3: 100-106), Cola styles himself Servant and Knight of the Holy Ghost (see Gabrielli, *Epistolario,* p. 49, l. 3; Burdach and Piur, p. 101, l. 1) and Candidate of the Holy Ghost (Gabrielli, *Epistolario,* p. 49, l. 11; Burdach and Piur, p. 101, l. 11) for the first time. The latter seems to have appealed more to the mystic temperment of the Tribunus Augustus, for from this date on he regularly began his official letters with *Candidatus Spiritus Sancti.* Compare Gabrielli, *Epistolario* 24, pp. 18-21, 24. See also Frugoni, "Cola di Rienzo."

34. Compare Virgil, *Aeneid* 6.794.

35. Laelius' full name was Lello di Pietro dei Stefaneschi dei Tosetti. The members of his house held a very prominent place among the Roman nobles and were close adherents of the Colonna. Laelius himself was one of the numerous courtiers in the Avignon household of Cardinal Giovanni Colonna. These facts alone would suffice to make him harbor ill-will against Cola; but we call attention to a document that seems to have been overlooked by previous research on the period and that throws added light on Petrarch's statement. This is a letter of Clement VI addressed *Dilecto filio nobili viro Lello Petri Stephani de Tosettis, domicello Romano, Magistro hostiario et familiari nostro* (Theiner 2, no. 178, p. 181, dated October 5, 1347).

Various parts of the address strengthen our belief that this is Petrarch's friend. Laelius is called a Roman nobleman, or perhaps a Roman syndic (compare Charles du Fresne Du Cange, *Glossarium mediae et infimae Latinitatis,* 10 vols. [Paris: Osmont, 1937-1938], see *domicellus,* especially under no. 3), a friend of the pope, and *Magister hostiarius,* or *ostiarius,* which we translate Master of the Guards (compare Du Cange, *s.v. hostiarius and magister ostiariorum*). This last title is consistent with Laelius' known military character. We suppose that the guards mentioned here were the predecessors of the Swiss Guards and were in charge of the entrances and the gates of the papal precincts.

After some preliminary remarks the pope says:

> We clearly understand from the documents you have submitted that a short time ago the office of Syndic in the city of Rome was, as you assert, conferred on you by our beloved sons, the inhabitants of the city; and that our beloved son Cola di Rienzo, who administers the office of Rector in the Roman state in our name, has without any predetermined and conceivable reason caused you to be summoned throughout the city by the voice of a herald, in order that, under penalty of permanent debarment from office – to use his own words – and the confiscation of your property, you might appear in person within a specified time to render an account of your tenure of said office of Syndic and to answer certain points concerning which an investigation of your tenure was being conducted.

From what follows in the papal brief it appears that Laelius had first asked the pope, and then the Consistory, for permission to leave his post at Avignon and to appear before Cola and thus retain possession of his estates. But the pope pointed out to Laelius that Cola, in issuing such a summons, had not consulted his superior the pope in whose name he held office, and that consequently the summons itself was null and void. The letter continues with the pope absolving Laelius from the necessity of obeying the rector's summons and with his reassuring Laelius in the undisputed possession of the estates he then held and of those he would acquire in the future. In closing, the pope distinctly forbids Laelius from going to Rome under penalty of forfeiting the good graces of His Holiness and also of being discharged from the position that he then held at the papal court.

In conclusion, we think that it was this personal reason, in addition to reasons of birth, that made Laelius so ready and so keen to receive bad news about Cola and to dispatch such news so eagerly to Petrarch, who was setting out on his Roman pilgrimage.

36. Petrarch here (Fracassetti, *Epistolae* 1: 373) makes a general statement *Immortale decus est, immortalis infamia*; in his translation Fracassetti wrongly gives *Immortale t'avrai o l'onore, o l'infamia*, applying the words directly to Cola (Fracassetti, *Lettere* 2: 190).

37. Terence, *Eunuchus* 1.1, 11 (or according to the consecutive numbering, vs. 56).

CHAPTER 10

AVIGNON, NOVEMBER 18 & 24, 1351

Cola's fortune reached its zenith with the successful battle fought on November 20, 1347. Intoxicated with his success, he began to behave in a way more and more uncertain, inconsistent, and questionable. The surviving barons allied themselves with Cardinal Bertrand. Cola, threatened with excommunication, resigned the office of podestà; and in his efforts to reconcile himself with the church eagerly embraced the title of Rector of the Pope again. While it is beyond the purpose of the present volume to detail the causes of Cola's fall, we should note Cola's increased unpopularity among the people as a result of the barons' embargo on the city, his new salt tax, and the political and diplomatic isolation that followed his alliance with King Louis of Hungary.[1] The resulting strain on the tribune's resources, political capital, and intellectual energies soon proved too much for him. Consequently, on December 15, 1347, after a riot instigated by the Colonna in the neighborhoods under their control, Cola quietly descended the Campidoglio, the stage from which he had brought visions of the ancient days of glory to the Romans and the world. Both he and the Romans wept as he was escorted to the protection of the Castel Sant' Angelo.[2]

We can follow Roman events only briefly. Papal power was almost immediately restored, and Cola fled to Naples, hoping to find refuge with the king of Hungary who had just captured that city on January 24, 1948. The dreadful plague of that year, however, forced the king to return across the Alps, and Cola fled to the inaccessible mountains of the Abruzzi, hunted down and pursued at every turn by the ban of the church. Here he found refuge among the Fraticelli on Monte Maiella.[3] At Rome, Bertoldo Orsini and Luca Savelli, the two senators appointed by the papal delegate, proved unequal to the situation that faced them.

The Black Death[4] that so depopulated Europe and interrupted all normal structures and patterns did not affect Rome as drastically. To make the misery complete, however, earthquakes followed one another in rapid succession, at times destroying entire cities, overthrowing towers, palaces, churches, and basilicas everywhere, leaving a heap of indescribable ruins. Such events were widely understood as the visitations of the Creator's wrath on the sinful population of Europe, a dire punishment for its unbounded licentiousness and for the wreckless destruction of all barriers in political and social relations. The Jubilee of 1350, therefore – the declaration which was in great part due to the efforts of Cola di Rienzo seven years before – came at a very opportune moment.[5] Downtrodden by political tyranny, orphaned by the ravages of the plague, and made homeless by the convulsions of nature, Italians were seized by a contagious enthusiasm. They turned to the Scriptures with the holy and irresistible faith of the early martyrs. From the pilgrimage to Rome humanity promised itself and confidently expected the recovery from all its ills and the regeneration of the world. Countless pilgrims must also have spread an atmosphere of holiness and sanctity on their return from the Jubilee city. There was, however, a loud note of discord; the addition of St. John Lateran as a third pilgrimage church for the Jubilee could hardly compensate for the pope's absence in France; and the papal benediction that served as a seal to the pilgrimage was not administered from the loggia of the mother of churches but from one of the far-off towers of the palace by the Rhone.

The artificial truce established by the Jubilee came to an end even before the echoes of the pilgrim's choruses had grown faint. New senators were constantly appointed, one representing the interests of the Colonna, the other those of the Orsini. All were doomed to ignominious failure. Cardinal Bertrand de Déaulx had been succeeded by Cardinal Annibaldo di Ceccano, legate for the Jubilee year. This cardinal so irritated the Romans that an attack was made on him. Shortly afterward he was visited by the cardinal of St. Chrysogonus, an eminent French prelate who then happened to be in Rome. To comfort Annibaldo for the attempt on his life, the latter said to him[6]: "He who would wish to restore Rome to order, would be obliged to destroy it utterly and then to rebuild it anew." De Sade[7] declares this story false. Whether true or false, the anecdote gives a true picture of the almost insurmountable difficulties facing Annibaldo. When he fled, the cardinal delegated his powers to Ponzio Perroto, bishop of Orvieto.

The question of giving the unruly and recalcitrant Romans some permanent form of government now became a problem of paramount importance to the pope and his cardinals. Finally, in 1351 Clement VI appointed a commission of four cardinals with power to settle this question to the best of their ability. They turned to Petrarch for expert consultation, and the poet immediately took the opportunity extended to him, writing a lengthy *ex cathedra* exposition that he forwarded to the cardinals in these two letters.[8] "Both letters, which redound to Petrarch's honor as a patriot, are manifestos of the democratic principle which governed the cities at the time.... Petrarch, questioned as to the best constitution for Rome, resembles Rousseau, placed in a similar position with regard to the Corsicans and Poles."[9] The first of these letters, *Familiari* 11.16, follows immediately. The second, *Familiari* 11.17, which was written at Avignon one week later and serves as a postscript to the first, follows on pages 117-19.

PETRARCH TO THE FOUR CARDINALS APPOINTED
TO REFORM THE GOVERNMENT OF ROME
(*FAMILIARI 11.16*)

A weighty burden is placed on my weak shoulders by one to whom I can deny nothing and in behalf of that city for which refusal is impossible. The love that governs my inner being commanded me to heed the request. The safety of our common country and mother was at stake; and he who is not moved by the woes of his dear mother is not a true son. In addition to this debt that humanity in general owes, there is added a certain special claim that the city of Rome has on my services for its former favors: by extraordinary privilege she elected me her citizen.[10] It may not be the least mark of her favor at this crisis, when her name and her glory are waning, that she places some hopes of assistance in me. In short, Rome has always deserved well of me. If her welfare were at stake, silence on my part would not only be disgraceful, but inhuman and ungrateful.

I wished to preface these remarks so that no one may consider me mad or forgetful of myself, charging that I have undertaken a task beyond my powers and that, contrary to the advice of the sage, I have aimed too high and too presumptuously. Let no one be roused to indignation if he hears the liberties of Rome championed in affectionate and respectful words, even though he may consider them lowly at one moment, prosaic the next, and, perhaps, even irrelevant. The obligation resting on me is, I confess, one of great responsibility; my conclusions are to be discussed in the presence of prominent men and are to be submitted to the supreme pontiff. I am conscious of my own insignificance; but an inborn devotion to the cause of Rome gives me courage to speak. Therefore, most reverend fathers to whom the reordering of the state has been entrusted,[11] if, as I hope, you are favorably disposed to accept this excuse for my boldness, give respectful attention, I beg you, to words spoken in good faith. Charitably consider not who I am but the motives that prompt me. Consider not the form but the substance of my speech. Judge not so much what I say as what I should wish to say, and what could be said on so pregnant a topic.

In the first place, I presume the following idea to be deeply rooted in your minds: that no group of words strikes a more responsive chord in the human heart than these, the Roman Republic. No region of this earth, no barbarian nation will deny it. The entire world would unanimously proclaim it, if it had a tongue to speak. It would openly acknowledge Rome as its head, even though she is now miserably unkept, forlorn, and unadorned.[12] Therefore, even though Rome were only a name, the name still would be that of a city once queen of the world and consequently, in my opinion, a name to be spoken with a certain degree of reverence. It would always represent, I say, that city that omnipotent God had adorned with many, marked favors of both temporal and spiritual dominion; the city where he set the cradle of the true faith, the rock of his church, and the supreme seat of empire.

But ample provision has at last been made that Rome may be something more than a mere name, that she may become the object of our hopes or our fears. The Roman pontiff has chosen you in particular from among the entire number of the Sacred College. He has shouldered this glorious and incomparable burden on you. It is a burden that must seem very heavy to those who are keenly alive to the pressing needs of the case. As we meditate on his action, we come to the conclusion that his selecting you four in particular was not without cause or design but was inspired by heaven. Three of you are endowed with most profound wisdom and vast learning. In addition, experience has given you an intimate knowledge of Roman affairs. The fourth member of your board is not merely of Roman origin but, according to some, traces his ancient ancestry to that most renowned and ancient family of the Cornelii. Therefore it is not without divine inspiration that this man, a noble example of true patriotism and sweet love of country, should now bravely champion and plead the rights of the defenseless plebeians against the proud nobles and protect the cause of oppressed liberty.[13] Appointed by the Lord to judge this cause, give no occasion to charges of indolence and have no regard for the requests and power of anyone.

But briefly to express my opinions on the question before us, I shall say that this is a repetition of the old Roman struggle. If only today's tyrants were no worse than those of old! This dastardly, self-satisfied nobility, spurning and despising all things, abuses the excessive meekness of the Roman plebeians and drags them to a shameful triumph, just as if they were so many Carthaginians or Cimbri taken in war and sent under the yoke. Yet no law sanctions such proceeding; no tradition warrants it, nor has anyone ever been heard to say that Romans triumphed over subjugated fellow Romans.

That no one may suspect my words to be prompted by even the slightest malice, it may not be inappropriate to mention here, by way of parenthesis, that of the two families from which all this trouble arises, I do not hate the one; whereas, needless to say, I do not merely love, but have cherished the other through a long period of almost familiar intercourse. In fact, I wish to state here that none of the princely families of this world has been dearer to me than the latter. Nevertheless, the public welfare is even dearer to me. Dearer is Rome, dearer is Italy, dearer the peace and the security of the upright.

Speaking with peace to the living and to the dead, it was to attain this security that God and man and fortune toiled and strove harmoniously. Their aim was to make Rome a stupendous city, fit to be the seat of both church and empire, and not the petty principality of a few citizens. Indeed, if I may speak the whole truth with your gracious leave, I shall correct my statement and shall say that Rome was not meant to be the prey of men who are not even Roman citizens and who do not even love the name of Rome. I shall not delay in order to review the origin of both these families. It is common knowledge and is sung by the shepherds in the valleys of the Rhine and of Spoleto. The queen of nations has sunk into abject misery. To none is she an object of compassion. She has been torn and mangled, not by the hands of her own children – as in the past – but by those of strangers. No longer can she derive consolation from those old lines:

> Our war no interfering kings demands,
> Nor shall be trusted to barbarian hands:
> Among ourselves our bonds we will deplore,
> And Rome shall serve the rebel son she bore.[14]

Is there any doubt that we should amend these wrongs? But no thought is given to what should have demanded our first attention, namely, with what carefully chosen penalties we should punish these public robbers or, at any rate, in what way these enemies of liberty can be most completely prevented from holding office in a free state. Strange to relate, this is the question that people are now debating: whether or not the Roman people, who once ruled the universe, should be restored to some degree of liberty; whether or not they may today participate to any extent with their home-grown tyrants in the government of their own city; and whether they are to have any voice on that very Capitol from which they drove the flames and the power of the Senonian Gauls, where they once beheld captured kings chained to triumphal chariots, where they listened haughtily to the suppliant envoys of foreign nations and from which they hurled proud citizens as well as enemies to headlong destruction.

Kind Jesus, to what have we come? Do you observe these things, Savior? Perhaps you are offended by our sins? Where have you turned your usually merciful eyes? Have mercy on us and wipe away the stains of our deep disgrace.

Have we fallen so low then? Was this, I ask, to be the end of all our woes that in public and, what is far worse, in the presence of Christ's vicar and of the successors of the apostles the question should be raised whether or not is it proper for a Roman citizen to be elected senator?

And this notwithstanding the fact that for so many years we have witnessed on the Capitol the rule of foreign-born tyrants and of so many proud Tarquins? This is the question that four heavenly hinges are laboring to solve![15]

For my part, if consulted, I should not hesitate to answer that according to Roman custom the Roman Senate should necessarily be composed of Roman citizens; that foreigners should all be barred from the threshold, not merely those born in a far-off land but also the Latins and those peoples inhabiting the country near and even adjacent to that of the Romans, peoples having, so to speak, the very same body with the Romans. I add that these foreigners should be excluded not merely by word or by pen but, if necessary, even by the sword. Let the example of Aulus[16] Manlius Torquatus suffice. When the Latins once asked that the high council and half the Senate be chosen from their number, he was so stirred with indignation as to swear that he would enter the Senate house in arms and would destroy all the Latins he might find there with his own hand.[17] How would Torquatus have felt to see the entire Senate composed of men hailing from the banks of the Rhine or from Umbria, he who so indignantly received the proposal of the Latins that only half the Senate should become non-Roman?

Our present foreigners do not want to appear to exercise their mad power without just cause. They give this defense for their usurpation of the senatorial privilege: that they are the stronger and consequently more capable of bearing the burden of so high an office. What is this power they boast of, a power that is never demonstrated except to the detriment of the state? From where is it derived, great or small though it be, except from the blood of the people and from the very vitals of the republic? But even granting that their power is great, and that it is just; what bearing, I ask, has that on the problem before us? Surely, when the above-mentioned embassy of the Latins came to Rome, Latium was described as flourishing in arms, men, and resources. Nonetheless their proposal was rejected because, relying on their power, they had aspired to undeserved honors, and because the Romans would not grant to the caprice of fortune honors that are the reward of virtuous conduct.

To tell the truth, if the senatorial dignity at Rome were to be the reward of mere brute force,[18] and if no regard were to be had for either

birth or conduct, then ancient Macedonia and Carthage and other powerful nations of the earth today could present a far more just and better
claim than the Roman barons. In excusing their usurpation, even the
barons will retort: "We are Romans; we have become Roman citizens
by our long and exclusive tenure of office and by the suppression of
liberty." I would consider it no slight victory if I had caused these most
haughty spirits to wish to be real citizens and not the plague of citizens. I should not then bar them from an honorable career with the
inflexibility of Manlius Torquatus.

In the name of God who takes pity on the affairs of this world, fathers most kind, and if you yourselves are moved by any compassion
for the Roman name, I ask whether you honestly believe that these
barons have seized the reins of government with the purpose of bringing their resources to the aid of the poverty-stricken city? If only they
had this in mind! I should then forgive them their generous ambition
and should admit them as candidates for office no matter what their
origin. But, believe me, they cherish far different aims. They plan not
so much to appease their insatiable and gluttonous hunger but to whet
it with the remnants of the ruined city. Perhaps they will dare deny
even this palpable fact. They will wish to veil with a general barefaced
denial the long series of crimes committed throughout their lives and
known to the whole world. They will desire to be called Roman citizens
and lovers of Rome. But not so! To call these barons citizens, to call them
human instead of princes and gods, constitutes a mortal offense.[19]

Although I have impartial judges, nevertheless I am arguing a case
under very unfavorable circumstances. I shall concede, therefore – but
merely for the sake of peace – a thing that it would be most easy to
refute: that these barons are citizens, and peaceable citizens at that.
Though unworthy, let them gain office, provided only that they do not
exclude the most deserving. If strangers compete against native Romans, and if all are to be designated by the common name of Romans,
why should only those be elected to office who enjoy the name of
Romans on sufferance, as it were; indeed why should they be given
preference over their fellow-citizens in anything at all? Is it because of
their nobility? But the essence of true nobility is still a moot point. The
barons will realize how noble they are only when they likewise realize
how virtuous they are.

Perhaps the barons claim superiority and preference because of their riches? I do not desire to belittle the extent of their wealth here. I warn them of this, however – that they should not for that reason despise those who are poorer than they; that mere wealth adds absolutely nothing to persons of good moral character; and that, remembering that riches are only of this world, they should use the wealth that they have sucked from the breasts of mother church with moderation. If they are so inclined, however, and if their dull intellects do not rise to the level of these higher concepts, let them enjoy their wealth as though it were an everlasting boon, provided they observe this one restriction: not to employ the riches they have amassed through the people's generosity for the destruction of the people.

But if they consider private wealth a necessary qualification for public honors, I would want them to answer the following questions. How much wealth did Valerius Publicola possess when he aided Brutus in expelling the proud kings, or when in his first consulship he triumphed over the Etruscans, and in his third consulship over the Sabines? Indeed, he died so poor that he was buried at the public expense. Again, how rich was Menenius Agrippa when he cemented the discordant and divided republic with words of divine inspiration? Or Quinctius Cincinnatus, who, abandoning his meager farm, saved Rome from defeat and freed a Roman consul and a Roman army from a siege?[20] What wealth did Curius possess, or Fabricius, when they overthrew the standards of King Pyrrhus and the Samnites? Or Attilius Regulus, who vanquished the legions of Carthage? Or Appius Claudius, who, though deprived of sight, continued to rule the republic wisely?

It would be an endless task to gather all the examples of glorious poverty. Nevertheless, I dare affirm – though the rabble may cry out against me – that the greatest obstacle to true virtue is overabundant wealth. Without trying to pluck out fixed ideas that are very deeply rooted, I dare assert what the writings of the ancient authors most clearly show: that riches conquered Rome, the conqueror of nations. It is beyond the shadow of a doubt that foreign vices and foreign evils entered Rome by one and the same gate through which poverty had left.

But to return to our barons. They believe, or – as I think more likely – they pretend to believe that wealth will be of the very greatest advantage to them, though it has always been the greatest bane of rulers. It remains for us to inquire into the real cause of their desire to rule. We do not have to search far. I shall not mention avarice. Though it might be suspected from many indications, my sense of decency forbids me to mention it in this discussion. It would be the foulest disgrace for avarice to dwell in noble hearts. On the contrary, it is always banished far from them. But now I am speaking of nobility in the general sense of the word! I shall merely point out with Sallust that pride is the evil common to all nobles.[21] It is not, therefore, a new disease that now infests the state. It attacked the ancient Romans, the true Romans, and the deadly poison crept stealthily among the noblest virtues. It was always checked, however, by the dignified resistance of the humble, as now, I hope, it is to be crushed by your decisions, most worthy fathers. But my statements seem to require amplification.

From the very beginning the Roman plebeians were wronged most cruelly. They demanded magistrates of their own to assert and protect their uncertain liberty. The nobility opposed their demands in a bitter struggle, and hence the first secession to the Sacred Mount. The plebeians, with justice on their side, finally overcame the pride of the nobles; and though the patricians protested in vain, for the first time there came into existence the Tribune of the People, the one spur and curb to the nobles' violence. After some time the plebeians demanded that this officer be elected in their own assembly, that is to say in the Tribunician Assembly. Again they were victorious, though opposed by Appius Claudius, the keenest of the patricians.

Thereafter a new struggle arose. The upper class with proud disdain refused to recognize the intermarriage of plebeians with patricians. In this way the most sacred bond of society was torn apart, and the state was split in half for the second time. The indignant plebs offered vigorous opposition, and with the reluctant consent of the nobles a new law was passed recognizing such intermarriage as legal. The priestly duties, the office of decemvir, the quaestorship, and the curule aedileship were still reserved to those of patrician birth. The plebeians realized that they were being made sport of. They rose in their might and secured the privilege of sharing in these offices too.

Here I must not pass over that brief anecdote related by Titus Livy, of small importance in itself but most clearly revealing the pride of the patricians and the plebeians' love of liberty. Gnaeus Flavius, the son of a scribe, a man of humble fortune but keen and well-spoken, had been elected curule aedile. This election so stirred the resentment of the nobles, who shrank back at the novelty of the appointment, that very many of them, grieving over his election as over a personal loss, laid aside their golden rings and other ornaments. Flavius, on the contrary, was not at all disturbed at this but met their insolence with a serene firmness and perseverance. Later it happened that Flavius visited his colleague who lay sick in bed. As he entered the room several young patricians who were present, obeying the contempt they all harbored, did not rise to offer him a seat. Flavius immediately ordered his curule chair to be brought in.[22] Thus he more nobly reduced the scorn of the youthful nobles to nothing; for now he looked down on them as they consumed themselves with envy, not from the bench of a private citizen but from the chair of office. In my opinion, this one act proved him most worthy to fill the office not only of aedile but even of consul.

I have purposely reserved the office of consul until the end, because the two senators who alone survive from the great number of conscript fathers who once constituted the Roman Senate can be considered the successors of the two consuls. The tenure of office both of our modern senators and of the consuls of old is a limited one; the senatorial dignity in ancient Rome, however, was enjoyed for life. If I were even to begin to rehearse the countless, bitter struggles over the consulship, I should put off even longer the end of this letter, toward which I am hastening. Suffice it to know this: that when the Roman plebs sought to gain admission to this, the highest magistracy, the patricians considered that such an outcome would be to their lasting disgrace and so opposed it with all their power. Finally, however, they were conquered as on previous occasions. Many disagreements followed, and at first this compact was made: that there should be no more consuls, but that four military tribunes with consular power should be created. The ambitions of the plebeians were not yet satisfied, and at last they won through the might of right what the swollen pride of the patricians had so long denied them: that a plebeian consul should sit by the side of a patrician one and should, with equal majesty, rule the common fatherland and the territory gained through common hardships.

If all this is true, and if it is truly recorded by all the most illustrious historians, why doubt any longer, most prudent fathers? Or why seek further encouragement? If you have pity for the misfortunes of the Romans, if you have resolved to prop the gigantic ruins with your patriotic shoulders, follow the examples of the time when Rome grew from nothing until her head touched the stars themselves. Do not heed the example of today, when she has fallen from the heights of so great a fortune almost into the lowest depths.

I trust you do not doubt that the city of Rome shelters many who are nobler and better than those who only boast of a noble name but who are a burden to heaven and earth. I shall not refuse to call them noble, if they will act accordingly; but surely not only I but Rome herself denies them the name of Romans. Let us grant that they are nobles, and Romans too. Are they still to be preferred to our ancestors, the defenders of justice, the protectors of the down-trodden, the conquerors of haughty nations and the builders of empire? Though their impudence is great, they will not dare to make this claim. If our ancestral Romans yielded then, do not let the barons feel shame yielding likewise to the plebeians, who justly demand that they shall not live in their own city as if in exile, and that they shall not be excluded from public office as if they were a diseased member of the body politic.

In this regard we might remember what Aristotle says. As in the case of those who straighten the plant that grows one-sided, so you must compel these nobles not only to share the senatorial and other dignities with the rest, but also to surrender unconditionally for a long period all the privileges that they have so long usurped through their own arrogance and the patient suffering of the plebeians. You must persevere along these lines until the republic, like the one-sided plant, will have bent in the opposite direction and have thus returned to its proper erect position.

These are my opinions, this I beg you on bended knee, this venerable Rome tearfully implores of you. If you display lack of energy in restoring her liberty, she will call you to account before the tribunal of the dreadful Judge. Christ orders you to reestablish her freedom, Christ, who will stand in your midst as you deliberate so that he may shield those he chose in the beginning to the very end. The apostles Peter and Paul entreat it, who inspired the Roman pontiff to confide this sacred duty to none other than to you. Heed the silent prayers of the saints, and you will find it very easy to spurn the hostile wishes and the pressure of all others. Finally, do not consider what may please the pride of others but only what best becomes your own integrity and what will be of the greatest advantage to Rome, to Italy, and to the world.

November 18, 1351.

PETRARCH TO THE FOUR CARDINALS APPOINTED
TO REFORM THE GOVERNMENT OF ROME
(FAMILIARI 11.17)

I know full well, excellent and most worthy fathers, that in judging between circumspect humility and unbridled arrogance you stand in no need of advice from an insignificant mortal like myself in order to render a just decision. But it pleases me to speak my mind on a question affecting the welfare of our common country and to shoulder my manly share of the burden.[23] Though I cannot contribute deeds, I shall contribute at least my pen to the defense of liberty. I shall speak, therefore, from purest conviction and in obedience to the dictates of my conscience, seeking neither glory nor praise from my words. I shall be quite unconcerned over whom my language may goad, provided it does not offend the sense of justice. It is, no doubt, a cruel necessity to rise against the mighty ones of this earth, especially when these are dear to one. Still, only he can consider himself a lover of truth who values it more highly than friends and all other possessions.

And so, thrusting aside my affection for those nobles who are very dear to me and whom I have long cherished,[24] I ask these foreign-born tyrants from where they have assumed such arrogant haughtiness in a foreign city? Three of you may perhaps wonder at this question, but the fourth will understand my meaning, I am sure.[25] If the barons laugh my charge to scorn, hoping that time has buried the origin of both houses in oblivion, Rome and Italy will both testify to the truth of my statement.

Astonishing and insufferable pride! Welcomed to the city as exiled strangers, they have long excluded the ancient citizens from all participation in the public offices, and they will continue forever to exclude them if not checked by the right hand of the supreme pontiff and by the measures that you will adopt. Our sins may, perhaps, have rendered us unworthy of your assistance, but assuredly the home of the apostles deserves to be freed from the violence of tyrants, the shrines of the saints deserve to be snatched from the clutches of the plunderer, and the soil consecrated by the lives of the martyrs deserves not to be defiled by the blood of its citizens. But none of these things can come to pass unless you repress the frenzy of the tyrants, and unless you bring timely aid to the wretched population.

There are some in this world who voluntarily put an end to their wrong-doing and return to the straight path, even though their repentance may be somewhat tardy; but there are some who never correct the error of their ways unless compelled to do so. It leads to the well-being of the latter class, therefore, to employ violence. Indeed, it is highly praiseworthy for a man to cultivate virtue and to flee from vice of his own accord; the next most commendable thing is to do so from compulsion.

Bring force to bear, then, on those unwilling barons. Do not heed their cries of protest, but wrench this baleful tyranny from their grasp. Not only admit the common people of Rome to a share in the public honors, but wrest from the present unworthy incumbents the office of Senator that they have always administered most abominably. Even if the barons were citizens, and good citizens, they could lay claim to only half the offices. As matters stand, they have conducted themselves in such a way as to be unworthy both of the city that they destroy and of the fellowship of the citizens whom they crush. How much more unworthy, then, are they of filling the highest office!

Pitiful, indeed, is their boast of noble birth and of wealth, relying on which they strut around in their pride, though lacking even a seed of virtue. It would take many pages to prove that the ancient Romans, who were endowed with a matchless and extraordinary virtue, were not successful in excluding the plebeians from office. It would be beyond my purpose to trace the particulars here. To state the question in its briefest outline, I shall say that, in almost every instance of a struggle for political office, the proud nobles were conquered by the humble plebeians.

CHAPTER 10, AVIGNON, NOVEMBER 18 & 24, 1351

I expounded this truth at greater length in the detailed letter that I recently wrote to you. If you agree to give that letter your undivided attention for one hour, I have hopes that you will follow in the footsteps of our ancestors, and that you will decree the salvation of the republic and of that fold especially dear to Jesus Christ. Though he had appointed trusty shepherds to keep watch over it, seeing them terror-stricken at the fierceness of the wolves, he himself, as you know, returned in person without hesitation to suffer for the second time the passion of the cross.

November 24, 1351.

NOTES

1. See *Vita* 1.22-23, 35-37; Wright, pp. 64-68, 87-91; Mollat, *Popes*, p. 151; Mollat and Wolff, p. 103.

2. *Vita* 1.38, Wright, pp. 92-94, Mollat, *Popes*, pp. 151-52.

3. Cola found refuge among the Fraticelli of Monte Maiella, whose Abbot Angelo, not the Spiritual leader Angelo Clareno, O.F.M., was an exponent of the group's Joachite prophesies of a last World Emperor and may, in fact, have been a disciple of Clareno. At any rate, Cola later tells the Emperor Charles IV that it was these Fraticelli who convinced him of his role in the apocalyptic events of the Last Days. See *Vita* 2.1, Wright, p. 126; Gabrielli, *Epistolario* 30, pp. 92-96; Burdach and Piur, Letter 49, pp. 193; Decima L. Douie, *The Nature and the Effect of the Heresy of the Fraticelli* (Manchester: Manchester University Press, 1932, rpt. ed., New York: AMS, 1978), 35. Paul Oskar Kristeller, *Renaissance Thought* (New York: Harper & Row, 1961), 154-55, n. 28, maintains that Cola's contribution to Renaissance ideas stem more from his training as a notary than from any Joachite influence, which, he asserts, Cola met only after this flight. Cola may well have known the Fraticelli of Monte Maiella before 1348, however. Mollat, *Popes*, pp. 148-49; Mollat and Wolff, p. 99; and Gordon Leff, *Heresy in the Later Middle Ages*, 2 vols. (New York: Barnes & Noble, 1967), 1: 6, n. 2 see his Joachimism as an essential part of his political program. Marjorie Reeves seems ambivalent on the issue. Discussing the Last World Emperor, she notes that Cola got his Joachite ideas from the Fraticelli only after fleeing to Monte Maiella. See *The Influence of Prophesy in the Later Middle Ages* (Oxford: Clarendon Press, 1969), 318-19. In her section on the Babylonian Captivity, however, she argues that Cola's imagery was Joachite from as early as 1343. See pp. 420-21. She seems to reconcile these views somewhat in *Joachim of Fiore and the Prophetic Future* (London: SPCK, 1976), 70-71.

There were, of course, Fraticelli in Rome from the beginning of the fourteenth century. See Douie, *Fraticelli*, pp. 64-65; Lydia von Auw, *Angelo Clareno et les Spirituels italiens* (Rome: Edizioni di Storia e Letteratura, 1979), 78-81, 293-98 et passim; and Renzo Mosti, "L'eresia dei Fraticelli nei territorii de Tivoli." *Atti e memoriale della Società Tiburtina di storia e d'arte* 38 (1965): 41-110. In addition, Cola had ample opportunity to be exposed to Joachite ideas in several of the popular religious movements of the first half of the century, including that of Fra Venturino da Bergamo, whose penitents reached Rome in 1335. See Dinora Corsi, "La 'crociata' di Venturino da Bergamo nella crisi spirituale di metà Trecento," *Archivio storico italiano* 147.4 (1989): 697-747; Alvaro Grion, "Legenda Beati Fratris Venturini O.P.," *Bergomum*, n.s. 30.4 (1956): 11-110; Clara Gennaro, "Venturino da Bergamo e la peregrinatio romana del 1335," *Studi sul medioevo cristiano offerti a Raffaelo Morghen* (Rome: Istituto Storico Italiano per il Medioevo, 1974), 1: 375-406; her "Movimenti religiosi e pace nel xiv secolo," in *La pace nel pensiero, nella politicà, negli ideali del Trecento. Convegni del Centro di Studi sulla Spiritualità Medievale* 15 (Todi: CSSM, 1975), 91-112; and her "Venturino spirituale," *Rivista di storia e letteratura religiosa* 23.3 (1987): 434-66. The series of political paintings that Cola had created for his propaganda campaign before his revolution in 1347 certainly contained vivid apocalyptic imagery. See *Vita* 1.2, Wright, p. 35; 2.4, Wright, pp. 37-38; and the works by Antoine, Belting, Schwarz, and Sonnay already cited.

4. For recent accounts of the Black Death see Larner, *Italy*, pp. 257-67; and Philip Zeigler, *The Black Death* (New York: Penguin Books, 1969). The classic contemporary account, of course, is that of Boccaccio in the *Decameron*, Preface to the Ladies.

5. On the Jubilee of 1350 see *Vita* 2.1, Wright, pp. 97-99; Pietro Fedele, "Il Giubileo del 1350," *Roma* 11 (1933): 193-212; Larner, *Italy*, pp. 245-46; Clara Gennaro, "Movimenti"; idem, "Giovanni Colombini e la sua 'brigata'," *Bollettino del Istituto Storico Italiano per il Medioevo e Archivio Muratoriano* 81 (1969): 237-71; and G. Miccoli, "Giovanni Colombini," in *Storia d'Italia* 2.1 (Turin: Einaudi, 1974), 914-24. On the importance of pilgrimage to the Roman economy, see Mario Romani, *Pellegrini e viaggiatori nell' economia di Roma dal xiv al xvii secolo* (Milan: Vita e pensiero, 1948); and Brentano, pp. 53-57.

6. *Vita* 2.2, col. 883; Wright, pp. 99-101.

7. *Mémoires* 3: 224.

8. *Familiari* 11.16, dated November 18, 1351, Bernardo 2: 120-27; and 11.17, dated November 24, 1351, Bernardo 2: 128-29. For background to these letters see Wilkins, *Life*, pp. 110-11. On dating see Wilkins, "Petrarch in Provence, 1351-1353," in *Studies*, pp. 81-181.

9. Gregorovius 6.1: 330, n. 1.

10. The word "privilege" used by Petrarch (Fracassetti, *Epistolae* 2: 145) is the same word that occurs in the document conferring Roman citizenship on him: *Privilegii laureae receptae a Francisco Petrarcha exemplar* (*Opera omnia* 3: 6). The sentence actually declaring him a Roman citizen runs as follows (p. 7):

> Furthermore: on account of his extraordinary intellectual endowments, and on account of the well-known devotion that he

cherishes for the city and for our state – a devotion to which common report and his own deeds and words bear witness – we hereby make, pronounce, decree, and declare said Francesco Petrarch a Roman citizen, honoring him with the name and also with the privileges, both old and new, of Roman citizenship.

11. The four cardinals to whom this letter was addressed are Bertrand de Déaulx, Gui de Boulogne, Guglielmo Curti, and Niccola Capocci (De Sade, *Mémoires* 3: 157; Wilkins, *Life*, p. 110). They formed a very wisely appointed commission, each having had practical experience in Roman affairs.

Of these four cardinals, Bertrand de Déaulx was the senior member, having been created cardinal of St. Mark by Benedict XII. His direct acquaintance with Roman conditions had begun as early as 1335, when he had been delegated to the city in an attempt to establish peace between the Colonna and the Orsini, who were then at war. See Chapter 2, pp. 27-28, n. 13. As we have seen, Clement VI also entrusted to him the negotiations with Cola di Rienzo. In fact, he was considered the most astute diplomat in the Sacred College (Jean Baptiste Christophe, *Histoire de la Papauté pendant le xive siècle* [Paris: Librairie de L. Maison, 1853], 2: 183), which after December 17, 1350 consisted of twenty-six members. See De Sade, *Mémoires* 3: 146; Mollat, *Popes*, pp. 294-310.

Gui de Boulogne was born of a very noble family; in fact, he was related to the royal house of France, for his niece, Jeanne d'Auvergne, was married to King John of France on September 26, 1349 (De Sade, *Mémoires* 3: 51 and n. a; but compare the marginal note on p. 150, which gives the date as September 24, 1349). The cardinal, moreover, was a friend and relative of Emperor Charles IV. For these reasons he was appointed ambassador plenipotentiary to the king of Hungary, to which country he traveled in 1349 to reconcile King Louis and Queen Giovanna of Naples. The following year he was ordered to Italy for the Jubilee and met Petrarch at Padua in February 1350. Gui de Boulogne is generally supposed to be the one who solicited Petrarch's opinion and to whom Petrarch, whose friendship with him dated from Avignon, could deny nothing. See De Sade, *Mémoires* 3: 51, 52, 150, 157; and Mollat, *Popes*, p. 306.

Guglielmo Curti, like Bertrand de Déaulx, had been created cardinal during the pontificate of Benedict XII (De Sade, *Mémoires* 3: 146). For further information regarding him, see Carlo Segrè, *Studi Petrarcheschi* (Florence: Le Monnier, 1903), 216-19.

Niccola Capocci was one of the twelve cardinals created by Clement VI on December 17, 1350 (De Sade, *Mémoires* 3: 146). He and Rinaldo Orsini, the former papal notary, were the only two Italians promoted to the rank of cardinal on that occasion (De Sade, *Mémoires* 3: 148). Petrarch tells us here that Capocci traced his descent from the Cornelii of republican Rome. See Gregorovius 6.1: 263, n. 1, and p. 682, n. 2, where reference is given to Capocci's *Vita*; and Wilkins, "Petrarch and Cardinal Niccola Capocci," in *Studies*, pp. 182-92.

Fracassetti, *Lettere* 3: 292, agrees with De Sade in assuming that Cardinal Talleyrand was one of the three judges later appointed to try Cola di Rienzo and adds that he was also one of this commission of four cardinals appointed to reform the government of Rome, in fact, that Talleyrand was the one who solicited Petrarch's opinion. On p. 99, however, Fracassetti had accepted De Sade's list of four cardinals, among whom Talleyrand does not appear. He had also accepted De Sade's identification of Gui de Boulogne as the cardinal who solicited Petrarch's opinion. In the midst of these contradictions, we prefer to adhere to the Abbé de Sade, who is generally quite accurately informed on papal matters.

12. Petrarch knew what he spoke about. In 1350 he had been one of the countless thousands who made the pilgrimage to Rome. There he witnessed with his own eyes the ravages of the Black Death of 1348 and the ruins caused by the earthquakes of 1349. Six months before this letter to the four cardinals, he had written to his dear friend Socrates, sadly describing the results of those catastrophes. The letter gives so faithful a picture of the terror that seized people's minds and presents so peculiar a blend of Petrarch's religious feelings with his patriotic concept of *Roma caput mundi,* that we cite it in full (*Familiari* 11.7; Bernardo 2: 99-101):

> What shall I do first? Shall I voice my laments or my fears? There is cause for grief everywhere; and all the present woes promise deeper woes to come. Yet I can scarcely conceive what worse evils can possibly be expected. The world has been destroyed and brought to an end by the madness of men and by the avenging hand of God. We have sunk to such depths of misery that no new species of misfortune comes to mind. Indeed, whoever narrates the present state of humanity to posterity – provided any descendants survive us – will seem to be recounting fables. Nor will it be right to grow indignant if we should be less believed in matters that we ourselves do not believe from others. As for myself, I frankly confess that the present times, in which humanity has experienced every conceivable evil, have made me more prone to believe many things of which I had been skeptical.
>
> I shall pass over those floods and hurricanes and conflagrations by which cities that were flourishing one moment perished root and branch the next. I shall also pass over those wars raging throughout the world and attended by endless human carnage. I shall touch only lightly, furthermore, on the heaven-sent plague, unheard of through the ages. They are matters well known to all. The depopulated cities and the fields deprived of their tillers bear witness to them; the face of the earth, afflicted and almost turned into a desert – yes Nature herself, so to speak, sheds tears of sorrow. These facts, I repeat, are abundantly known in the lands of the setting sun as well as those of the rising sun; in the regions of Boreas, and in those of Auster.

CHAPTER 10, AVIGNON, NOVEMBER 18 & 24, 1351

But as you know, in many places the Alps were shaken to their very foundations recently. From that the earthquake proceeded; and – oh, unusual and dire warning of things to come – a great portion of both Italy and Germany were simultaneously rocked. Evils followed that we cannot recollect without tears, that are beyond our power to enumerate. Very recently the insignificant few of us who seemed to have been snatched from the universal shipwreck hoped that the deadly visitation had abated its ravages and that the wrath of the Lord had been appeased. But look – you may still be ignorant of this, perhaps – Rome herself was so violently shaken by the strange trembling that nothing similar to it had ever been known there in the two thousand years and more since the city's founding.

The massive structures of the ancients fell in ruins, structures that, although neglected by the citizens, brought amazement to the stranger. That famous tower called the Torre dei Conti, unique in the world, was split by enormous cracks and fell apart; and now, with its summit lopped off, it looks down and sees the glory of its proud head strewn on the ground. Finally, that positive proofs of divine wrath may not be lacking, the appearance of many churches speaks loud in testimony. Above all, the ruined appearance of a large portion of the church of St. Paul the Apostle and the fallen roof of the church of St. John Lateran saddened the fervor of the Jubilee and made the pilgrims shudder. Nature dealt more kindly with the church of St. Peter, however.

These occurrences are unprecedented – and they justly depress many. For, if the trembling of the limbs warned of such dread calamities, what is not threatened now by the trembling of the head? Yes, let those who judge themselves to have some authority fume and fret; let them murmur their disapproval. Nonetheless, Rome is the head of the world. Though grown old and unkept, Rome is undoubtedly the head of all nations. Could it speak to me with one voice, the world itself would not deny this. And if the world should not acknowledge it on good authority, it would be won over by written proofs.

So that I may not be judged a most malignant prophet of evil in the hour of adversity, however, or be thought to have created unfounded fears, I shall free myself from such charges by citing examples of recent ills that have befallen us and by appealing to the authority of Pliny, a writer ranked among the very highest. To avoid even the suspicion of warping his statements, I shall quote him verbatim (*Naturalis historia* 2.84[86].200): "Indeed, the evil is not free from complications, nor does the danger lie only in the earthquake itself, but it is a portent of an equal or of a greater danger. Never has the city of Rome trembled without its being the omen of some future disaster." These are Pliny's words. Why therefore, should I now remain silent? Or why repeat them? I am speaking to you like this because you belong to those of our generation who dearly love the Roman Republic. What does it matter, to tell the truth, where you first drew breath? Instead, I consider your disposition, which our friendship has rendered quite distinctly Italian.

Therefore, my dear Socrates, give me your close attention. I feel deep concern for the highest welfare of the republic, and sad forebodings make me tremble not so much for Rome as for the whole of Italy. I fear not so much the convulsions of Nature as the upheavals of men's minds. I am terrified by many things but above all by that ancient prophecy uttered so long before the city was founded and inserted not in any minor writings but in the Sacred Scriptures themselves. Though I was then entirely absorbed in secular literature and not familiar with the Scriptures, I confess that when I first read it I shuddered, and the blood in my heart grew cold and chilled. The utterance is in the final words of the last prophecy of Balaam. I shall quote it here to relieve you of the labor of running through the pages. So, then, is it written (Num. 24: 24): "They shall come in galleys from Italy, they shall overcome the Assyrians, and shall waste the Hebrews, and at the last they themselves also shall perish."

Some may hold that this prophecy has long since been fulfilled in the fall of the Roman Empire; but I trust that this recent trembling of the city does not portend a second overthrow of peace and liberty. But steady your faltering spirits on the strong foundation of your virtues and firmness. In spite of quaking earth, may you remain unshaken in your secure home, may you be like him of whom Horace speaks (*Carmina* 3.3.7-8, Addison trans.):

> Should the whole frame of Nature round him break
> In ruin and confusion hurled,
> He, unconquered, would hear the mighty crack,
> And stand secure amidst a falling world.

I wrote this letter to you while I was still at Padua, but my lack of a messenger delayed sending it until today. I am pleased to dispatch it to you from this city for no other reason than to humor this mutual friend of ours, who refused to go to you without bearing a letter from me. For that matter, there was no need of either messenger or letter, since I myself am just about to follow him. When, therefore, you read this letter, know that I am already near. You will give me pleasure, indeed, if you came to meet me at the Fountain of the Sorgue. Remember me always, and farewell.

At Piacenza, June 11, 1351.

13. Petrarch wants to emphasize that it was only natural for Capocci to champion the right of the defenseless plebeians against the nobles. He has already stated that Capocci was a native Roman boasting a descent from the Cornelii. Hence Capocci inherited the native, Italian antagonism to the foreign-born nobles who, as Petrarch has already said time and again, hailed from the valley of Spoleto, from the banks of the Rhine, or from some other obscure corner of the world.

14. Lucan 8.354-56 (Rowe trans.).

15. A play on words, connecting the word "cardinals" with the very literal meaning of the Latin *cardo*, the hinge of a door or gate. This, in fact, has a long tradition in ecclesiastical theory. See Walter Ullmann, *The Growth of Papal Government in the Middle Ages* (London: Methuen & Co., 1970), 320-21.

16. Petrarch was mistaken about the *praenomen* of this Torquatus, which should be Titus.

17. The story is given in Livy 8.5.7.

18. The passage is reminiscent of Cicero, *In Catilinam* 2.9.19.

19. It is hardly necessary to point out that passage after passage of this letter harks back to similar lines in Letter 2 above.

20. Petrarch's original reads (Fracassetti, *Epistolae* 2: 151): *deserto rure, inopi victu Romam et obsidione consulem romanum atque exercitum liberaret*. Fracassetti translates (*Lettere* 3: 91): *mosse a liberare il console e Roma dall'assedio e dalla sconfitta*. We have altered the punctuation of the Latin by placing the comma after *inopi*, thus translating the first three words together, "abandoning his meager farm." In fact, Rome was not under seige at the time, and Livy 3.26.27 clearly states that Cincinnatus "freed from a siege a Roman consul and a Roman army."

21. Sallust, *Iugurtha* 64.1: *superbia, commune nobilitatis malum*. Fracassetti (*Lettere* 3: 92) places his *come narra Sallustio* after the statement that pride is not a new disease in the state. The impression, therefore, is that this is also from Sallust, who merely says, however, that pride is the evil common to all nobles.

22. Livy 9.46.8, 9, 12.

23. Compare Livy, *Praefatio* 3; and Chapter 4, p. 43, n. 12.

24. This is an unmistakable reference to the members of the Colonna family. Petrarch seems to have had some misgivings as to the effect of the preceding letter on the commissioners, all of whom, being cardinals and residents of Avignon, had personally known Cardinal Giovanni Colonna and other members of the family. Everyone, of course, knew of Petrarch's intimacy with the Colonna, and hence our patriot reiterates here his love for the Colonna as individuals and his unavoidable hatred for them as members of a foreign and invading feudal order.

25. The fourth member referred to is Niccola Capocci, of course. See n. 11 above.

CHAPTER 11

VAUCLUSE, AUGUST-NOVEMBER 1352

The cardinals' commission named to reform the government of Rome failed to accomplish anything in spite of Petrarch's suggestions. Their deliberations continued with due gravity and solemnity, while the Romans patiently waited for the solution to their pressing problems. At last, wearied by the inaction of the responsible authorities, the Romans faced the situation squarely and provided their own solution. On December 26, 1351 they gathered at the church of Santa Maria Maggiore and declared the plebeian Giovanni Cerroni absolute head and master of the city. This act immediately relieved the deep embarrassment of both the cardinals and the pope; and though the Romans had not seen Petrarch's two letters, it is evident that their solution was quite in accord with Petrarch's suggestions.

The children of Mars, however, continued to be as unruly and as warlike as ever. Cerroni was shortly obliged to flee the city, and his flight renewed the party strife of Colonna and Orsini. In sheer desperation, and because they recalled the relatively peaceful and glorious days of 1347, on September 14, 1353 the Romans at last gave control of the city to Francesco Baroncelli,[1] second tribune of Rome. But what of Cola di Rienzo? What had now become of the people's former idol?

During many of those months of turmoil, Cola had been living the quiet life of a monk on Monte Maiella, in the company of the Fraticelli.[2] Finally, spurred on by dreams of power and by the prophecies of the hermit, Fra Angelo, he journeyed to Prague, the capital of the Bohemian king and emperor of the Holy Roman Empire. His intention was to place schemes before the emperor for establishing the claims of the empire independent of papal pretensions. In short, Cola had become a Ghibelline. The Bavarian claimant to the empire, the "inveterate enemy of the evil days gone by," would have welcomed Cola, "the son of Belial," with open arms. But unfortunately for Cola, Lewis the Bavarian was dead, and Charles IV was now without a rival. Charles IV, it will be remembered, had submitted to the demands of the church on all issues. To assure himself the support of the church in his candidacy for the empire, he had promised at Avignon to be the pope's humble servant. After the consummation of this bargain, he had promised to enter Rome for the coronation, to leave the City of the Apostles on the very same day, and never again to enter the territory of the church. The eagle of the Ghibellines had by this time become the tame and docile dove of the Guelphs.

When, therefore, Cola reached Prague in July 1350, the scholarly emperor decided to give him an audience, spurred chiefly by a sense of curiosity to see the ex-tribune by whom he had been so boldly summoned three years before. Cola now began to write to the emperor, to the chancellor of the empire, and to the archbishop of Prague those lengthy letters of self-defense to which we have already referred.[3] The strongly Catholic emperor grew increasingly alarmed at Cola's bold language and finally cast him into prison. He sent news of his actions to his sponsor at Avignon. Clement VI at once began to urge the emperor to surrender Cola. In a letter of August 17, 1350[4] the pope begs Arnest von Parbubitz, the archbishop of Prague, either to send Cola to Avignon immediately or else to be sure to keep close guard over him. On February 1, 1351 Pope Clement again writes the emperor,[5] rehearsing the well-known fact that Cola had been declared a heretic by Cardinal Bertrand de Déaulx and Bishop Annibaldo di Ceccano of Tusculum. The tone of this letter is one of reproach and complaint, because, in spite of repeated demands, Cola had not yet been dispatched to Avignon. Cola's continued residence in the North caused the pope serious worry over the harmful influence of Cola's religious and political preachings. As Gregorovius says[6]: "The Tribune in chains at Prague was more dangerous to the Papacy than he had been when at the height of his power on the Capitol." On February 24, 1352, consequently, the pope wrote a general letter to the archbishops and bishops of Germany and Bohemia[7] instructing them to inform their flocks of Cola's heresy and to warn them to shun him accordingly. Finally by brief of March 24, 1352,[8] Clement VI gave very specific instructions for Cola's surrender:

> Clement, Bishop, etc., to his very dear son in Christ, the illustrious Charles, king of the Romans, greetings.

In a separate communication, we are sending instructions to our venerable brother Arnest, archbishop of Prague, to the effect that, without causing any disturbance, he be good enough to deliver Cola di Rienzo, the Roman citizen condemned of heresy, to our intimate acquaintances and bearers of the present [letter], namely, to our venerable brother Giovanni, bishop of Spoleto, and to our beloved son Roger de Moulinneuf, Master of the Guards, and to Hugue de Charlus, in order that the said Cola di Rienzo be conducted before us. Therefore, we earnestly beg your Serenity that, in so far as it lies in you, you may lend your efficient aid to the said archbishop in order that he may successfully fulfill our instructions in this regard.

Given at Villeneuve (-lès-Avignon), in the diocese of Avignon, on the 24th of March, and in the tenth year of our pontificate.

Cola di Rienzo himself was glad for the coming change. His transfer to Avignon would release him from the cold and damp dungeon in which he had been confined for months and would offer him the long-desired opportunity to defend himself in person against the charge of heresy. His journey from the representative of the temporal to that of the spiritual power was one continued ovation. Cola's anonymous biographer condenses this journey to Avignon, his trial, and his acquittal into one short chapter[9]:

> After some time Cola asked a favor of the emperor that he might go to Avignon to appear before the pope and submit proofs that he was neither a heretic nor a Patarine.[10] The emperor was very hesitant that he should go, but finally he agreed to humor his desire. Cola di Rienzo kept saying, "Most Serene Emperor, I am going before the Holy Father willingly. Therefore, provided that you are not sending me under compulsion, you will not be breaking your promise to me."[11] On his journey the inhabitants of all the countries through which he passed rose up in a great commotion. Great crowds went out to meet him with great shouting and uproar. They took him and said that they wanted to rescue him from the pope's hands, that they did not want him to go to Avignon. To all he answered, "I am going willingly and not under compulsion,"

and he would thank them. And so he passed from city to city. Solemn honors were paid him all along his route. When the different peoples saw him they marveled and went along with him. And this is how he traveled to Avignon.

When Cola di Rienzo reached Avignon, he spoke in the pope's presence. He presented his defense, that he was not a Patarine, and that therefore he was not affected by the sentence [of excommunication] passed on him by the cardinal [Annibaldo di Ceccano] and by Messer Bruno [Bertrand de Déaulx, once bishop of Embrun]. He expressed his willingness to undergo a trial. The pope remained silent at these words. Cola di Rienzo was imprisoned in a strong and spacious tower; a heavy enough chain secured his foot. The chain was fastened to the vaulted ceiling of the tower room. There Cola remained, clothed in decent enough robes. He had many books; he had his Livy, his histories of Rome, the Bible, and many other books. He studied incessantly. The pope's kitchens provided him with food in abundance; it was given him out of charity in the name of God. His acts were examined, and he was found to be a faithful Christian. Then the trial was annulled, and the sentence of Messer Bruno and of the Cardinal di Ceccano was revoked, and he was absolved. He fell into the pope's good graces and was saved.

The medieval biographer's condensation has caused us to jump ahead a bit. It appears that Cola was surrendered to the papal emissaries in July 1352.[12] Since the distance between Prague and Avignon was much greater than that between Rome and Avignon, we calculate that if Cola left in the early days of July he must have reached Avignon in the early days of August. A few days later, perhaps a whole week later, Petrarch wrote a long letter from Vaucluse,[13] in which he described to his friend Francesco Nelli both Cola's arrival and the strange rumors that were being spread about him.

PETRARCH & COLA DI RIENZO

PETRARCH TO FRANCESCO,
PRIOR OF THE HOLY APOSTLES
(FAMILIARI 13.6)

What do you expect to find in this letter?[14] Do you think that I shall complete the mournful though ridiculous tale of my last letter to you?[15] Surely, there is nothing more important to do just now. Rather, there are many such tasks, but lack of time forbids me from giving attention to those of greater importance.[16] What little time I have is not at my own disposal but is clogged with truly remarkable interruptions. Even I am constantly on the go; I find myself in the middle of turmoil and confusion. I am here and there at once, so that I never really get anywhere. This is the familiar evil attending all wanderers. But recently I left Babylon and halted at the Fountain of the Sorgue, the well-known refuge from the storms that beset me.

Here I am waiting for some traveling companions and for the end of autumn, or at least that season described by Virgil,[17] when "the days are shorter, and the heat milder." In the meantime, therefore, so that my stay in the country may not be altogether fruitless, I am bringing together the scattered fragments of previous meditations. My daily effort is, if possible, to add a little to the larger works that I have in hand or to put the finishing touches on some of the minor ones. Learn from this letter, then, the task that I have set myself for today.

Poetry, a divine gift bestowed on only a few, begins to be the common property of the mob. This is putting it mildly, for I might well say that poetry is now desecrated and degraded. There is nothing that stirs greater wrath inside me; and if I have come to know your tastes, my friend, I am sure that there is no way that you too can tolerate such an affront. Never in Athens or in Rome, never in Homer's or Virgil's time, was there so much prattle about poets as there is today along the banks of the Rhone. Yet I am positive that in no place and at no time was there such profound ignorance on the subject of poetry. Appease your wrath with laughter, please, and learn to be merry in the middle of sorrow.[18]

There recently came to the Curia or, rather, he did not come but was led here a prisoner, Cola di Rienzo, formerly the widely feared Tribune

130

of Rome, today the most wretched of men. He has now touched the very lowest depths of misfortune; for, though he is extremely miserable, I do not know whether he is to be pitied by any means. He might have died a glorious death on the Capitol; but he has submitted to the chains first of a Bohemian, and then of a Limousin – to his everlasting disgrace and in mockery of the Roman name and republic.[19]

The constant praise and exhortations that so busily engaged my pen are, perhaps, better known than I should like at present. I loved his virtues, praised his aims, and marveled at the man's courage. I congratulated Italy; I foresaw the empire of the bountiful city and anticipated the peace of the entire world. I could not repress the joyous feelings springing from such numerous causes, and it seemed to me that I should share in his glory, if I goaded him on in his course. Indeed, his messengers and letters to me bear witness that he esteemed my words as very potent incentives. The heat of my enthusiasm became more intense in turn. I racked my brain to devise means to inflame his already glowing spirit. I knew full well that nothing enkindles a generous heart more readily than praise and the prospects of glory; hence I constantly introduced words of high praise that appeared extravagant to many but to me seemed justly deserved. I praised the deeds already performed and urged him to perform others.

Several letters that I wrote to him survive, letters that even today I am not displeased to have written. I am not used to predicting the future. I wish that he, too, had not been addicted to prophecy! To tell the truth, the deeds that he was performing and that he gave promise of performing when I wrote fully deserved not only my praise and admiration but all humanity's. I hardly think that all those letters should be destroyed for this one false step: that he chose to live in shame rather than to die in glory. But it is a waste of time to deliberate on the impossible. Though my desire to destroy them should be great, I am now powerless. They have gone out into the world and are no longer subject to my control.

But to resume my story. Rienzo entered the Curia, humbled and despised, he who once made the wicked of this world tremble and fear, and who had filled the upright with most joyful hopes and expectations. Once upon a time he was attended by the whole people of Rome, and in his train the princes of the Italian cities followed. Today the unhappy man proceeded on his way, hemmed in on this side and that by two guards, while the rabble eagerly rushed forward to gaze on the face of the man whose illustrious name they had only heard of. He was being sent to the Roman pontiff by the king of the Romans! Strange traffic indeed.[20] I do not dare to commit to writing the thoughts that now rush to my brain. I did not intend that even this much should escape me; and so I shall continue with the story that I began.

Upon his arrival, then, the supreme pontiff immediately appointed three princes of the church to try his case, with instructions to discover the most suitable punishment for the man who desired the freedom of the republic.[21] O *tempora, o mores.*[22] Alas, how often must we utter this exclamation in our age! In a certain sense, I admit that no penalty is too severe for Cola; first, because he did not persevere in his aims as steadfastly as he should have, and as the condition and the needs of the state demanded; and second, because, having once declared himself liberty's champion, he should not have permitted the enemies of liberty to depart under arms when he could have crushed them all at a single blow, an opportunity that fortune had never offered to any ruler. Fatal and dreadful darkness, which often obscures the sight of men as they struggle over projects of supreme importance![23]

He used to style himself "severe and clement." To tell the truth, he should have decided to put into practice only the second part of this title and not that other part that was quite necessary because of the republic's disease. I say if he had determined to show only mercy to the traitors of their country in sparing their lives, he should at least have deprived them of all means of doing harm, and especially he should have driven them from their frowning strongholds. In this way those who had previously been enemies of Rome would have become her citizens. At any rate, those who had been a source of constant fear would have become an object of contempt. I remember having written to him a well-pondered letter on that occasion.[24] Had he heeded its substance, the republic would now be in a far different condition. Today Rome would not be the slave of others, nor he a prisoner.

I cannot forgive this, nor do I see how his subsequent actions can very well be excused. Although he had assumed the protection of all good citizens and the extermination of all wicked ones, it was only after a short interval that he unexpectedly changed purpose and manners, began to favor the wicked and place his whole trust in them, greatly to the dismay and detriment of the upright. Rienzo himself may perhaps know the motives for his actions, for I have not seen him since; but surely the excuse for a misdeed, though an eloquent man may always frame it readily, never can have the ring of truth. At least he should not have chosen the very lowest of the low. I wrote him once again on the subject, at a time when the republic had not yet fallen but was already tottering.[25]

But enough. I am speaking with too much ardor and, as you see, I dwell sadly on the different stages of my story. Naturally so, for I had placed my last hope for the liberties of Italy in that man. I had long known him and cherished him; but when he began to attempt that most glorious enterprise, I allowed myself to love and to worship him beyond all other mortals. Therefore, the more I hoped in the past, the more I now grieve at the destruction of these hopes. I frankly confess that, whatever the end of it all may be, even now I cannot help admiring his glorious beginning.

But to return once more to my story. He came, but not in chains. This alone was missing from his public disgrace; as for the rest, he was so carefully guarded that there was no hope of escape. As soon as he reached the city gate, the poor unfortunate inquired whether I was in attendance at the Curia, perhaps hoping that I might be of some assistance to him – which, to my knowledge, I can not be – or else simply because he was reminded of an old friendship formerly contracted in that city.[26] Now, therefore, the life of that man, in whose hands the safety and the welfare of so many nations rested, hangs on the nod of strangers. His life and his name are both at stake. Do not be surprised at the outcome; men are now wavering in their opinions; and you will be sure to hear one of two sentences: either that he has been deprived of all legal rights, or that he has been condemned to death.[27] The clay of any moral creature, even of the most sacred and pure, can indeed be destroyed; but virtue fears neither death nor reproach. Virtue is invulnerable and survives all calumny and attack uninjured.

If only he had not stained his honor by his own lethargy and change of purpose! He would have nothing to fear from the sentence hanging over him except physical injury. Yet even today his fame is not in danger among those who judge right and wrong, glory and shame not according to the general opinion but according to certain and more reliable tests. His fame rests secure with those who measure people's greatness by considering the noble qualities they have displayed and not the success that has attended their undertakings.

That this is so results most clearly from the nature of the charge brought against him. No account is taken of the many errors all upright citizens upbraid him for. He is accused for what he did at the opening of his career and not at all for what signaled its close. He is not accused of embracing the cause of the wicked, nor of deserting the standard of liberty, nor of fleeing from the Capitol although in no other place could he have lived more honorably or died more gloriously. What then is the charge, you may ask? This is the one great crime for which he is brought to trial. If he is condemned for this, I shall consider him marked not with infamy but with eternal glory: he has dared to entertain the hope that the republic should be restored to safety and to freedom and that questions of the Roman Empire and the Roman dominion should be settled at Rome.[28] This, a crime, worthy of the gallows and its waiting vultures, indeed! This, surely, is the sum and substance of the accusation and it is for this that punishment is demanded: that a Roman citizen should have voiced his grief at seeing his country, the rightful queen of the universe, the slave of the vilest men!

Now at last listen to what first prompted me to write, and you will have good cause for laughter after the sad recital that has preceded. While the trial is in this unsettled state, I learn from the letters of friends that one hope of safety still remains – the rumor that has spread abroad that Rienzo is a most famous poet! Consequently it seems an act of sacrilege to do violence to a man so worthy and dedicated to so sacred a study. The magnificent phrases that Cicero addressed to the judges in defense of his teacher Aulus Licinius Archias are now on everyone's lips.[29] Many years ago I brought back that speech from far off Germany, where I had roamed impelled by my youthful desire to visit those regions. The following year I sent it on to you all at Florence, who were so eagerly expecting it. I do not stop to cite the passage; for I can readily see from your letters that you still prize that famous oration and still read it with care.[30]

What shall I say of this strange rumor? I heartily rejoice. I consider it a cause for endless congratulation that the Muses are held so much in honor even today. The following is even more astonishing: that the mere mention of the Muses should be powerful enough to bring safety to one who is hated by his very judges, men who are quite unacquainted with their civilizing influence.

What greater victory could the Muses have scored under Augustus Caesar, an age when they were most highly honored and when poets assembled at Rome from every land to view the noble face of the man who was at once an unparalleled prince, the friend of the poets, and the master of the universe? What greater tribute, I ask, could have been paid to the Muses in those days than what we witness today? A man undoubtedly hated – though how just or unjust the hatred I do not stop to prove – and entirely free from all guilt – yet pronounced guilty and convicted – considered worthy of capital punishment by the unanimous vote of his judges – this man is then snatched from the very jaws of death by an appeal to the Muses. Again, I rejoice and congratulate both him and the Muses. I congratulate him because the Muses have been his shield. I congratulate the Muses because of this honor so freely bestowed. I do not begrudge him that the rumor of his being a poet should bring him salvation in his hour of extreme need and when the trial has assumed such a doubtful aspect.

If you were to ask me my private opinion, however, I should answer that Cola di Rienzo is a very fluent speaker, possessing great convincing powers and a decided vein for oratory. As a writer he is pleasing and elegant. His diction, though not extensive, is charming and brilliant. I suppose he has read all the poets, at least all those who are generally known. But he is no more a poet for that reason than he would be a weaver for robing himself with a mantle woven by another's hands. The mere production of verses is not sufficient to merit the composer the name of poet. Horace's words are very true[31]:

> For one certainly should never say this, "I know it's
> Quite enough to give lines their six feet," or suppose
> Those true bards who, like me, write what's much
>   more like prose.

As for Cola, never, to my knowledge, has he managed to write a single line; nor has he devoted the slightest study to the subject of poetry, and without application nothing can be well done, no matter how easy it is.

I wanted to acquaint you with these facts, that you may grieve over the fate that has befallen the former deliverer of a people, that you may rejoice at his unhoped-for freedom, and third that you may, at the same time, weep and laugh over the reason for his safety, even as I do now. Stop to consider for a moment. If Cola escapes uninjured from such great perils under the shield of poetry – and may it so fall out! – what dangers would Virgil not escape.[32] If tried by the judges of this generation, Virgil, however, would perish for other reasons: for today he is considered not a poet but a sorcerer. Indeed, I will now tell you something that will increase your mirth. Even I, the most inveterate enemy of both divination and sorcery that ever was, even I at times have been pronounced a magician by these most worthy judges – and all because of my intimacy with Virgil. Look how low our studies have fallen! Look at what hateful and ridiculous trifles they are reduced to.[33]

I shall relate to you one other remarkable absurdity so that you may become better acquainted with the trend of things by a comparison of several cases, and that you may form an adequate idea of what the people's condition must be from considering the example set by those in high station.

I have a dear friend in Babylon, a man whose acquaintance deserves to be cultivated with great care. I call him "friend" only because I employ the ancient and candid style of speech, writing in the same spirit in which Cicero addressed Pompey the Great as "Friend," or in which Pliny the Elder sent familiar greetings to Vespasian. If I were to adopt today's slavish and cringing speech, I would be compelled to see in my friend only an excellent and revered master. Whatever may be the proper title, this much I can assert in all honesty: that he is one of the few, a prince among princes, and foremost among the highest; a man who reflects honor on his office of Roman cardinal; a man of rare foresight, whose wisdom, it would seem, is easily capable of ruling the world; a man, finally, of lofty intellect and of wide reading.[34]

But after all, Sallustius Crispus is right in saying[35]: "Intellect displays its power only in those things to which attention has been given." This great man frequently honors me by admitting me to his conversation with intimate friends. Often enough there is mention of someone or other who has learned to put together a few words in making a public address, or perhaps has learned to compose a letter with great difficulty. In each and every instance my friend would turn to me with great eagerness – not to say stupefied amazement – and would ask me: "Is this man a poet?" I, on the other hand, would remain silent. What else could I do?

Finally, one day he put that question once too often, this time regarding certain rhetoricians who through long practice rather than ability could manage to write some stupid and nauseating stuff.[36] I repressed a smile with difficulty. Being a very sharp man, he noticed my changed expression at once. Consequently, he pressed me urgently and more urgently to tell him the reason for this. Then, in obedience to his repeated requests, I took advantage of the familiarity with which I always speak to him. I rebuked him – with all due respect, however – for the crass ignorance of so noble a subject in a man of such lofty genius. I pointed out that he did not comprehend even the elementary and fundamental principles of an art to which formerly the masters of the earth, burdened down as they were with affairs of state, certainly had devoted their profound intellects with such longing and earnestness. I cited several examples (which you, of course, do not need) and concluded by proving to him that the number of poets was far smaller than he thought. I spoke hastily, briefly, and superficially, discoursing on the origin of poetry, on its nature and on its aims, but especially on the incredible scarcity of poets, the last subdivision of the learned mentioned by Cicero in his work *De oratore*.[37] That great man listened to my words in wrapt attention; for, though learned in other matters, he was quite ignorant of the subject under discussion. He seemed to be thirsty for information. When I was finished speaking he asked many questions on the separate points of my discourse; and since that day he has carefully avoided making inquiries on the subject of poetry.

As for you, may you live happily and well. Unless you think otherwise, when you are through reading today's letter and yesterday's, send them on to our dear Zanobi at Naples, so that both he and my Barbato may share our mirth and our indignation – provided, of course, that

Barbato has left his haven at Sulmona by now and has returned to the stormy waters of Parthenope.

At the Fountain of the Sorgue, August 10.[38]

NOTES

1. For the events of 1352 and 1353, see Gregorovius 6.1: 328-55; and Mollat, *Popes*, pp. 152-53.

2. See above Chapter 10, pp. 119-20, n. 3; and Mollat, *Popes*, p. 153.

3. See also Mollat, *Popes*, p. 153.

4. Theiner 2, no. 200.

5. Theiner 2, no. 204.

6. Gregorovius 6.1: 346.

7. Theiner 2, no. 217.

8. Theiner 2, no. 218.

9. *Vita* 2.13; Wright 4.2, pp. 127-28.

10. The pope's comparison may have been apt. Though often accused of Manichean heresy, the Patarines were an orthodox but revolutionary group that reached their height in Milan in the 1060s and 1070s. Spurred by the emerging Gregorian Reform, they called for the moral renewal of the clergy, boycotting sacraments administered by priests living in sin. Largely poor working people, they found themselves allied with the papacy against the higher clergy and nobility of the city. Though the movement was short-lived, the fears of social upheaval that it inspired long survived it. See Rosalind and Christopher Brooke, *Popular Religion in the Middle Ages. Western Europe 1000-1300* (New York: Thames and Hudson, 1984), 53-54, and bibliography on p. 161.

11. The chapter of the *Vita* preceding this says that the emperor had reassured Cola not to entertain any fears whatsoever regarding his powerful enemies. For background see Jaroslav Ludvíkovsky, "List Karla IV Colovi di Rienzi do Vézení [The Letter of Charles IV to Cola di Rienzo in Prison]," *Studia minora facultatis philosophicae universitatis Brunensis. Series Archeologica et Classica* 24 (1981): 117-21.

12. Gregorovius 6.1: 350.

13. *Familiari* 13.6, Bernardo 2: 193-98; Wilkins, *Vaucluse*, pp. 132-40; Bishop, *Letters*, pp. 115-18. See also Wilkins, *Life*, pp. 117-18; and his *Studies*, pp. 193-212.

14. Fracassetti wrongly adopted July 1351 as the date of Cola's journey to Avignon. In this he followed Papencordt, and he was consequently forced into several misunderstandings. For instance, he argues that Cola's journey could not have taken place in July 1352, because in such case it would be difficult to believe that he could have reached Avignon as soon as August, and that the trial could already have been ended by August 10, when all fear of Cola's conviction had vanished, and when there was already talk of acquitting him on the strange plea of his being a poet (*Lettere* 3: 237). Fracassetti furthermore assumes that a

considerable period of time elapsed after Cola's arrival at Avignon before the pope appointed the three cardinals who were to judge him. He also assumes the usual delays of the law, all in an attempt to bridge the gap between the supposed date of Cola's arrival in July or August 1351 and August 10, 1352, the date of *Familiari* 13.6. Finally, and for the same reason, he places Petrarch's letter to the Roman people (*Sine Titulo* [*Nomine*] 4, Piur, pp. 173-84) chronologically ahead of this letter to Nelli (*Familiari* 13.6).

The papal briefs already cited prove beyond possibility of doubt that Cola's journey from Bohemia to Avignon took place during July 1352. Consequently, the letter to Nelli was in fact written shortly thereafter and Petrarch's "recently" (*nuper*, Fracassetti, *Epistolae* 2: 234) must be taken in its literal sense, and not (as Fracassetti says, *Lettere* 3: 237) in a rather broad and liberal sense. It follows, therefore, that *Familiari* 13.6 must be earlier than *Sine Titulo* [*Nomine*] 4. The internal evidence of *Familiari* 13.6 refutes Fracassetti's assumptions.

We shall take up the various points in their proper order. There was no delay in appointing the three cardinals who were to judge Cola. Petrarch distinctly says that they were appointed immediately after Cola's arrival – *Ut ergo* [sc. *Nicolaus*] *pervenit, illico pontifex maximus tribus e numero principum ecclesiae causam eius discernendam dedit* (Fracassetti, *Epistolae* 2: 236). All fear of Cola's conviction had not vanished, for Petrarch says: first, that Cola's safety was still in the hands of strangers – *Nunc ergo viri salus...de manibus pendet alienus* (p. 237); second, that he learns from the letters of friends that only one hope for Cola's acquittal remains – *unam sibi relictam spem salutis* (p. 238); and third that Cola is in his hour of extreme need – *in extremis casibus* (p. 239; compare *in extremis* 3: 501 and *dum licet* 3: 503). Finally, as Petrarch continues to speak of Cola's acquittal as a matter that had been unhoped for but that was still to be realized – *de insperata gaudeas salute*; and he adds: "if Cola escapes uninjured from such great perils" – *si...Nicolaus e tantis periculis evaserit* (2: 240). All the above citations prove, we think, not only that the trial was not over by August 10 but, indeed, that it had been only recently launched. For this reason, as well as from the internal evidence offered by *Sine Titulo* [*Nomine*] 4, we reach the conclusion that the letter is to be dated later than *Familiari* 13.6, and perhaps not earlier than the middle of September 1352.

15. In *Familiari* 13.5 (Bernardo 2: 187-92; Wilkins, *Vaucluse*, pp. 124-31; Bishop, *Letters*, pp. 112-15), which precedes the present letter in his correspondence, Petrarch relates that his friends had warmly offered to him the office of apostolic secretary, and that, in the presence of the pope himself, they had remarked that the only drawback was his style, which would prove to be too noble and too elevated for the position offered to him. Petrarch could hardly believe them serious in offering him a post of such honor; indeed he judged that their criticism of his style was meant very much as satire. The assurances of the assembly, however, restored his confidence in the sincerity of their proposal. He was then given a theme on which to compose something extemporaneously.

Petrarch, who dreaded the mere thought of tying himself down to such steady employment and who considered any encroachment on his time as nothing short of slavery, saw his opportunity here and he made the most of it. He assures Nelli that, though the theme suggested to him was in no way worthy of the Muses and Apollo, he so exerted his every power as to rise to heights to which his listeners could not follow. The verdict of the assembly was that Petrarch should be allowed time in which to learn the barbaric style characteristic of the chanceries of the day. Breathing freely once again, Petrarch concludes the letter congratulating himself on his narrow escape from the threatened servitude.

16. Robinson and Rolfe, *Petrarch*, p. 342, translate "although there are plenty of trifling duties." The main original reads (Fracassetti, *Epistolae* 2: 233): *Nil certe nunc maius habeo quod agam: Immo vero multa: sed maioribus incumbere breve tempus vetat.* Similarly we do not think that *Babylone ultimo digressus* (Fracassetti, *Epistolae* 2: 234) means "Having left Babylon for the last time." It so happens that after his departure for Italy on May 1, 1353 (Fracassetti, *Lettere* 1: 181), Petrarch never again set foot on French soil. But surely he could not have known this when writing the present letter to Nelli on August 10, 1352; for Vaucluse was only 15 miles from Avignon, and the slightest call from the pope or from one of his many friends in the Sacred College would have brought him back immediately. Were any further proof necessary we would find it in a letter that Petrarch wrote in 1361-62, in which he describes to Cardinal Talleyrand the motives that urged him to leave Avignon at about this time – December 1352 or January 1353. Petrarch says (*Seniles* 1: 3, p. 739, quoted below in n. 33) "Therefore, at the time that he [Innocent VI] ascended the sacred chair [December 30, 1352], I left Avignon not knowing whether or not I should ever return" – *nescio an umquam reversurus inde abiens.*

17. *Georgics* 1.312.

18. In a letter to Pietro, abbot of St. Bénigne, written in the same year as the present letter, Petrarch expresses himself on this subject with greater freedom and playfulness (*Familiari* 13.7; Fracassetti *Epistolae* 2: 245-46; Bernardo 2: 199-203; Wilkins, *Vaucluse*, pp. 145-49; Bishop, *Letters*, pp. 118-22):

> Until now, well-meaning young men, eager to further their own interests and those of their friends, were used to drawing up papers that pertained to their own property, or to their business affairs, or to the noisy debates of the echoing law courts. But now we are all plying the same trade. Now the words of Horace are verified to the letter [*Epistolae* 2.1 117], "But verses all men scribble, wise or fools."
>
> It is only a poor form of consolation to have found so many to share one's burdens. I would prefer to grow ill alone. As matters stand, I am preoccupied by my own faults as well as by those of others; and even if I should wish to pause and to regain my breath, I

am not permitted to do so. Daily, and from every corner of the world, epistles and odes are showered on my head. Nor does this satisfy my foreign correspondents. I am overwhelmed by a perfect avalanche of letters not only from France, but also from Greece and Germany and England. I am called on to be the arbiter of all talents, though unaware of possessing any myself. Were I to answer each and every one of these letters, I would be the busiest of men. Were I to condemn the fruits of their labors, I would be pronounced an envious critic; were I to praise them, a false flatterer; and were I to express no opinion at all, I should be judged insolent and haughty. They are afraid, I suppose, that I am aging too slowly. Thanks to their incitements and to my ever-feverish passion for writing, I may gratify their wishes.

But this was nothing. Who would believe it? The disease has been spreading and very recently it fastened on the Roman Curia itself. What do you suppose the lawyers and the physicians are now discussing? They no longer study their Justinian and their Aesculapius, they no longer heed the voices of their clients or the groans of their patients. They have become deaf, smitten with prophetic fury by the names of Homer and Virgil. They rove in the wooded valleys of Cirrha and linger by the murmuring fountain of Aonia. But why do I dwell on these minor portents? Wagon-makers, fullers, and farmers have abandoned the plough and the other tools of their trades and chatter about the Muses and Apollo. It is inconceivable how far this pestilence has spread. Only recently it was confined to a few.

If you require a reason for all this, it is simply that poetry is a most delightful thing; but it is really understood only by men of rare talents, for poetry demands an utter disregard and contempt for all mortal things, an elevated mind that can withdraw itself from the things of the world, and suitable natural endowments. Therefore, both experience and the authority of the most learned men teach us that in none of the arts is progress less due to study than in that of poetry.

It may be laughable to you, perhaps, but to me it is a disgusting fact that one can stumble over poets at every street corner, but can scarcely see one on Helicon. All men taste the Pierian honeycomb with the tips of their tongues, but not one can digest it. Imagine, I beg you, how powerful and how delightful a gift poetry must be to its true possessors, when it gives such great pleasure to these idle dreamers; when, in spite of their occupations and their greed, in spite of the countless vanities of our age and the many hours spent in frivolities, it has caused these men to forget their affairs and to neglect the accumulation of riches!

For one reason I congratulate the fatherland: that in the midst of the miserable tares and barren oats [Virgil, *Eclogue* 5.37; *Georgics* 1.154] scattered throughout the world young men of greater ability are rising, young men who, unless my love deceives me, will drink at the Castalian spring and not in vain. I congratulate you all, Mantua beloved by the Muses, Padua, Verona, Umbria, my dear Sulmona, and Parthenope, home of Virgil. For I behold these new bands of poetasters far away from you, roaming far and wide in uncertain bypaths and tormented by a parching thirst that they can never quench.

19. The references are, respectively, to the Bohemian king, Emperor Charles IV; and to Clement VI, whose family name was Pierre Roger and who was a native of Limoges.

20. Robinson and Rolfe omit these words (Fracassetti, *Epistolae* 2: 236, l. 1) to *In hoc statu* (p. 238); and again from the words O *nugas* (p. 240) to the end of the letter. These two omissions constitute almost exactly one-half of the entire letter.

21. Here again we are indebted to Abbé de Sade, who seems to have been so well informed on matters dealing with the Sacred College. He admits that the three judges appointed to try Cola di Rienzo are not known but proposes the following cardinals: Gui de Boulogne, Talleyrand, and Bertrand de Déaulx (*Mémoires* 3: 233).

22. Cicero, *In Catilinam* 1.1, 2.

23. Petrarch refers to the arrest of the barons at the banquet given by Cola on September 14 and to their release on September 15, when Cola, as if to make amends for his boldness, showered honors and offices on them. The arrested barons included several members of the Colonna, and even more of the Orsini. Their names are given in detail in the anonymous *Vita*, which consequently became their chief source for identification. According to the *Vita* (1.28, col. 821, Wright, pp. 74-75), the Colonna were Stefano the Elder, the venerable head of the house; Pietro d'Agapito Colonna, lord of Genazzano, formerly provost of Marseilles, and senator of Rome during the first half of 1347; and Giovanni Stefano Colonna, grandson of Stefano the Elder, and at this time a youth of twenty years, who had, a few days before, been appointed by Cola captain of the Campagna. The Orsini were Roberto, son of Count Bertoldo, and likewise senator of Rome during the first half of 1347; Giordano of the Orsini del Monte; Rinaldo of the Orsini of Marino; Cola, lord of Castel Sant' Angelo; and Count Bertoldo, lord of Vicovaro. This makes a total of three Colonna and five Orsini; and the biographer adds (*Vita*, col. 823; Wright, p. 75): "and many others of the foremost barons of Rome."

In Cola's letter to Rinaldo Orsini (*Epistolario* 23, dated Rome, September 17, 1347, p. 61; Burdach and Piur, Letter 40, 2.3: 145, ll. 15-17) we have practically the same list. Among the Colonna there is no mention of Pietro, son of Agapito;

among the Orsini we do not find Senator Roberto, but instead there is mention of Orso, brother of Giordano del Monte and son of Jacopo Orsini, Among those who were honored with offices, di Rienzo gives (*Epistolario* p. 63; Burdach and Piur, p. 146, ll. 39-45) the same list as on p. 61, with the addition of Cola Orsini.

Petrarch thinks that Cola di Rienzo missed his opportunity here. Cola's biographer considers him guilty of neglecting a second opportunity after the battle of November 20, 1347, when Cola broke the power of the barons. After an excursus on the famous conversation between Hannibal and Maharbal after the battle of Cannae, he says (*Vita* 1.36, cols. 857, 859; Wright, p. 90):

> And now to the point. If Cola di Rienzo, the Tribune, had followed up his victory and had advanced on Marino, he would have taken the castle of Marino and would have utterly destroyed the power of Messer Giordano, who could never again have raised his head. And the people of Rome would have lived unmolested in the enjoyment of their liberty.

24. In Chapter 9, p. 90, we already pointed out the dearth of material for the period of time between the writing of *Familiari* 7.1 and *Familiari* 7.7. The former letter, addressed to Marco Barbato, is dated Avignon, September 11, 1347; the latter, addressed to Cola, is dated Genoa, November 29, 1347. Of course, Develay (*Lettres à Rienzi* 2: 90) is absolutely wrong in identifying the "well-pondered letter" mentioned here with Letter 2. Letter 2 was written when Petrarch first heard of Cola's elevation, and all agree that the letter must be dated to the end of June or the beginning of July. It is clear from our preceding note that the "well-pondered letter" that Petrarch mentions here must have been written when he became acquainted with the arrest of the barons on September 14 and with their release on September 15. Cola sent a full account of these events to the papal notary Rinaldo Orsini on September 17 (see n. 23). According to our calculations, this letter must have reached Avignon about October 3. But by this time the pope must have heard only of the arrest of the barons, for we find him writing on October 4, 1347 and interceding with Cola for the pardon of the nobles in the name of the reverence due to the pope and the apostolic see (Theiner 2, no. 177). Someone, evidently, had hurriedly sent a dispatch to the pope on the evening of September 14. The "well-pondered letter" that Petrarch wrote on that occasion, therefore, must likewise have been written in October, but unfortunately such a letter is not to be found in the extant correspondence.

25. The letter referred to now is *Familiari* 7.7, the spirit of which is clearly summarized in the present paragraph.

26. It will be remembered that Cola and Petrarch had become intimate friends at Avignon in 1343, on the occasion of the second embassy of the Romans to the newly elected pope, Clement VI. See Chapter 1, pp. 1-8.

27. The original Latin is very uncertain here: *Non advertes ante vibrante sententia* (sic) *vel intestabilem illum audies vel extinctum* (Fracassetti, *Epistolae* 2: 237). Just

143

like Fracassetti *(Lettere* 3: 231), we have tried to divine the meaning of this passage, for it was impossible to translate it. Bernardo 2: 195 reads: "Do not be surprised if you hear him declared in a ringing judgment guilty of infamy or sentenced to death"; Wilkins, *Vaucluse,* p. 136: "The decision is in the balance: do not be surprised if you hear that he has been convicted of infamy or put to death." Bishop, *Letters,* p. 116, offers: "Don't be surprised if, when the sentence is proclaimed, you learn that he is degraded or capitally punished."

28. These are the two charges on which Cola was to be tried: his declarations that Rome was a free city, and that the rights of the Roman Empire were in the sacred possession of the Roman people only. These two statements, therefore, constituted a declaration of war against the two principles that so fundamentally ruled the Middle Ages, represented by the Guelphs and the Ghibellines: the supremacy in Italy of the Roman church as embodied in a pope, and the supremacy of the Holy Roman Empire as embodied in the emperor of German origin. The former declaration assailed the temporal claims of the papacy over Rome; the latter, those of Charles IV. According to Petrarch's testimony, then, Cola's lengthy trial reduces itself to a political one, purely and simply. The religious trial – that is to say the question of Cola's heresy and the subsequent excommunication inflicted on him – must have been hushed or previously dealt with as quickly and as concisely as its description by Cola's anonymous biographer: "His deeds were examined, and he was found to be a faithful Christian."

29. Cicero, *Pro Archia* 8.

30. Petrarch says (Fracassetti, *Epistolae* 2: 238): *illa quidem praeclara sententia iam in vulgus effusa, qua pro Aulo Licinio Archia praeceptore suo apud iudices usus est Cicero; quam non apposui.* The *quam* surely refers to *sententia,* and the sentence *quam non apposui* should be translated: "I do not stop to cite the passage" *(quam,* i.e. *sententiam).* Compare: "But I need not add a description of the oration" (Robinson and Rolfe, p. 345). Similarly, Petrarch's *orationem...vobis optantibus transmissam* (Fracassetti, *Epistolae* 2: 239, l. 1) surely indicates that the oration was eagerly desired by all of Petrarch's Florentine friends, including Nelli, as is proved by the plural *vobis* instead of a *tibi,* and by the plurals *habetis* and *legitis* instead of a *habes* and a *legis;* hence the oration was not sent in response to the desires of your friends" (Robinson and Rolfe, p. 345), but "to you all at Florence, who were so eagerly expecting it."

Petrarch gives a brief account of his discovery of the oration *Pro Archia* in a letter written to the papal secretary Luca della Penna (*Seniles* 16.1, *Dabis veniam,* dated Arquà, April 27, 1374, p. 948 in the Basel ed. of 1582; Bishop, *Letters,* pp. 292-99, especially 295-96):

> At about the twenty-fifth year of my life [1329], while hurriedly traveling among the Belgians and the Swiss, I reached the city of Liège. On hearing that the city contained a good number of books, I stopped there and detained my companions until I was in possession of two

orations of Cicero, one copied by the hand of a friend, the second by my own. The latter oration I afterward spread throughout Italy; and to make you smile I tell you that it was quite a considerable task to find some ink in so fine a barbarian city and then when it was found, it was much the color of saffron.

31. *Saturae* 1.4, 40-42 (R.M. Millington trans.).

32. Petrarch says (Fracassetti, *Epistolae* 2: 240): *cogitesque: si (quod utinam accidat) sub clypeo poetico Nicolaus e tantis periculis evaserit, unde non evasurus esset Maro?* Robinson and Rolfe (p. 347) translate as follows: "and will wonder, if Cola – which God grant! – can, in such imminent peril, find shelter beneath the aegis of the poet, why Vergil should not escape in the same way."

33. There is a passing reference to this accusation against Petrarch in *Familiari* 9.5; Fracassetti, *Epistolae* 2: 18-19; Bernardo 2: 13-23, dated Avignon, December 8, 1352:

> I say I may now appear to many to be a necromancer and enchanter, because to tell the truth I am frequently alone and because – it is something that has justly dispelled my wrath with laughter – I read the works of Virgil, as those most learned men say. And I do not deny it; I have read them. See the cause of their suspicions! See the disrepute cast on our studies.

The above letter continues with some very interesting remarks on the vanity of human wishes. But the details of the incident are given in a letter written years later, in 1361 or 1362, to Cardinal Talleyrand, and they are mentioned in connection with the post of the Apostolic Secretary that had been offered to him (*Seniles* 1.4, *Litteras pridem;* 1.3 of the Basel edition of 1581, p. 739; see Wilkins, *Life*, pp. 180-82; and Ugo Dotti, "Il primo libro delle 'Senili' di Francesco Petrarca," *Giornale storico della letteratura italiana* 169.546 (1992): 228-39 for background). A new translation of the *Seniles* has appeared as *Letters of Old Age, Rerum senilium libri* I-XVIII, Aldo S. Bernardi, Saul Levin, and Reta A. Bernardo, trans. (Baltimore: Johns Hopkins University Press, 1992).

> It was with reverent joy but with amazement, most loving father, that I read your letter and the commands of His Holiness that it contained. The great hurry of your messenger did not allow me the time necessary for an adequate answer. Nevertheless, I answered as best I could, very briefly, but clearly. What I had not time to put down in writing, I was content to confide to your trusted messenger. But look, I am now overwhelmed again by more messengers and by more letters on the same subject, at which both my astonishment and my joy increase.
>
> For who, I ask, would not be amazed, and who would not rejoice at becoming the friend of the Vicar of Jesus Christ, at becoming the friend of that man who not merely suspects, but actually affirms

that I am a magician? Who would not rejoice that he has now suddenly laid aside this suspicion of me, a suspicion that he had so falsely entertained and that until now he had always defended so stubbornly against your eloquent objections and against those of many who desired to root it out? Why should I not rejoice? Not only has he now laid aside such suspicion, but he has replaced it with an opinion so utterly the opposite that he offers to me the post of Apostolic Secretary and beseeches with gifts and with prayers the faithful services of the very man at whose conversation and presence he once seemed to shudder! Great is the power of truth; it may be crushed and prostrated by falsehood, but it cannot be destroyed. After lying prostrate for a time, of its own strength truth will rise to greater and brighter heights.

May God, however, forgive him who was so falsely the author of that suspicion [Cardinal Pierre Desprez]. He was a great man indeed, for he was not the least among those of your order [he had been vice-chancellor since 1325]; in addition, he was a most learned jurist (which makes his error all the more remarkable), a man of the most varied experience [cardinal since 1320] and of very advanced years [born c. 1280]. But perhaps his was not an error at all but merely evidence of his hatred....

Whatever may have been the cause, he pronounced me a magician, and he did not blush to allege as his reason for the fact that I read the works of Virgil, or had read them. And he found men to believe him [among others, Cardinal Etienne Aubert of Limoges]. Look at the intellects to which the control of the highest matters is entrusted!

You truly know how often we joked over these accusations, several times even in the presence of the one whom my accuser had persuaded [Cardinal Aubert]. But when at last he [Cardinal Aubert] had been raised to the papal see [as Innocent VI], then the accusation ceased to be a joking matter, and it began to turn to your anger and to my grief. Not that I especially desired anything of him, for all my desires are well known to you. But since Benedict [XII] had judged my youth, and Clement [VI] my manhood, and since they had found me, I do not say innocent, but at any rate opposed to base studies and injurious arts, I could not help grieving that my old age had been suspected by Innocent. Therefore at the time that he ascended the sacred chair [December 30, 1352], I left Avignon not knowing whether or not I should ever return. Although, in compliance with even his wishes, you had desired to take me to him that I might bid him farewell, I refused, lest my magical arts should annoy him, or lest his credulity should annoy me.

You know that I speak the truth when I say that you tried time and again, and in vain, not to have me set out without having paid my respects to him. See what the venomous tongue of a single man brought on me, a man who had no earthly reason for hating me! But nothing happens without a reason; he [Desprez] hated me not indeed for myself, but because of that man with whom he remembered I had lived on the most intimate terms [Cardinal Giovanni Colonna, who died on July 3, 1348]. Yes, because of that same man he hated you too; but, being conscious of fostering an unjust hatred, he feigned friendship for both of us, consummate hypocrite that he was! I mention facts that are well known to you; though that man had been laid to rest, as if not appeased by his death, he [Desprez] had declared war on his very ashes....

The pontiff, indeed, can scarcely believe that the man whom he desires as his secretary is a magician. Nor can he suppose that the man whom he considers worthy of the secrets of his inner councils and fit to perform the duties of his sacred correspondence devotes his labors to abominable incantations and sorceries. For these great honors I render him thanks; nor do I render him lesser thanks for having rid himself of his delusion....

34. These would seem to be sufficient evidence to identify Petrarch's "dear friend," and yet such identification is impossible at present. Develay's statement that the cardinal referred to is Giovanni Colonna (*Lettres à Rienzi* 2: 103) is, of course, the wildest kind of guess; for Cardinal Giovanni Colonna died of the plague in Avignon on July 3, 1348. Fracassetti (*Lettere* 3: 238) advances the hypothesis that the cardinal in question may have been one of the three cardinals appointed to try Cola.

35. Sallust, *Catilina* 51.3.

36. Petrarch's meaning and words, *pingue quiddam et rancidum* (Fracassetti, *Epistolae* 2: 241), are reminiscent of the words spoken by Cicero with similar purpose, *pingue quiddam sonantibus atque peregrinum* (*Pro Archia* 10.26).

37. The original Latin is misleading: *quem novissimum articulum in Oratore suo Tullius attigit* (Fracassetti, *Epistolae* 2: 241). Petrarch undoubtedly refers to the *De oratore* 1.3. That chapter speaks first of the philosophers. Cicero says it would be difficult to enumerate the large number of eminent ones. It then speaks of the mathematicians, all of whom seem to attain what they earnestly desire; third, of musicians and of grammarians, who are able to master the whole range of their sciences, though they are almost infinite. Finally Cicero says (1.3, 11):

I think I may truly say this: that of all who have occupied themselves with the studies and the principles of the most liberal arts, the number of those who have risen to eminence is smallest among the poets. And in the number of the learned....here will be found far fewer good orators than good poets.

38. There is a strange inconsistency among authors in regard to the date of this letter, which is August 10, 1352 (Fracassetti, *Lettere* 1: 110, 3: 227, 236; *Epistolae* 2: 242). Papencordt, who prints part of this letter to Nelli among his Documents (no. 28), dates it Vaucluse, August 12, 1352 (p. lxxviii), but correctly prints *ad fontem Sorgie* IIII *Id Aug.* on p. lxxxi, and gives August 10, 1352, on p. 254, n. 1. Filippini, citing and perhaps misunderstanding Papencordt, gives August 12, 1351 (*Studi storici* 10: 254, n. 2), changing it without any explanation to August 12, 1352 in the continuation of his article (*Studi storici* 11: 11, n. 2). Gregorovius likewise using Papencordt, says August 12 on one page (6.1: 351, n. 2) and August 10 on the next (352, n. 1; compare also Maurice Faucon, "Note sur la détention de Rienzi à Avignon," *Mélanges d'archéologie et d'histoire (École française de Rome)* 7 (1887): 53-58, esp. pp. 53 and 55). The reason for Papencordt's slip, which they all follow, was an error on the day on which the Ides of August fell. Since these fell on August 13 and not on August 15, according to the Roman method of calculating dates, four days before the Ides would be August 10. A further proof of the correctness of this date is to be found in Petrarch's closing statement referring to another letter to Nelli written on the preceding day. This letter is extant (*Familiari* 13.5) and is dated *V Ides Augusti* (Fracassetti, *Epistolae* 2: 233), that is, August 9. For this letter see above n. 15.

CHAPTER 12

AVIGNON, OCTOBER 1352

Cola's trial advanced with all the usual delays of the law. Indeed, not much attention was paid to the former tribune after the excitement of his arrival had abated. The first mention of Cola in papal expense books is found under the date of August 14, 1352, where the interesting fact is recorded of the purchase of a bed for the imprisoned tribune.[1] The next entry is under the date of October 21, 1352, and it records the payments made by Michel de Pistoie (Michele di Pistoia?), the sergeant-at-arms in charge of Cola, for other purchases intended to satisfy Cola's needs.[2] In the meantime in his vaulted prison chamber, Cola calmly read his Bible and his Roman historians, perhaps feeling quite certain of his ultimate freedom.[3] If Gui de Boulogne were really one of the three cardinals appointed to try Cola, then his mission to Paris in the early part of September 1352 caused a vacancy in the board of cardinals, and an unavoidable delay in the trial must have ensued. Again, the illness of Pope Clement VI and his death on December 6, 1352 must further have brightened Cola's prospects of ultimate acquittal. Under the new pope, Innocent VI, who had not been directly harmed by Rome's former rector, Cola's custody must have become very light and easy.

The time for an appeal to the Romans was propitious: interest in the prosecution of Cola's trial had abated; the outburst of the poetic mania in Provence also favored Cola's chances; there may still have been a vacancy on the board of judges; and the pope's illness had reduced the urgency for Cola's conviction. Petrarch's lack of interest in Cola's fate, the coldness evident in the preceding letter, began to change under these favorable circumstances. His patriotism, which he had thought dead so far as Cola was concerned, was stirred again. It irresistibly urged him to take up his pen so that his voice, as in the golden days of the *Hortatoria*, might be heard again, though from a distance, and that he might again perform his duty as a Roman citizen and an Italian patriot.

PETRARCH TO THE ROMAN PEOPLE
(SINE NOMINE 4)

Invincible people, conqueror of the universe, my people! It is you whom
I address anonymously.[4] I must discuss matters of the highest importance with you, and briefly. Give me your attention, I beg and beseech
you, most illustrious people. Your interests are at stake. It is a question,
I repeat, of great importance, no, of the greatest importance, one to
which all other earthly questions must give way. Perhaps you are eager
to learn the facts; consequently I shall torment you with suspense no
longer, nor shall I try to magnify with mere words a question that by its
very nature is a most momentous one. Without further preamble, then,
I come to the facts themselves.

Your former tribune is now – oh melancholy sight – the prisoner of a
stranger. Like the man who steals under the cover of darkness, or like
an ordinary traitor, he pleads his cause in chains. Though brought before the arbiters of the world and the dispensers of justice, he is denied
the privilege of presenting a legal defense – a right that has never been
denied to even the most sacrilegious wretch.[5] But perhaps his suffering
such a treatment is not altogether undeserved; for, at the very moment
when his enterprise gave promise of most glorious success, he abandoned the flourishing republic that had been planted and had taken
deep root, so to speak, in his genius and his hands. Most undeserved,
however, is the penalty inflicted on Rome. Formerly her citizens were
inviolable and exempt from punishment under the protection of their
laws. But today they are dishonored and outraged everywhere in obedience to the cruel caprices of everybody and anybody. The offenders,
moreover, not only incur no infamy for their crime but, on the contrary, receive high praise as men of virtue!

Illustrious people, no longer be ignorant of the charges preferred
against him who was once your head and ruler but who is now – shall
I say your fellow citizen or exile? You will hear facts that may or may
not be known to you but that will surely fill you with wonder and indignation. He is accused not of neglecting, but of defending, the cause of
liberty. He is pronounced guilty not for having deserted, but for having

mounted the Capitol. This, finally, is the chief charge against him, a crime to be atoned for on the scaffold: that he has had the presumption to affirm that even today the Roman Empire is at Rome and at the disposal of the people of Rome.

Ungodly age! Grim envy! Unheard-of hatred! What are you doing now, Christ, infallible and incorruptible judge of all things? Where are your eyes, with which you dispel the mists of human misery? Where have you turned your gaze? Why don't you end this infamous trial with your forked lightning?[6] Though we are unworthy, look on us and take pity. Look how our enemies – your enemies as well – have multiplied! See with what unholy hatred they hate us, and you! Judge, we beseech you, between two causes so utterly unlike. Finally let your presence pronounce judgment, and let your eyes behold justice.

Surely, there is no cause for indignation or for wonder that any nation, or that all nations – as we have seen – should have desired freedom from the yoke of Rome, just and easy though the yoke was. For there dwells in the human heart an innate love of liberty, which is often inconsiderate and rash. Often a false sense of shame forbids humans from obeying their superiors, and those who would have played their role better in subordinate positions often rise unfit to positions of command. Consequently the world becomes confused and chaotic. Hence it is that, in the place of dignified command, we often find shameful servitude; and in the place of just subjection, unjust command. Were it not so, human affairs would be better ordered; and the world would be in better health, if Rome, its head, were still uninjured.

If my words are unconvincing, then believe past experience. When, I ask, was there such peace, such tranquillity, such justice; when was such tribute paid to honesty, when were the good so readily rewarded and the evil punished; when were human affairs so well administered as when the world had only one head, and that head was Rome? At what time did God, the lover of peace and justice, condescend to be born of the Virgin and to visit the earth?[7] Every living creature possesses only one head; and the world, which the poet calls the Great Body,[8] should be content with only one temporal head. It would be monstrous and unnatural for any creature to possess two heads. How much more portentous, then, is an animal with a thousand different heads biting and tearing one another in turn? Even granting that several heads are possible, surely none ought to doubt that one of these should curb and hold all the others in check so that the peace of the body as a whole may remain undisturbed.

We have countless proofs, and the authority of the most learned scholars as well, to the effect that unified rule has always been of the greatest advantage both in heaven and on earth. Omnipotent God has declared in many ways his will that this supreme head should be none other than Rome.[9] He has ennobled her with the glories of peace and of war and has made her a matchless wonder, excelling in all the virtues.

The human mind rejoices daily in its own perversity. Notwithstanding the truth of the above, if then, any nation, as I have already said, should have preferred a dangerous and doubtful liberty to the safe and wholesome authority of the common mother, some indulgence could be offered for its arrogance – or for its ignorance. But who can hear with unruffled brow that learned men are discussing the question whether or not the Roman Empire should be at Rome? I suppose we are to assume that the empires of the Parthians and the Persians and the Medes are respectively in the power of the Parthians and the Persians and the Medes. Will the Roman Empire alone, then, have no fixed abode? Who can stomach this insult? Who would not rather vomit it out and cast it off completely?

If the Roman Empire is not at Rome, pray, where is it? To tell the truth, if it is to be found elsewhere, it is no longer the empire of the Romans but of those among whom fickle fortune has placed it.[10] Roman generals surely often fought to defend the needs of the empire in the lands of the extreme East and in those of the extreme West; they often fought in the regions ruled by Boreas and in those ruled by Auster. But the Roman Empire itself, in the meantime, remained firmly fixed at Rome. It was Rome that judged whether Roman generals were to be praised or censured. On the Capitol it was decided who should be honored and who punished, who should enter the city as a private citizen and who should receive an ovation or a triumph. It is a positive fact that, even after the tyranny – or monarchy if we so prefer – of Julius Caesar, the Roman emperors, although already assigned a place in the council of the gods, sought sanction for their deeds either from the

Senate or from the Roman people. According to whether this sanction was given or withheld, they accomplished their undertakings or abandoned them. Emperors, therefore, may roam about; but the seat of the empire remains firm and immovable.

We must suppose, therefore, that Virgil was speaking of the perpetuity of the Roman Empire and not of the temporal existence of the Romans themselves, when he said:

> While Capitol abides in place,
> The mansion of the Aeneian race,
> And throned upon that moveless base
> Rome's father sits sublime.[11]

For by these words Virgil was promising to the two youths[12] not one hundred nor one thousand years of glory, but immortality itself. That no one may consider my words mere flattery, unworthy both for me to speak and for you Romans to hear, I shall now make a necessary digression.

I am well aware that, in this matter of empire, Virgil was rebuked by St. Augustine in a certain passage, and not unjustly. But presently, and in the same passage, he is most justly excused by the same St. Augustine. When the poet represents Jove as speaking of you, Romans, he says:

> Then, with his nurse's wolf-skin girt,
> Shall Romulus the line assert,
> Invite them to his new-raised home,
> And call the martial city Rome.[13]

Adding the element of perpetuity to the prophecy of the Roman origin, the poet continues:

> No date, no goal I here ordain:
> Theirs is an endless, boundless reign.[14]

At this point St. Augustine rightly remarks: how, indeed is he [Jove] able to grant an endless empire, who never has granted nor can grant anything whatsoever, having no power beyond that of any other wretched mortal, and being not honored, but burdened down and oppressed by the false belief in his divinity? But I pass over the question concerning the author of the Roman Empire, for it is certain that it

was granted by none other than Omnipotent God, who rules with undisputed sway both in heaven and on earth, and from whose power all
other authority is derived. St. Augustine next inquires where this empire is situated: "Has it its abode in heaven or on earth? Undoubtedly
on earth," he answers; "and even were it in heaven, heaven and earth
shall pass away,[15] which God himself has created. How much sooner,
then, will what Romulus has founded pass away."[16]

So speaks St. Augustine denying Virgil's statements. It is very certainly very clear that all kingdoms and whatever else appears grand
and magnificent to our eyes, even though not sooner, will inevitably
fall into ruin when heaven and earth are shaken from their foundation
by the arm of their creator who will call into being a new heaven and a
new earth.[17] For, being truth itself, he does not lie,[18] as Jupiter does. His
is the kingdom without beginning and without end, of which it is written: "And of his kingdom there shall be no end."[19]

Virgil may, perhaps, have been ignorant of this prophecy, for though
God had endowed him with a surpassing genius and power of expression, he had denied him the knowledge of those truths that were hidden from the wise and were to be revealed to little ones.[20] But surely
Virgil clearly understood that all the kingdoms of the earth, having a
beginning, are destined to perish. He was consequently extremely cau-
tious. If in any passage of his works he promised immortality to the
Roman Empire, it will be observed that he was not speaking in his own
person, but that he placed the words in the mouth of Jove, so that the
lying prophecy and the false promise are both to be attributed to the
lying god.[21] In other words, Virgil falsely employed the falsehood of
another to gratify the vanity of the Roman people. But elsewhere, when
he wished to voice his personal opinion in this regard, that same Virgil
did not remain silent on the truth but spoke of the "great Roman state
and kingdoms destined to perish."[22]

Who does not clearly realize the immense chasm between an endless reign and kingdoms destined to perish? In the latter passage Virgil
was the spokesman; in the former, Jove; in the latter, the man of genius; in the former, the false and lying god. It is to this effect, though in
different words, that St. Augustine first accuses and then excuses Virgil.
The things that I have already said and those that I am about to say are
in harmony with this judgment.

It was also a Roman who wrote: "All that is born must perish and, in the very process of gaining added strength, advances toward decay."[23] Hence all things will waste away, if they continue to exist. If the end of all things is old age, then surely all things will become weak and aged, unless they are already so. All that now stands in vigor will likewise fall, and if old age does not precede the fall, it will at least attend it. There is no possible exception to this rule, whether the things of this world be granted a long or a short existence. Sooner or later all created things will waste away and die. Fickle Fortune will turn her wheel without stop and will whirl ephemeral kingdoms from people to people. In compliance with her every whim, she will make kings of slaves, and slaves of kings, and she will hurl her irresistible might against the city of Rome and against the world of the Romans.

For a long time and in lamentable ways, excellent people, Fortune has directed her power chiefly against you, who may have become an object of compassion to many, though no one has hastened to offer assistance. Fortune will continue to vex you. I am positive of this, and I grieve over it. I am more angered at that than one could believe possible; but I do not know what else I can do. I do not feel particularly distressed that Fortune has exercised her privileges over you as over the rest of humanity and that, in order to prove herself absolute mistress of human affairs, she has not feared to assault the very head of the world. I, too, have known her violence; I, too, have known her fickle moods.

Yet I can ill tolerate the vain bragging of certain so-called invincible nations whose heads are raised in such wanton insolence, though their necks still bear the traces of the Roman yoke. Now – shame and tale incredible! – to pass over many other serious wrongs, now the question is raised whether or not the Roman Empire is at Rome! In truth, where the wild forests now rule, there may some day arise the palaces of kings; and where there are now halls resplendent with the glow of gold, the eager flocks may some day go out to pasture, and the wandering shepherd may roam in the apartments of kings. I do not underestimate the power of Fortune. As she has destroyed other cities, so can she totally overthrow, with equal ease but with greater ruin, the very queen of cities, a thing, alas! that she has already accomplished in great measure. This she can never bring to pass, however: that the Roman Empire be anywhere else than at Rome. The moment it begins to reside elsewhere, that very moment it ceases to be Roman.

Your wretched fellow citizen does not deny having made such assertions and continues to adhere to his previous statements. This is the terrible crime for which his life now hangs in the balance. He adds – and I believe that he speaks the truth – that he reached these conclusions only after consulting many wise men; and he demands that counsel and the opportunity to present his defense be given to him. This is denied him: and unless divine mercy and your good will intercede on his behalf, it is all over. Innocent and without counsel, he will surely be condemned. A great many feel pity for him. Truly, there is hardly one who does not, except those for whom it would be proper to pity and to pardon the sins of others and not to envy them their virtues.

In this city there is no lack of prominent jurists who maintain that, according to civil law, this maxim of the illustrious prisoner could be proved in the clearest way. There is no lack of others who say that, were they permitted to speak freely, they could add many reliable examples from the pages of history that would corroborate that same maxim. But no one dares murmur a syllable now, except in a remote corner, or in the darkness, or in fear. I myself, who am writing to you, should not refuse, perhaps, to die for the truth, if my death would seem to be of any advantage to the state. Yet I too remain silent, nor do I affix my name to this letter, supposing that the style will be sufficient to reveal the writer. I add only this: that it is a Roman citizen who addresses you.

If the case were being tried in a safe place, and before a just judge, and not at the tribunal of our enemies, I feel confident that, with truth illuminating my soul and with God directing my tongue and my pen, I could speak convincing words, words from which it would result clearer than day that the Roman Empire, though long exhausted and oppressed by the blows of Fortune, though seized at various times by Spaniards, Africans, Greeks, Gauls, and Germans is still – however limited it may be – at Rome and nowhere else than at Rome. These words, I repeat, would clearly prove that there the Roman Empire will remain, though nothing were left of the stupendous city but the bare rock of the Capitol. Furthermore, I should prove that, at the time when Rome was not yet at the mercy of the barbarian hands and when the Roman Caesars ruled the world, even then all the rights of empire rested not with the emperors, but on the citadel of the Capitol and with the Roman people. I should clearly prove, finally, whether or not it is truly a fundamental principle of government that rulers who do not possess the confidence of their subjects shall not dictate the laws of the land.[24]

Time glides along, and everything is still in an unsettled state, a delay, perhaps, that has been granted from on high so that a question of such great importance may be decided in the light of day.[25] This is a favor for which only recently you did not even dare to hope. Consequently it has been impossible for me to check one request that seems to concern your dignity and that of the Roman name most deeply. The faith that makes me entwine you and your city with an unparalleled love and veneration urges me to write. I therefore beg and beseech you, illustrious people, not to abandon your fellow citizens in his hour of extreme need. Send a formal embassy, point out that he belongs to you, and claim him as your own. Though they may try to wrest all claim to the empire from you, they have not as yet reached that degree of insanity as to dare deny that you have the right of jurisdiction over your own citizens. To tell the truth, if this man has sinned, it is at Rome that he has sinned. There can be no doubt that you should pass judgment on sins that are committed at Rome – unless the common rights of law are torn from you who are the very founders and organizers of law, and who once framed laws for the nations of the world.

Where, indeed, can crimes be punished with greater justice than in that region where they were committed? There the very scene calls back the crime to the mind of the transgressor – itself no small part of the punishment and the sight of the penalty meted out either soothes or terrifies the spectators. Many, or rather all, right-minded people hold that your tribune deserves to be rewarded and not punished. If this is so, where will he receive his reward more appropriately than in that city where he performed the deeds that have earned it for him? In no other place is reward more worthily given than on the very scene of brave actions, in order that the beholders may be moved by the reward to follow the good example.

Have confidence, then, and demand the return of your citizen. You will make no new or unjust demand; on the other hand, you will be guilty of a positive wrong if you remain silent. If the plea of a common country is advanced in defense of his being punished in the city where he is now held captive, how much more truly is Rome his common country, the city where he was born and reared and where he performed all the deeds of which he is now accused? Here, on the contrary, he has done absolutely nothing deserving either praise or blame.

If, however, contrary to the traditions of your ancestors, your courage fails you in the hour of adversity; if the times have become so degenerate that those whose fathers considered no difficulty insurmountable now consider it an act of rashness to demand justice, then at least ask for what can always be asked of any barbarian nation where laws exist: insist that your citizen be given a public trial and that he not be denied the right of counsel. Demand that he, whose every action was performed in the light of day and who shed as much splendor on this earth as is humanly possible, not be condemned in the darkness. Make it perfectly clear, finally, that you will not forsake the cause and the fortunes of your fellow citizen. Resist the injustice; forbid the completion of such an unspeakable crime. Protect him if you judge him innocent; pass sentence on him if you judge him a criminal or culprit; but at least avoid the possibility of his being sentenced according to the caprice of anyone who may so desire.

Bring what aid you can and should bring to your tribune or, if that title has lost its spell, to your fellow citizen who deserves well of the republic. Foremost among his claims is the fact that he has revived an important question, a question of great interest to the world but that has been forgotten and buried in the sleep of many centuries, the question that alone can lead to the reformation of the state and can usher in the golden age. Aid this man. Do not treat lightly the safety of that one who, in your behalf, has exposed himself to a thousand dangers and to everlasting hatred. Think of his plans and purposes; remember in what condition your city was and how suddenly, through the wisdom and efforts of a single man, not only Rome but all Italy rose to great hopes. Remember how quickly the Italian name and the glory of Rome were restored to their ancient splendor. Recollect the deep fear and the grief of your enemies, the exultant joy of your friends, the lofty expectations of nations; recollect how the course of events was changed, how the face of the earth was altered, how different human desires became, and how everything beneath the vault of heaven assumed a different look. So marvelously and rapidly was the world changed!

He held the reins of government no longer than seven months, so that I can scarcely conceive a greater or nobler attempt in the history of the world. Had he continued to the end as he began, his work would have seemed that of a god rather than of a mortal. For that matter, anything well done by man is divinely done. As all know, this man worked to enhance your glory and not to gratify his personal ambitions. He therefore deserves your unhesitating favor. Fortune must be blamed for the outcome. If any listlessness followed his enthusiastic beginning, attribute it to the inconstancy and the frailty of human nature. While you still can, protect your fellow citizen against a grave wrong, you who formerly and with great peril to yourselves defended the Greeks against the Macedonians, the Sicilians against the Carthaginians, the Campanians against the Samnites, and the Etruscans against the Gauls.

Your resources, I know, are sadly depleted; but never were your fathers imbued with greater courage than when Roman poverty, the mother of virtues, was held in honor. I am fully aware that your power has dwindled; but believe me, if a single drop of the old blood still courses through your veins, you possess no slight majesty, no indifferent authority. Dare something, I earnestly ask you, in memory of your past history, for the ashes and the glory of your ancestors, in the name of the empire, out of mercy for Jesus Christ, who commands us to love our neighbors and to aid the afflicted. Dare something, I beseech you, the more so that any demand on your part is honorable, whereas silence is dishonorable and disgraceful. Dare something, if not for his safety, then at least to preserve your own self-respect – if you desire to be held in any esteem.

Nothing is less Roman than fear. I predict to you that if you are afraid, if you despise your own worth, many will likewise despise you, and no one will fear you. But if you begin to make it clear that you will not be spurned, you will be respected far and wide, a fact that was frequently made clear in ancient times and again recently when he of whom I speak governed the republic. Be unanimous in your demands; let the world realize that the voice of the Roman people is united. No one will then deride or mock you; everyone will either respect it or fear it. Be sure to exact the return of this prisoner or to demand justice. The latter, surely, will not be denied. You who once with an insignificant embassy freed a king of Egypt from the siege of the Syrians,[26] now liberate your fellow citizen from undeserved imprisonment.

NOTES

1. Faucon, p. 56.

2. Faucon, p. 57.

3. See *Vita* 4.2; Wright, pp. 127-28.

4. This is *Sine Titulo [Nomine]* 4. Piur, pp. 173-84. See also Coogan, pp. 53-64. Wilkins, *Life*, pp. 119-20, dates it to Avignon in October 1352, a date that the present editor accepts. The word used by Petrarch, *clam* (Fracassetti, *Epistolae* 3: 493), must refer simply to the fact that the author himself included the present letter to the Roman people in the group *Sine Titulo [Nomine]* because of its outspoken sentiments. In those letters Petrarch thought it safer to suppress the names of the addressees, deleting his own name as well. Hence the word *clam* must mean "anonymously," and hardly "in confidence" (Robinson and Rolfe, p. 348). This is proved by Petrarch's statement (Fracassetti, *Epistolae* 3: 500), *neque his ipsis ad vos scriptis meum nomen adiicio,* on the grounds that the style would be sufficient to reveal the writer.

5. De Sade, *Mémoires* 3: 234, remarks: "Je ne comprens pas pourquoi cette grace qu'on accorde à tous les criminels lui fut refusée sous le Pontificat le plus doux." But Robinson and Rolfe note (p. 349): "Rienzo was accused of heresy, and it was quite in accord with the jurisprudence of the inquisition to refuse him counsel."

6. From this sentence it is again clear, as we have already shown in Chapter 11, pp. 138-39, n. 14, that the trial was not over by August 10, 1352. According to the calculations made there the present letter is later than Letter 13; and Cola's trial had not ended, even at the writing of this letter.

7. Dante, in *Convivio* 4.5, expounds at great length on the medieval theme that the birth and the unparalleled growth of Rome were both predestined "in the most high and divine Consistory of the Trinity." Speaking of Rome, he concludes: "I, surely, am of the firm opinion that the stones in her walls are worthy of reverence, and that the soil on which she rests is more worthy than what is said and proven by men."

8. Virgil, *Aeneid* 6.727.

9. To add still another example to the many already cited, we shall give the following lines from a letter written to Emperor Charles IV (*Familiari* 23.2; Fracassetti, *Epistolae* 3: 193): "Yes, Rome is the mother country of all; she is the head of the universe, the queen of the world and of cities, abounding in so many noble examples that, once seen, she readily inspires the soul." Compare *Familiari* 11.7, printed in full in Chapter 10, pp. 122-24, n. 12. See also C.C. Bayley,

CHAPTER 12, AVIGNON, OCTOBER 1352

"Petrarch, Charles IV and the 'Renovatio imperii,'" *Speculum* 17 (1942): 323-41. On Petrarch's political ideas of empire, see Von Wilhelm Kölmel, "Petrarca und das Reich. Zum historisch-politischen Aspekt der 'studia humanitatis,'" *Historisches Jahrbuch* 90 (1970): 1-30.

10. In the *Africa* Scipio grieves at hearing that the honor of the empire was one day to fall into barbarian hands; but his father consoles him by saying (2.287-89; compare Bergin and Wilson, pp. 32-33, ll. 376-79): "Stop your crying, I beseech you, and lay aside your fear: the glory of the Latins will live, and the empire will always be called by the same name, the Roman Empire."

But Petrarch might have cited papal authority for this statement of fact. In a letter that is supposed to have been addressed to Francesco Nelli and to have been written in Milan in 1357, Petrarch tells the following interesting story of Pope John XXII (*Sine Titulo [Nomine]* 17, *Quo te cumque converteris*; 15 in the Basel ed. of 1581, pp. 727-28; Piur, *Sine Nomine* 17, pp. 219-28; Coogan, pp. 79-89):

> Our own listlessness is responsible for these cowards' daring. They take unholy joy in our patience, and at the same time they hate us. Indeed, so that you may be most profoundly astonished, know that they have an inward fear of those for whom they outwardly show contempt. The latter is merely feigned, the former really exists. There are a thousand proofs of their hatred and terror. I shall now relate an anecdote that will serve to prove both at once. Though this story was at first kept secret, ultimately it got around, so that it became known not only in Babylon but even in more distant lands.
>
> The incident occurred when that supreme pontiff [John XXII] had organized a decrepit expedition of the priestly soldiery with the purpose of reducing Italy to the condition of a province, and above all, of destroying the city of the Milanese. It was at the time, I repeat, when the Father of the Christians was rendered so extremely furious by his thorough and complete hatred of this Christian land and Christian city that one would not have thought this land Italy, but Syria or Egypt; and this city not Milan, but Damascus or Memphis.
>
> For the accomplishment of this holy and pious undertaking the pontiff chose one of the fathers of the Sacred College [Beltram de Poggetto], his own son as many said. Indeed, in addition to his physique [compare Gregorovius 6.1: 188, n. 1, and reading with him, *secundum formam* instead of the Basel *famam*], a strong resemblance and the ferocity of his character strengthened the belief. He did not equip himself in the manner of an apostle but in that of a robber; not with the signs of the virtues and with the power of working wonders but with the ensigns of the camps and with wonderful legions. Thus equipped he sent him into these lands not as a second Peter but as a second Hannibal. In the war that ensued Omnipotent

God, according to his way, humbled the proud and raised the humble and fought openly on the side of justice.

There was in that same troop of cardinals a certain man who also nourished an insatiable hatred for us. He was a man of boundless arrogance whom I – at that time a mere boy – knew by sight and whose character I execrated with all the energy of my feeble youth. This man was dear to the pontiff beyond all others. One day, entering the papal cabinet, he found the pope dismayed and distressed by the reports of the war. In fact, the onslaught of the war had, contrary to expectations, been checked on the very threshold of this city [Milan], which was not then even defended by walls but, indeed, by what constitutes the very best kind of wall, extraordinary soldiers and very brave commanders. And so the besieged had frequently put the besiegers to flight; the prisons were overflowing with the hordes of captives; and the fields were being fattened by the blood of the slain.

While matters were in this state, therefore, and since he saw the pope more downcast than usual, relying on his great intimacy with the pope, he addressed him and said: "I wonder, most Holy Father, why it is that, though you are very clear-sighted in other matters, your vision is limited in that one question that is of special and highest importance to us."

At these words the pontiff raised his head, which had been weighed down by heavy cares, and said, "Continue. What do you mean?"

Then that excellent counselor replied: "I know that you desire nothing as ardently as the destruction of Italy. To this end we are devoting all our strength, our resources, our counsels, to this end we have now squandered nearly all the riches of the church. Unless another way is tried, we have ventured into a labyrinth with no escape. See now our magnificent war preparations! The edge of our power is being blunted at the very gates of Milan, a city that your cringing sycophants asserted was like any one of our cities, but which experience has found to be superior to them all. If we are conquered by a single Italian city, when shall we conquer the whole of Italy? But, if you wish, there is a far easier way to accomplish this end."

"What way," exclaimed the pope, "speak, and more quickly. For this is what I am laboring over, this is what I desire, this is the one thing for which I would be willing to sell both body and soul."

And the other: "You can do all things. Whatever you order is accomplished. Why, therefore, do you not deprive the city of Rome and Italy of both the papacy and the empire? Why don't you transfer that empire to Cahors, our native place, that is to say, to Gascony? [John xxII had been born Jacques d'Euse, of Cahors.] It is not a difficult task; speak, and it will be done. There is no need of arms, in which we are greatly their inferiors. By a single word you will triumph over your enemies. Thus, by transferring the very summits of power to our country, you will distinguish us with new honors, and you will deprive that hateful people of its double glory."

At these words the pontiff raised his head and, smiling in the midst of wrath, replied: "You have deceived me up to now. I had not yet known you to rave like a madman. Don't you know, you fool, that according to the way you thought you had so subtly devised, both I and my successors become merely bishops of Cahors, and that the emperor, whoever he may be, becomes a prefect of Gascony? Don't you know that they who rule at Rome in spiritual and in temporal matters would be, respectively, the real pope and the real emperor? So, while thinking to overthrow the Italian name, you are elevating it to its former dignity. Therefore, while heaven permits, let us hold fast the reins of the Roman pontificate, and let us bend our every energy to this: that Italian hands may never grasp what is theirs by right. But it is an uncertain matter how long this event can be delayed. Let us not haggle about mere names; for whether we will it or not, the head and center of all things will still be Rome."

On hearing these words, that sagacious fool blushed scarlet. I, in truth, disapprove of the pope's intentions but am obliged to approve his good sense. For, though he was consumed with undeserved hatred for us, he nevertheless remembered and knew full well what the lofty structure from whose summit he exhibited his pride had been founded on. He clearly realized that to impair the foundations would bring on ruin. He therefore decided that it was best to remain quiet and to enjoy the papacy in silence, like an object obtained by theft.

I do not know whether others have recounted this tale. I have given it in detail so that, if you have already heard it you may know that I too am acquainted with it; if you have not yet heard it, you may learn it from me, and being acquainted with the past, you may not be ignorant of the present.

11. *Aeneid* 9.448-49, Connington trans., p. 304. After these verses Robinson and Rolfe omit a selection from the words *Neque enim* (Fracassetti, *Epistolae* 3: 496) to *Certe romanus* (p. 498); they give two lines and then, without indicating the fact, omit the following fifteen lines, from *Senescent ergo* (p. 498) to *Nec me angit* (p. 499). Again, there is an omission from *Si verum* (p. 500) to *Ferte quam potestis* (p. 502). These omissions constitute one-third of the letter.

12. Nisus and Euryalus.

13. *Aeneid* 1.276-77.

14. *Aeneid* 1.278-79.

15. Matt. 24: 35; Mark 13: 31; Luke 21: 33.

16. St. Augustine, *Sermo* 105 (alias 29, *De verbis Domini*), in Migne, *Patrologiae Latinae Cursus Completus* 38: 618. Chapter 10, entitled *Terreno regno aeternitas adulatorie promissa*, reads as follows (col. 622-23):

> Those who have promised eternity to the kingdoms of earth have not been led to do so by the truth but have lied from a sense of adulation. A certain pagan poet represents Jove as speaking and says of the Romans [Virgil, *Aeneid* 1.278-79]:

> No date, no goal I here ordain:
> Theirs is an endless, boundless reign.

> But this does not quite answer to the truth. You [Jove], who have granted nothing, does this reign, which you have granted, endless and boundless, have its home in heaven or on earth? Undoubtedly on earth. Even if it were in heaven, heaven and earth shall pass away [Luke 21: 33]. Those things shall pass away that God himself has created; how much sooner, then, will what Romulus has founded pass away?

> If we wanted to take Virgil to task for this and revile him for having made such a statement, he would perhaps take us to one side and say to us: "I, too, know its falsity; but what was I to do to please the Romans except to employ this flattery and to promise them something that I knew to be false? And yet I was cautious in doing so. When I said: 'Theirs is an endless, boundless reign,' I brought their own Jove on the scene to speak those words. It was not in my own person that I spoke the falsehood, but I shouldered the character of liar on Jove; for just as he was a false god, so he was also a false prophet. Indeed, do you want to feel certain that I was aware of this? In another passage, and when I did not represent a Jove of stone as speaking but when I spoke in my own person, I said 'the great Roman state and kingdoms destined to perish' [*Georgics* 2.498]. You will observe that I said 'kingdoms destined to perish,' I actually said 'kingdoms destined to perish.' I did not remain silent."

> And so Virgil, when speaking the truth, did not conceal the fact that kingdoms of the earth were destined to perish. But when flattering the Romans he promised them an endless reign.

This citation demonstrates that Petrarch follows St. Augustine fairly closely. But where he says, "At this point St. Augustine rightly remarks," what follows is not a direct quotation from St. Augustine, who after the verses from the *Aeneid* simply says: *Non plane ita respondet veritas. Regnum hoc, quod sine fine dedisti, o qui nihil dedisti, in terra est, an in caelo?* Therefore, the first three lines printed in italics in Fracassetti's Latin edition belong to Petrarch himself and should not have been printed in italics, which inevitably imply a direct quotation from St. Augustine. See Fracassetti, *Epistolae* 3: 497.

17. Is. 65: 17; 66: 22; 2 Pet. 3: 13; Apoc. 21: 1.
18. Num. 23: 19; John 3: 33, 8: 26; Rom. 3: 4.
19. Luke 1: 33.
20. Matt. 11: 25.
21. Compare Dante *Inferno* 1.70-72, where the shade of Virgil says (Longfellow trans.):

> Sub Julio was I born, though it was late And lived at Rome under the good Augustus, During the time of false and lying gods.

22. *Georgics* 2.498.
23. Sallust, *Iugurtha* 2.3.
24. Petrarch's republicanism contrasts sharply with his frequent praise of princes. Yet his one political goal was the unification of Italy and the restoration of Rome by whatever agency seemed available. On Petrarch's ideas of just rule and political freedom see Rodolfo de Mattei, *Il Sentimento politico del Petrarca* (Florence: G.C. Sansoni, 1944); Foster, pp. 9-13, Kohl and Witt, *The Earthly Republic*, pp. 25-78; and Mann, pp. 32-42. Kohl, p. 27, incorrectly dates Cola's revolution to 1343.
25. Unfortunately the three extant letters written by Cola while he was confined at Avignon are not dated. These are Gabrielli, *Epistolario* 47; Burdach and Piur, Letter 73, 2.3: 415-19, to the archbishop of Prague; and Gabrielli, *Epistolario* 48 and 49 to the Roman people; Burdach and Piur, Letter 74, 2.3: 419-20; and 75, 2.3: 421-22. The trial may have dragged on (see *dies trahitur,* Fracassetti, *Epistolae* 3: 500) for any one of many reasons. Among them we point out the departure of Gui de Boulogne, one of the presumed judges, in the early part of September 1352 (Fracassetti, *Lettere* 3: 254). This cardinal was then sent to Paris in an attempt to bring about a peace between the kings of France and England, who had already fought the battle of Crécy and who were renewing their war preparations after the enforced truce caused by the Black Death. See Edouard Perroy, *The Hundred Years War* (New York: Capricorn Books, 1965), 127-29.
26. In 168 B.C. ambassadors from Ptolemy and Cleopatra, rulers of Egypt, reported to the Roman Senate that Alexandria was being besieged by Antiochus, king of Syria (Livy 44.19, 9). The Senate immediately appointed an embassy composed of C. Popilius, C. Decimius, and C. Hostilius (44.19, 13), instructing these envoys to visit both kings and to reestablish peace. The envoys met Antiochus at Eleusin, four miles away from Alexandria; and the unbending severity of Popilius compelled Antiochus to make peace at once (45.12). In the same year envoys of Ptolemy came to the city to thank the Romans, whose intervention had saved the Egyptians from a very wretched siege (45.13, 5: *per quos obsidione miserrima liberati essent*).

CHAPTER 13

Petrarch's correspondence that directly treats the Roman revolution of Rienzo comes to an end with the letter *Sine Titulo [Nomine]* 4. We have dated this letter to October 1352. Neither the political career of Rienzo, however, nor Petrarch's reflections on that career ended this early. In fact, Petrarch never did quite forget Rienzo. Only two years before his own death, he could still draw a moral from the unhappy fate of the tribune, and in the calm of his advanced years he could still feel the flame that had been fanned so vigorously in 1347. This concluding chapter, therefore, proposes to follow briefly through Petrarch's life the thin thread of his blasted hopes in Rienzo.

As we have already seen,[1] after the fiasco of the commission of four cardinals appointed to reform the government of Rome, the citizens of the Urbs had on St. Stephen's day, December 26, 1351, declared the plebeian Giovanni Cerroni absolute head and master of the city. His rule came to an end when he fled in September 1352. This flight threw Rome into a state of utter chaos, a period during which it is difficult to reconstruct the true course of events.

In this inextricable tangle it appears that the Romans returned to the time-worn system of senators and elected to that office Count Palatine Bertoldo Orsini and Stefanello Colonna. The pope in distant Avignon, however, does not seem to have ratified the choice of the Romans, and he nominated instead Giovanni Orsini and Pietro Sciarra Colonna as senators for the year 1353. In other words, in January 1353 there must have been four senators in Rome, two representing the interests of Avignon, the other two the wishes of the Romans themselves. It is therefore safe to assume that until February 15, 1353 the control of affairs really rested with the people's choice, Bertoldo Orsini and Stefanello Colonna.

Stefanello was the grandson of Stefano the Elder. We have already pointed out the attachment to the Colonna of Petrarch's friend, Laelius.[2] During his period of supremacy Stefanello seems to have asked Laelius for advice. In fact, Laelius' friendship for the Colonna and his present intimate relations with the young Stefano were so well known at Avignon that the pope and the Curia considered all the rebellious acts of the unratified senators due to Laelius' suggestions. This information we gather from a letter of Petrarch to Laelius.[3] Considering its historical content, this letter must be assigned to January or to the beginning of February 1353.

We should recall that Cola was still under guard at Avignon, and that the broken-hearted Petrarch placed no more hopes in his shattered idol. But now, on the contrary, the alliance of a Colonna and of Laelius – a Roman nobleman by birth – raised new hopes in the poet for a rejuvenated Rome under the rule of a native Roman. He did not yield to this new ray of hope at once nor with full enthusiasm. Yet, with as much self-restraint as was possible for his optimistic nature, he expressed his personal belief that Laelius had sufficient strength to restore the Roman republic provided only that the Romans would listen to his counsels, and that Laelius would devote himself wholeheartedly to the welfare of the city. Petrarch, referring to Laelius' enemies, continues as follows[4]:

> Regarding those men, finally, there is no advice that I need to give you. You know everything. One thing, however, I would wish that you never forget, the statement that we have so often heard from the lips of that venerable old man who, though of opinions hostile to ours, nevertheless had a great soul and wide experience. The saying is worth remembering, not so much for the elegance of its diction as for the truth of its content. That experienced man used to say, and excellently so, that the Roman church always loves the powerful. Nothing could be more concise, nothing more true.
>
> Therefore, Romans, if you desire to be great among the nations and, what is desired even more, dear to God, practice virtue, love your religion, and observe justice. Employ your ancient arts: spare the conquered and subdue the proud.[5] But, on the contrary, if you desire to be loved by this church, all that you need is power, without which, I assure you, you will be held in no esteem, no matter how great your virtues are. With respect to you, Romans, I will make only one remark. There are two men who have in our times seized the reins of government. To one of them [Cola di Rienzo] I wrote numerous letters; to the second [Giovanni Cerroni] I wrote not a word. The reason for my course was that the former led me

to entertain great, though premature, hopes; while the latter did
not arouse in me any hopes whatsoever. As for you, Laelius, if you
retain your power, if you do not fear the menacing hissing of ser-
pents, there flash through my mind many and varied thoughts
destined to energize in due time. Let it suffice for the present to
have given you this warning: to those who enter on this career
excess patience and excess zeal are both sources of danger. You
have before your eyes native and recent examples of both. As Ovid
says, you will be safest in the middle course.[6] Farewell; and since
you are a man, see to it that you prove yourself a man.

Laelius, however, was not permitted to continue long in the role of
mentor. The turbulence of the Romans proved to be the undoing of
the senators whom they themselves had chosen. Because of the scarcity of grain and the resulting high prices the Roman populace gathered in the marketplace of February 15, 1353; the slogan of rebellion
was again heard. Of the senators, Bertoldo Orsini was stoned to death,
while the younger and more vigorous Stefanello managed to escape.[7]
Naturally, the Avignon candidates Giovanni Orsini and Pietro Sciarra
Colonna now ruled unmolested. Peace, of course, was bound to be of
short duration. On September 14, 1353 the Romans, temporarily wearied by their fratricidal strife, elected a Roman, Francesco Baroncelli,
second tribune of Rome.

The pope was, as ever, kept accurately informed of these kaleido-
scopic changes in the City of Peter. From the account of Rinaldi,[8] it
becomes clear that Cola's liberation was a direct consequence of
Baroncelli's elevation to the tribunate:

On being informed of these events by Hugo Harpaion, apostolic
internuncio, the pontiff [Innocent VI] conceived the plan of free-
ing from prison Cola di Rienzo, who was repeatedly promising
that he would be a most ardent champion for the maintenance of
papal supremacy. The pope hoped that other tyrants would be
crushed by Cola, whose name was still in good repute with many.
This is what the pope wrote to the above-mentioned Hugo:

"After carefully seeking a remedy for this evil, we have caused
our beloved son, the noble Cola di Rienzo, a Roman knight, to be

absolved from all the penalties and the judgments by which he had been overwhelmed; and, if God grant it, we shall quickly send him as a free man to the city, hoping that he may have gained understanding from his troubles; that, having utterly renounced the unjust and perverse endeavors of the malicious, he will sanely oppose his former fantastic innovations, drawing on his own activity and shrewdness, which is indeed great, and also on that of the inhabitants and of the many nobles of the said city who desire to live a quiet life and to enhance the general welfare; hoping, finally, that, with the assistance and the favor of God, he will resist the absorbing greed and the lawless, injurious desires of certain leaders.

Given at Villeneuve (-les-Avignon), in the diocese of Avignon, on the fifteenth day of September, and in the first year [of our pontificate]."

Here, at last, we have the first official mention of Cola's liberation. There were many suppositions and hypotheses. We have heard Petrarch asserting the Cola was likely to be set free because of the strange rumor that he was a poet. Rinaldi[9] says that Cola was freed because of his eloquence, but he does not clearly state whether he was absolved from the charge of heresy or from that of being a political rebel. Later in his annals, however, Rinaldi says[10]:

How Cola was brought to trial on the charge of heresy, and how, in spite of the fact that he had been condemned by two cardinal-legates, he cleared himself of that charge, was freed from his imprisonment, and finally slain and burned – all this will be narrated in its proper place.

The place indicated is the chapter that we have already quoted, which cites the papal brief to the internuncio Hugo Harpaion. The underlying cause of Cola's freedom, therefore, was not his innocence of heresy, not the papal forgiveness of his political offenses, but merely the skillful maneuvering of papal diplomacy. By this simple move of an insignificant and despised pawn Innocent VI checkmated the drastic but aimless efforts of the Romans. He counterbalanced the magic of Baroncelli's title by opposing to it the former irresistible sway of the first tribune who had sworn to uphold the papal cause. To the Spanish Cardinal Albornoz, who on June 30, 1353[11] had been appointed vicar-general in Italy and in the State of the Church, he thus added a source of strength greater than that of many legions. It remained for the pope to acquaint the Romans with his decision to set Cola free. Needless to say he would represent things in quite a different light. On the very next day after writing to Hugo Harpaion, the pope wrote the following letter to the Roman people.[12]

> Innocent, Bishop, to his beloved children the Roman people, greetings.
>
> Although many evil things concerning our beloved son, the noble Cola di Rienzo, your fellow citizen and knight, had been related to our predecessor of blessed memory, Pope Clement VI, and also to ourselves; and although both our venerable brother Bertrand, cardinal of Sabina (then presbyter-cardinal of St. Mark), and Annibaldo of good memory, bishop of Tusculum (then legate of the apostolic see) had instituted some legal proceedings against him; nevertheless, having been raised to the summit of the highest apostleship through the assisting grace of God, and considering that, although the said knight, who was then detained in our prisons, had transgressed in many things, he had nevertheless performed more good works worthy of reward; and reflecting that, according to the past and the present trustworthy reports of many, your unanimous will and universal love most ardently demanded the liberation and restoration of Cola to the city; and that, after a long period, he had been weakened by the inconveniences of his prison chamber, which, however, was quite respectable and within the walls of the palace; and hoping confidently that he who, out of love for the common weal and zeal for justice – which he is said to have administered during his regime without regard to person – exposed himself to many dangers and to the hatred of many who eagerly desired a tyranny and your subjugation and who sought their own gain in your loss and in that of others – confidently hoping, we say, that such a man will curb their criminal appetite with the bit of justice and that, having stifled all hatred

and rancor, he will, with the favor of God and with our aid, cause you and your compatriots to enjoy the prayed-for quiet and peace, we therefore have caused him to be absolved from all the judgments and the penalties by which he had been overwhelmed, and we have decided that he should be sent back to you a free man.

Therefore we request and urge you all, earnestly soliciting you to aid the above-mentioned knight, whom you have so eagerly sought, whom you desire to welcome joyfully, and who, with the grace of God, will strengthen your weakness and that of the state.

We solicit you to aid him unanimously, with timely and effectual good-will, in restoring your fallen conditions, in directing them toward a better state, and in enlarging your republic – objects that he himself is said to be especially desirous of attaining. We beg you to rival with your aid the wisdom of his plans so that you may check the ravenousness of your powerful fellow citizens and neighbors who are gnawing your sides both within and without the city, and so that you may break the lifted horns of the proud.

Given at Villeneuve (-les-Avignon), in the diocese of Avignon, on the sixteenth day of September, in the first year of our pontificate.

From this letter it is evident that the Roman people had asked for Cola's freedom and also for his return unless the passage in question is mere rhetoric on the part of the apostolic secretary. Petrarch's last letter to the Romans, consequently, was not altogether in vain. On September 24, 1353 the sum of 200 florins for traveling expenses was given to Cola.[13] He left Avignon on that day in order to overtake Albornoz, who must have left in the first half of August. Indeed, as early as September 14, 1353 Albornoz had entered Milan and had been met by Petrarch and by Giovanni Visconti. On this occasion Galeazzo saved Petrarch's life when the latter's horse was on the point of throwing him violently to the ground.[14]

In November 1353 Baroncelli fled Rome, and Cardinal Albornoz took possession of the city.[15] It was not until August 1, 1354 – the seventh anniversary of Cola's knighthood, of the famous citation, and of the proclamation of Rome as the capital of the world – that Cola reentered

the Urbs, but now as senator and ruling in the name of Innocent vi.
Only sixty-nine days later, on October 8, 1354, the sword of Cecco del
Vecchio put an end to the life of Cola di Rienzo:

> The mangled and headless corpse was dragged from the Capitol
> to the Colonna quarter, and was hanged outside a house close to
> S. Marcello. Two days the appalling figure remained; once in life
> the idol of Rome, now the target for the stones of street boys. By
> command of Jugurtha and Sciarretta Colonna, the remains of the
> Tribunus Augustus were burnt by the Jews on the third day, on a
> heap of dry thistles in the Mausoleum of Augustus. The scene of
> the last act of this curious tragedy had been specially chosen in
> mockery of Cola's pompous ideas concerning antiquity. His ashes
> were scattered like those of Arnold of Brescia.[16]

About a month and a half after this tragedy, Petrarch addressed
Charles iv, the Holy Roman Emperor, and reproached him for delaying
his descent into Italy, citing Cola's successes as an example of what
would be possible for the rightful emperor. These are his words [17]

> Would not your mere name, together with the assistance of the
> few good men who still love virtue and the empire, easily bring to
> a successful close any struggle against sluggish magnificence and
> unarmed pride? Do you wish me to prove and to demonstrate to
> you that things are as I say? Well, then. Very recently one of the
> lowly plebeians rose to power. He was not a Roman king, nor a
> consul, nor a patrician. He was a Roman citizen who was scarcely
> known – one who was not illustrious because of the glory and the
> images of distinguished ancestors, nor indeed because of any vir-
> tues of his own that had as yet appeared. Nevertheless he proclaimed
> himself the champion of Roman liberty. Dazzling declaration of
> an obscure person!
>   Immediately and eagerly, as you know, Tuscany joined hands
> with him and obeyed his orders. Gradually all Italy followed her
> example; and soon Europe, yes the entire world, was astir. But
> what need of many details? We have not read about these events,
> we have witnessed them with our own eyes. Justice and peace

CHAPTER 13, CONCLUSION

seemed to have returned in company with their handmaidens –
genial confidence and tranquil ease. In short, traces of the golden
age reappeared. In the very bloom of prosperity, however, he submitted to the counsels of another. I do not want to blame either of
them. I neither condemn nor acquit; I am not the judge, and I shall
keep my opinions to myself. He had assumed the title of Tribune,
the lowliest among Roman offices. And if the name of Tribune
was able to accomplish so much, what is impossible for one boasting the title of Caesar?

The next mention of Cola that Petrarch makes is found in his *De
remediis*, written between the years 1358 and 1366. In Book I, Dialogue
89, entitled "On coming out of prison," *De carceris exitu*, we find the
following strange conversation put into the mouths of the usual two
characters, Joy and Reason[18]:

Joy: I rejoice at having come out of prison.
Reason: Only recently you rejoiced at having entered the haven,
now you rejoice at leaving it. The prison has been a haven to many;
to many it has been a place of refuge, to many a source of safety.
The prison has spared in chains many who were destined to perish
when restored to liberty. What is bound fast and placed under lock
and key is more carefully preserved. In their blindness people do
not know what is to their best advantage. Consequently they keenly
desire their own evil; and when they have attained it, they rejoice
at a thing over which they will soon grieve. That you may not have
far to seek [for an example] you recently witnessed the spirited
and noble – rather than persevering – endeavors of that man [Cola
di Rienzo] who, in a time of adversity, dared to proclaim himself
the defender of the Roman Republic, taking the title of Tribune.
But fortune soon changed. Expelled from the city, he was imprisoned first by the emperor of the Romans [Charles IV] and then by
the pope [Clement VI]. In each case he was treated both well and
honorably. Unluckily he was set free. He was not merely slain, but
indeed he was mangled by the swords of his enemies. I believe
that in his dying moments he must have sighed for the safety of
his former prison.

The last mention of Cola in Petrarch's extant writings occurs in his *Invectiva in Gallum,* the fiery invective that the poet wrote against the monk Jean de Hesdin, who had defended the establishment of the Papal See outside Italy. Though this answer was written in 1371 or 1372 and therefore only shortly before Petrarch's death in 1374, it reveals all the vigor of his youth. It furthermore proves the undiminished sway wielded over him by memories of his idealized Cola. We cite from the *Invectiva*[19]:

And yet I do not speak blasphemy, as he has done, but something closely akin to blasphemy, when I say that he [Jean de Hesdin] rends the Holy City with his profane abuse. How great is the audacity of slaves! How great is their impudence, when they have once escaped from the fetters of their masters! Incapable of avenging themselves otherwise, they war against their former masters with curses and maledictions, pouring the wrath of their ulcerous souls out on the winds. They bark in their fear like feeble dogs. This barbarian mentions the ancient slavery of his race; and, though his neck still is callous from the Roman yoke, like a runaway slave he rails at his mistress from afar, quivering with fear. If omnipotent God were to grant peace and brotherly concord to the sons of Rome – to her barons, I say – and if Rome were aided, as formerly, by the united strength of the Italians, how quickly and how easily would she suppress the rebellious barbarians and impose on them that same yoke of ancient days! Had this been unknown until now, it became clearly manifest recently, when a single man of the most obscure origin and not possessed of riches – a man who, as experience proved, was endowed with greater spirit than constancy, dared to buttress the republic with his weak shoulders and to assume the defense of the tottering empire. How soon was all Italy aroused; how great did the fear and the fame of the Roman name spread to the furthermost countries of the earth! And with how much greater authority would it have spread, were it as easy to persevere as it is to make a beginning. I was then in Gaul, and I know very well what I heard, and what I saw, and what I read in the words and the eyes of those who were considered the greatest of men. They would deny it now, perhaps, for it is extremely easy to deny fear when its cause no longer exists. Then, however, consternation had filled every corner, so true is it that Rome is still something. But no more of this, lest I drive my barbarian to the brink of despair as he bitterly reflects on what Italy really is and on the uncivilized state of his own country....

To the last, then, Petrarch regarded Cola's uprising with feelings of unabated sympathy. Petrarch has been accused, and not only once, of having followed now this policy, now that. We frankly acknowledge that he wrote eulogistic letters to King Robert, the great champion of the Guelph cause in Italy; that he addressed verses to Benedict XII and to Clement VI, urging both to restore the Papal See to the City by the River; that he surrendered himself heart and soul to Cola; that he afterward addressed Emperor Charles IV with equal vigor and persistency; and that he finally turned again to Pope Urban V. But behind it all, actuating and giving strength to his every word, uplifting him in the hour of crushing disappointment, pouring balm on his wounded heart, and stirring even new hopes in his responsive soul, we discern the one great cause and sustaining faith of Petrarch's existence, a creed that was summed up in the single name "Rome."[20]

Petrarch's deep and concentrated studies had first awakened in him a belief in the rebirth of an Augustan Rome. The distracted and mangled condition of Italy had caused this belief to blossom into an overpowering and all-mastering passion. Whether addressing Cola the Tribune or King Robert, whether addressing the Venetian or the Genoese doge, whether addressing popes or emperors, the one thought supreme in Petrarch's mind was the establishment of peace and harmony among the Italian states and a hegemony under the leadership of Rome. He longed for a renewal of the golden days, of the universal esteem and veneration of Rome, of the days when the City of the Seven Hills centered within its walls the grandeur and the glory of human achievements. Petrarch was neither a Guelph not a Ghibelline, neither a Florentine nor a Roman; neither a bigoted churchman nor a Protestant reformer. He was, in a word, an Italian patriot who had conceived an ideal that his imaginative nature could not bring to a practical consummation. He was consequently doomed to disappointment in his

PETRARCH & COLA DI RIENZO

dealings with the mighty of the earth, a disappointment to which he
fortunately gave vent in the noblest and most glorious of all canzoni,
Italia mia, uttering words that were destined to become the rallying cry
of generations of patriotic Italians.

NOTES

1. See introduction to Chapter 11, pp. 126-29.
2. Chapter 9, pp. 103-4, n. 35.
3. *Familiari* 15.1, from Vaucluse. See Bernardo 2: 249-51.
4. Fracassetti, *Epistolae* 2: 309.
5. *Aeneid* 6.853.
6. *Metamorphoses* 2.137.
7. Gregorovius 6.1: 338; Fracassetti, *Lettere* 3: 340-41.
8. Ad annum 1353, chap. 5, p. 574, col. 1.
9. Ad annum 1347, chap. 21, p. 448, col. 2.
10. Ad annum 1350, chap. 5, p. 504, col. 2.
11. Gregorovius 6.1: 336. See Francesco Filippini, *Cardinale Egidio Albornoz* (Bologna: N. Zanichelli, 1933); Paolo Colliva, *Il Cardinale Albornoz, lo stato della chiesa, le "Constitutiones Aegidianae" (1353-1375)* (Bologna: Royal College of Spain, 1977); and Juan Beneyto Perez, *El Cardenal Albornoz: Hombre de iglesia y de estado en Castilla y en Italia* (Madrid: Fundación Universitaria Española, 1986).
12. Theiner 2, no. 257, p. 255, dated September 16, 1353.
13. Faucon, p. 58, n. 1.
14. Fracassetti, *Lettere* 1: 180-81; 2: 240.
15. Gregorovius 6.1: 358.
16. Gregorovius 6.1: 373.
17. *Familiari* 18.1, November 23, 1354; Fracassetti, *Epistolae* 2: 463-64.
18. Ibid., p. 243.
19. Basel edition of 1581, p. 1071.
20. On the consistency of Petrarch's political views see Chapter 12, p. 165, n. 24.

BIBLIOGRAPHY

PRIMARY SOURCES

PETRARCH

LATIN

Africa. Francesco Corradini, ed. Padua: Premiata Tipografia del Seminario, 1874.

Epistolae de rebus familiaribus et variae. Giuseppe Fracassetti, ed. 3 vols. Florence: Le Monnier, 1859-63.

Opera omnia. 3 vols. Basel: Henricus Petri, 1554; rpt. ed., Sebastian Henricpetri, 1581.

Opera omnia. Edizione Nazionale. Florence: G.C. Sansoni, 1926–.

Petrarcas "Buch ohne namen" und die päpstliche Kurie. Paul Piur, ed. Halle: M. Niemeyer, 1925.

De remediis utriusque fortunae libri duo, eiusdem De contemptu mundi colloquiorum liber quem secretum suum inscripsit. Rotterdam: Arnold Leers, 1649.

De viris illustribus vitae. Luigi Razzolini, ed. Bologna: Gaetano Romagnoli, 1874.

ITALIAN

Lettere di Francesco Petrarca delle cose familiari libri ventiquattro, lettere varie libro unico. Giuseppe Fracassetti, trans. and ed. 5 vols. Florence: Le Monnier, 1892.

Lettere Senili di Francesco Petrarca. Giuseppe Fracassetti, trans. and ed. 2 vols. Florence: Le Monnier, 1892.

Poesie Minori del Petrarca, sul testo latino ora coretto. Various trans. Domenico Rossetti, ed. Milan: Società Tipografica de' Classici Italiani, 1829.

Rime di Francesco Petrarca sopra argomenti storici, morali e diversi. Giosue Carducci, ed. Livorno: Vigo, 1876.

Le vite degli uomini illustri di Francesco Petrarca. Donato degli Albanzani da Pratovecchio, trans. Luigi Razzolini, ed. 3 vols. Bologna: Gaetano Romagnoli, 1874-79.

BIBLIOGRAPHY

FRENCH

Eglogues. Victor Develay, trans.and ed. Paris: Librairie des Bibliophiles, 1891.

Lettres à Rienzi. Victor Develay, trans.and ed. Paris: Librairie des Bibliophiles, 1885.

Lettres sans Titre. Victor Develay, trans.and ed. Paris: Librairie des Bibliophiles, 1885.

ENGLISH

Babylon on the Rhone: A Translation of the Letters by Dante, Petrarch and Catherine of Siena on the Avignon Papacy. Robert Coogan, trans. and ed. Madrid: Jose Porrua Turanzas; Potomac, MD: Studia Humanitatis, 1983.

How a Ruler Ought to Govern His State. Benjamin G. Kohl, trans. In *The Earthly Republic. Italian Humanists on Government and Society*. Benjamin G. Kohl and Ronald G. Witt, trans. and ed. Manchester: Manchester University Press, 1978, pp. 25-78.

Letters from Petrarch. Morris Bishop, trans. and ed. Bloomington, IN and London: Indiana University Press, 1966.

Letters on Familiar Matters. Rerum familiarium libri. Aldo S. Bernardo, trans. Vol. 1 (I-VIII), Albany: State University of New York Press, 1975; vol. 2 (IX-XVI), Baltimore and London: Johns Hopkins University Press, 1982; vol. 3 (XVII-XXIV), Baltimore and London: Johns Hopkins University Press, 1985.

Letters of Old Age. Rerum senilium libri I-XVIII. Aldo S. Bernardi, Saul Levin, and Reta A. Bernardo, trans. Baltimore: Johns Hopkins University Press, 1992.

The Life of Solitude of Francis Petrarch. Jacob Zeitlin, trans. and ed. Urbana, IL: University of Illinois Press, 1924; rpt. ed., Westport, CT: Hyperion, 1978.

On Remedies against Good and Evil Fortune. Conrad Rawski, trans. and ed. Cleveland: Western Reserve University Press, 1966.

Petrarch, the First Modern Scholar and Man of Letters. James H. Robinson and Henry W. Rolfe, trans. and ed. New York: Putnam, 1898.

Petrarch at Vaucluse. Letters in Verse and Prose. Ernest Hatch Wilkins, trans. and ed. Chicago: University of Chicago Press, 1958.

Petrarch's Africa. Thomas G. Bergin and Alice S. Wilson, trans. and ed. New Haven: Yale University Press, 1977.

BIBLIOGRAPHY

Petrarch's Book Without a Name. Norman P. Zacour, trans. and ed. Toronto: Pontifical Institute of Mediaeval Studies, 1973.

Petrarch's Bucolicum Carmen. Thomas G. Bergin, trans. and ed. New Haven: Yale University Press, 1974.

Petrarch's Letters to Classical Authors. Mario E. Cosenza, trans. and ed. Chicago: University of Chicago Press, 1910.

Petrarch's Lyric Poems. R.M. Durling, trans. and ed. Cambridge, MA: Harvard University Press, 1976.

Sonnets and Songs. Anna Maria Armi, trans. Intro. by Theodor E. Mommsen. New York: Grosset & Dunlop, 1968.

The Sonnets, Triumphs, and Other Poems of Petrarch. Various trans. London: Bohn's Illustrated Library, 1893.

COLA DI RIENZO

LATIN

Briefwechsel des Cola di Rienzo. Vol. 2 in Konrad Burdach and Paul Piur. *Vom Mittelalter zur Reformation*. 5 parts. Berlin: Weidmann, 1913-29.

Epistolario di Cola di Rienzo. Annibale Gabrielli, ed. Rome: Forzani e Compagnia, Tipografi del Senato, 1890.

Vita Nicolai Laurentii (sive di Cola di Rienzo), Tribuni Romanorum. Trans. from the Italian into Latin by Petrus Hercules Gherardius. Lodovico Antonio Muratori, ed. Vol. 7. Arezzo: Antiquitates italicae medii aevi, 1775.

ITALIAN

La vita di Cola di Rienzo, tribuno del popolo romano, scritta da incerto autore nel secolo decimo quatro. Zefirino Re, ed. Forli: Bordandini, 1828.

La vita di Cola di Rienzo. A.M. Ghisalberti, ed. Rome, 1928.

Vita di Cola di Rienzo. F. Cusin, ed. Florence: G.C. Sansoni, 1943.

Vita di Cola di Rienzo. Arsenio Frugoni, ed. Florence: Le Monnier, 1957.

Vita di Cola di Rienzo. Cronaca di anonimo romano. Giuseppe Porta, ed. Milan: Adelphi, 1979.

Anonimo romano. *Cronica, Vita di Cola di Rienzo*. Ettone Mazzali, ed. Milan: Rizzoli, 1991.

BIBLIOGRAPHY

ENGLISH

Letters 49 and 58. In *Visions of the End. Apocalyptic Traditions in the Middle Ages.* Bernard McGinn, ed. New York: Columbia University Press, 1979.

The Life of Cola di Rienzo. John Wright, trans. and ed. Toronto: Pontifical Institute of Mediaeval Studies, 1975.

OTHER SOURCES

Avena, Antonio. *Il Bucolicum Carmen e i suoi commenti inediti.* Padua: Società Cooperativa Tipografica, 1906.

Deprez, Eugene, ed. *Clément VII. Lettres closes, patentes et curiales interessant les payes autres que la France publiées ou analysées d'après les registres du Vatican.* Paris: A. Fontemoing, 1901

Rinaldi, Oderico, ed. *Annales Ecclesiastici.* vols. 25-26. Rome: Vitale Mascardi, 1643.

Theiner, Augustin. *Codex diplomaticus dominii temporalis S. Sedis. Recueil de documents pour servir à l'histoire du gouvernement temporel des États du Saint-Siège.* Extraits des Archives du Vatican. 3 vols. Rome: Vatican Press, 1861-62.

Villani, Giovanni. *Cronica, con le continuazioni di Matteo e Filippo.* Turin: Einaudi, 1979.

SECONDARY WORKS

Amargier, Paul. "Pétrarque et ses amis au temps de la verte feuillée." In Marie-Humbert Vicaire, ed. *La papauté d'Avignon et en Languedoc 1316-1342.* Cahiers de Fanjeaux 26. Toulouse: Privat, 1991, 127-40.

Anselmi, Gian Mario. "Il tempo della storia e quello della vita nella *Cronica* dell' Anonimo romano." *Studi e problemi di critica testuale* 21 (Oct. 1980): 181-94.

—. "La *Cronica* dell'Anonimo romano." *Bullettino dell'Istituto storico italiano per il medioevo e Archivio Muratoriano* 91 (1984): 423-40.

Antoine, Jean-Philippe. "*Ad perpetuam memoriam.* Les nouvelles fonctions de l'image peinte en Italie, 1250-1400." *Mélanges de l'École Française de Rome. Moyen Age et Temps Modernes* 100.2 (1988): 541-615.

BIBLIOGRAPHY

Aurigemma, Marcello. "Recenti studi sul Petrarca." *Cultura e scuola* 23.92 (1984): 7-14.

Avignon au temps de Pétrarque: 1304-1374. Avignon: Direction des Services d'Archives de Vaucluse, 1974.

Baldelli, Giovan Battisti (Boni). *Del Petrarca e delle sue opere, libri quattro.* Florence: Gaetano Cambiagi, 1797.

Barraclough, Geoffrey. *The Medieval Papacy.* New York: W.W. Norton, 1979.

Bartoli, Adolfo. "Il Petrarca e Cola di Rienzo." *Storia della letteratura italiana* 3 (1884): 113-34.

Barzini, Luigi. "Cola di Rienzo or the Obsession of Antiquity." In *The Italians.* New York: Atheneum, 1967, 117-32.

Bayley, C.C. "Petrarch, Charles IV and the 'Renovatio imperii.'" *Speculum* 17 (1942): 323-41.

Belting, Hans. "Langage et réalité dans la peinture monumentale publique en Italie au Trecento." In Xavier Barral i Altet, ed. *Artistes, artisans et production artistique au Moyen Age.* Actes du colloque internationale de Rennes, 1983. Paris: Picard, 1990, 3: 491-511.

Beneyto Perez, Juan. *El Cardenal Albornoz: Hombre de iglesia y de estado en Castilla y en Italia.* Madrid: Fundación Universitaria Española, 1986.

Bergin, Thomas G. *Petrarch.* Twayne's World Authors 81. New York: Twayne, 1970.

Berlan, Francesco. *Parma liberata dal giogo di Mastino della Scala addì 21 Maggio 1341.* Bologna: Gaetano Romagnoli, 1870.

Bernardo, Aldo S. *Scipio and the Africa. The Birth of Humanism's Dream.* Baltimore: Johns Hopkins University Press, 1962.

Blanc, Pierre. "La construction d'une utopie néo-urbaine. Rome dans la pensée, l'action et l'oeuvre de Pétrarque de 1333 à 1342." In Daniel Poirion, ed. *Jérusalem, Rome, Constantinople: L'Image et le mythe de la ville au Moyen Age.* Culture et civilisation medievale 5. Paris: Presses de l'Université de Paris, 1986, 149-68.

Brandi, Karl. *Cola di Rienzo und sein Verhältnis zu Renaissance und Humanismus.* Darmstadt: Wissenshaftliche Buchgesellschaft, 1965.

Braudel, Fernand. *The Mediterranean and the Mediterranean World in the Age of Philip II.* Sian Reynolds, trans. 2 vols. New York: Harper & Row, 1972.

BIBLIOGRAPHY

Brentano, Robert. *Rome before Avignon. A Social History of Thirteenth-Century Rome.* New York: Basic Books, 1974.

Brizzolara, Giuseppe. "Il Petrarca e Cola di Rienzo." *Studi storici* 8 (1899): 239-51, 423-63.

—. "Ancora Cola di Rienzo e Francesco Petrarca." *Studi storici* 12 (1903): 353-411; 14 (1905): 69-101, 243-77.

Brooke, Rosiland, and Christopher Brooke. *Popular Religion in the Middle Ages. Western Europe 1000-1300.* New York: Thames & Hudson, 1984.

Bulwer Lytton, Edward. *Rienzi, the Last of the Roman Tribunes.* London, 1835.

Carocci, Sandro. "Baroni in città: Considerazioni sull' insediamento e i diritti urbani della grande nobiltà." In Étienne Hubert, ed. *Rome aux XIIIe et XIVe siècles.* Collection de l'École Française de Rome 170. Rome: EFR, 1993, 137-73.

Castellani, Arrigo. "Note di lettura: La 'Cronica' d'Anonimo romano." *Studi linguistici italiani* 13 (1987): 66-84.

Cheyney, Edward P. *The Dawn of a New Era 1250-1453.* New York: Harper & Row, 1936; rev. ed., 1957.

Christophe, Jean Baptiste. *Histoire de la Papauté pendant le XIVe siècle.* Paris: Librairie de L. Maison, 1853.

Cipolla, Carlo. "Sui motivi del ritorno di Francesco Petrarca in Italia nel 1347." *Giornale storico della letteratura italiana* 47 (1906): 253-65.

Cola di Rienzo nel sesto centenario della morte. Rome: Unione storia ed arte. Memorie e conferenze romane. Vol. 1, 1955.

Colliva, Paolo. *Il Cardinale Albornoz, lo stato della chiesa, le "Constitutiones Aegidiane" (1353-1357).* Bologna: Royal College of Spain, 1977.

Contini, Cianfranco. "Invito a un capolavoro." *Letteratura* 4.4 (1940): 3-14.

Corsi, Dinora. "La 'crociata' di Venturino da Bergamo nella crisi spirituale di metà Trecento." *Archivio storico italiano* 147.4 (1989): 697-747.

Cosenza, Mario E. *Official Positions after the Time of Constantine.* Lancaster, PA: New Era Publications, 1905.

—. *The Study of Italian in the United States.* New York: Italy America Society, 1924.

—. *The Establishment of the College of the City of New York as the Free Academy, Townsend Harris, Founder.* New York: Associated Alumni of the College of the City of New York, 1925.

—. *Biographical and Bibliographical Dictionary of the Italian Humanists and the World of Classical Scholarship in Italy 1300-1800*. 5 vols. with supplement. Boston: G.K. Hall, 1962-67.

—. *Biographical and Bibliographical Dictionary of the Italian Printers and of Foreign Printers in Italy*. Boston: G.K. Hall, 1968.

—. *Checklist of Non-Italian Humanists 1300-1800*. Boston: G.K. Hall, 1969.

—, trans. Ettore Pais. *Ancient Legends of Roman History*. New York: Dodd Mead & Co., 1905.

—, trans. Amerigo Vespucci. *Quatuor Americi Vesputii navigationes*. Washington, DC: U.S. Catholic Historical Society, 1907.

—, ed. *The Complete Journal of Townsend Harris, First American Consul General and Minister to Japan*. Garden City, NY: Doubleday and Japan Society, 1930; rev. ed., 1959.

Costa-Zalessow, Natalia. "The Personification of Italy from Dante through the Trecento." *Italica* 68.4 (1991): 316-31.

Crémieux, Benjamin. "Sur la destinataire de la canzone 'Spirto gentil,' un témoignage du xvᵉ siècle en faveur de Cola di Rienzo." *Mélanges de philologie, d'histoire e de litterature offerts à Henri Hauvette*. Paris: Les Presses Françaises, 1934, 99-105.

D'Achille, Paolo, and Claudio Giovanardi. *La letteratura volgare e i dialetti di Roma e del Lazio. Bibliografia dei testi e degli studi*. Vol. 1: *Dalle origini al 1550*. Rome: Bonacci Editore, 1984.

D'Annunzio, Gabriele. *Vite di uomini illustri e di uomini oscuri: La vita di Cola di Rienzo*. Milan: Fratelli Treves, 1913.

Dardano, Maurizio. "L'articolazione e il confine della frase nella 'Cronica' di Anonimo romano." In Federica Albani Leoni, ed. *Italia linguistica: Idee, storia, strutture*. Bologna: Il Mulino, 1983, 203-22.

D'Arrigo, Giuseppe. "Ricordo di due grandi: Francesco Petrarca e Cola di Rienzo." In *Fatti e figure del Lazio medievale. Gruppo culturale di Roma e del Lazio*. Rome: Fratelli Palombi Editori, 1979, 511-16.

Davis, Charles T. *Dante and the Idea of Rome*. Oxford: Clarendon Press, 1957.

De Caprio, V. "La cultura romana nel periodo avignonese 1305-1377." In Roberto Antonelli, Angelo Cicchetti and Giorgio Inglese, eds. *Letteratura italiana: Storia e geografia*. Turin: Einaudi, 1987, 495-505.

De Mattei, Rodolfo. *Il sentimento politico del Petrarca*. Florence: G.C. Sansoni, 1944.

BIBLIOGRAPHY

De Sade, Jacques F.P.A. *Mémoires pour la vie de François Petrarque, tirés de ses oeuvres et des auteurs contemporains.* Amsterdam: Arskee et Mercus, 1764-67.

Dotti, Ugo. *Vita di Petrarca.* Rome: Laterza, 1987.

——. Il primo libro delle 'Senili' di Francesco Petrarca." *Giornale storico della letteratura italiana* 169.546 (1992): 228-39.

Douie, Decima L. *The Nature and the Effect of the Heresy of the Fraticelli.* Manchester: Manchester University Press, 1932; rpt. ed., New York: AMS, 1978.

Du Cange, Charles du Fresne. *Glossarium mediae et infimae Latinitatis.* 10 vols. Paris: Osmont, 1937-38.

Duncalf, Frederic, and August C. Krey. "The Coronation of Cola di Rienzo." In *Parallel Source Problems in Medieval History.* New York: Harper & Row, 1912, 177-237.

Duprè-Theseider, Eugenio. *I papi di Avignone e la questione romana.* Florence: Le Monnier, 1939.

——. *Roma dal comune di popolo alla signoria pontificia, 1272-1377.* Bologna: C. Cappelli, 1952.

——. "L'attesa escatologica durante il periodo avignonese." In *L'Attesa dell'età nuova nella spiritualità della fine del medioevo.* Convegni del Centro di Studi sulla Spiritualità Medievale. Todi: CSSM, 1962, 65-126.

Faucon, Maurice. "Note sur la détention de Rienzi à Avignon." *Mélanges d'archéologie et d'histoire de l'École Française de Rome* 7 (1887): 53-58.

Fedele, Pietro. "Il Giubileo del 1350." *Roma* 11 (1933): 193-212.

Felici, Lucio. "'La Vita di Cola di Rienzo' nella tradizione chronachistica romana." *Studi romani* 25.3 (1977): 325-43.

Ferguson, Wallace. *The Renaissance in Historical Thought.* Boston: Houghton Mifflin, 1948.

Filippini, Francesco. "Cola di Rienzo e la Curia Avignonese." *Studi storici* 10 (1901): 241-87, 11 (1902): 3-35.

——. *Il Cardinale Egidio Albornoz.* Bologna: N. Zanichelli, 1933.

Fiorentino, Francesco. *Scritti varii di letteratura, filosofia e critica.* Naples: Domenico Morano, 1876.

Fleisher, V. *Rienzo: The Rise and Fall of a Dictator.* London: Aigion Press, 1948.

Folena, Gianfranco. "Varia Fortuna del Romanesco." *Lingua nostra* 52.1 (1991): 7-10.

BIBLIOGRAPHY

Forcellini, Vincenzo. *"L'horrendurn tripes animal* della lettera 3 del libro v delle familiari di Petrarca.*" In *Studi di storia napoletana in onore di Michelangelo Schipa.* Naples, 1926, 167-99.

Foresti, Arnaldo. "Sognando la riforma del governo di Roma." In *Aneddoti della vita di Francesco Petrarca. Studi sul Petrarca* 1. Padua: Antenore, 1977, 263-67.

Foster, Kenelm. *Petrarch: Poet and Humanist.* Writers of Italy 9. Edinburgh: Edinburgh University Press, 1984.

Frugoni, Arsenio. "Cola di Rienzo 'tribunus sompniator'." In *Incontri nel Rinascimento.* Brescia: La Scuola, 1954, 9-23.

Gaspary Adolf. *Geschichte der italienischen Literatur.* 2 vols. Berlin: Robert Oppenheim, 1885-88.

Gennaro, Clara. "Mercanti e bovattieri nella Roma della seconda metà del Trecento." *Bollettino dell'Istituto storico italiano per il medioevo e Archivio Muratoriano* 78 (1967): 155-203.

—. "Giovanni Colombini e la sua 'brigata'." *Bollettino del Istituto Storico Italiano per il Medioevo e Archivio Muratoriano* 81 (1969): 237-71.

—. "Movimenti religiosi e pace nel XIV secolo." In *La pace nel pensiero, nella politica, negli ideali del Trecento.* Todi: CSSM, 1975, 91-112.

—. "Venturino da Bergamo e la peregrinatio romana del 1335." In *Studi sul medioevo cristiano offerti a Raffaelo Morghen.* 2 vols. Rome: Istituto Storico Italiano per il Medioevo, 1974, 1: 375-406.

—. "Venturino spirituale." *Rivista di storia e letteratura religiosa* 23.3 (1987): 434-66.

Graf, Arturo. *Roma nella memoria e nella immaginazione del Medio Evo.* Turin: E. Loescher, 1915.

Gregorovius, Ferdinand. *History of the City of Rome in the Middle Ages.* Annie Hamilton, trans. 8 vols. in 13. London: George Bell & Sons, 1894-1900; rpt. ed., New York: AMS, 1967.

—. *Rome and Medieval Culture. Selections from History of the City of Rome in the Middle Ages.* Karl F. Morrison, ed. Chicago: University of Chicago Press, 1971.

Grion, Alvaro. "Legenda Beati Fratris Venturini O.P." *Bergomum*, n.s. 30.4 (1956): 11-110.

Hale, J.R. *Renaissance Europe 1480-1520.* London: Collins, 1971.

BIBLIOGRAPHY

Höfele, Karl Heinrich. *Rienzi, das abenteurerliche Vorspiel der Renaissance.* Munich: R. Oldenbourg, 1958.

Hubert, Étienne. *Rome aux xiiie et xive siècles.* Collection de l'École Française de Rome 170. Rome: EFR, 1993.

Joubert, M. "Rienzi and Petrarch." *The Contemporary Review* 166 (July-Dec. 1944): 34-42.

Kelley, Donald R. *Renaissance Humanism.* Twayne's Studies in Intellectual and Cultural History 2. Boston: G.K. Hall, 1991.

Kölmel, Von Wilhelm. "Petrarca und das Reich. Zum historisch-politischen Aspekt der 'studia humanitatis.'" *Historisches Jahrbuch* 90 (1970): 1-30.

Krautheimer, Richard. *Rome. Profile of a City, 312-1308.* Princeton: Princeton University Press, 1980.

Kristeller, Paul Oskar. *Renaissance Thought.* New York: Harper & Row, 1961.

Kuhn, Fritz. *Die Entwicklung der Bündnisplane Cola di Rienzos im Jahre 1347.* Berlin: Denter & Nicolas, 1905.

Larner, John. *Italy in the Age of Dante and Petrarch, 1216-1380.* New York: Longman, 1980.

Leff, Gordon. *Heresy in the Later Middle Ages.* 2 vols. New York: Barnes & Noble, 1967.

Ludvíkovsky, Jaroslav. "List Karla iv Colovi di Rienzi do Vézení [The Letter of Charles iv to Cola di Rienzo in Prison]." *Studia minora facultatis philosophicae universitatis Brunensis. Series Archeologica et Classica* 24 (1981): 117-21.

Macek, Josef. "Les racines sociales de l'insurrection de Cola di Rienzo." *Historica* 6 (1963): 45-107.

—. "Pétrarch et Cola di Rienzo." *Historica* 8 (1965): 5-51.

Maire-Vigueur, Jean Claude. "Cola di Rienzo." *Dizionario Biografico degli Italiani* 16. Rome: DBI, 1982, 662-75.

Mann, Nicholas. *Petrarch.* Past Masters Series. New York: Oxford University Press, 1984.

Mariani, Marisa. "Cola di Rienzo nel giudizio dei contemporanei fiorentini." *Studi romani* 8 (1960): 647-66.

Mazzei, Francesco. *Cola di Rienzo: La fantastica vita e l'orribile morte del tribuno del popolo romano.* Milan: Rusconi, 1980.

BIBLIOGRAPHY

Mazzotta, Giuseppe. *The Worlds of Petrarch*. Duke Monographs in Medieval and Renaissance Studies 14. Durham, NC: Duke University Press, 1994.

Miccoli, G. "Giovanni Colombini." In *Storia d'Italia* 2.1. Turin: Einaudi, 1974, 914-24.

Miglio, Massimo. "Gruppi sociali e azione politica nella Roma di Cola di Rienzo." *Studi romani* 23.4 (1975): 442-61.

—. "Gli ideali di pace e di giustizia in Roma a metà del Trecento." *La pace nel pensiero, nella politica, negli ideali del Trecento*. Convegni del Centro di Studi sulla Spiritualità Medievale 15. Todi: CSSM, 1975, 175-97.

—. "'Et rerum facta est pulcherrima Roma.' Attualità della tradizione e proposte di innovazione." In *Aspetti culturali della società italiana nel periodo del papato avignonese*. Convegni del Centro di Studi sulla Spiritualità Medievale 19. Todi: CSSM, 1981, 311-69.

—. "Il progetto politico di Cola di Rienzo ed i comuni dell'Italia centrale." *Bollettino dell' Istituto Storico Artistico Orvietano* 39 (1983, act. 1988): 55-64.

Mollat, Guillaume. *The Popes at Avignon, 1305-1378*. New York: Thomas Nelson, 1963.

Mollat, Michel, and Philippe Wolff. *The Popular Revolutions of the Late Middle Ages*. London: Allen & Unwin, 1973.

Morghen, Raffaello. *La formazione della storiografica sul medioevo 2: Cola di Rienzo*. L. Gatto, ed. Rome: Ateneo, 1955.

—. *Cola di Rienzo Senatore*. L. Gatto, ed. Rome: Ateneo, 1956.

—. "Il mito storico di Cola di Rienzo." In his *Civiltà medioevale al tramonto*. Rome & Bari: Laterza, 1971, 165-93.

Mosti, Renzo. "L'eresia dei Fraticelli nei territorii de Tivoli." *Atti e memoriale della Società Tiburtina di storia e d'arte* 38 (1965): 41-110.

Musto, Ronald G. "Queen Sancia of Naples (1286-1345) and the Spiritual Franciscans." In *Women of the Medieval World. Essays in Honor of John H. Mundy*. Julius Kirshner and Suzanne F. Wemple, eds. Oxford: Basil Blackwell, 1985, 179-214.

Musumarra, Carmelo. "Petrarca e Roma." *Critica Letteraria* 18.1 (1990): 155-67.

Oizon, René. *Dictionnaire géographique de France*. Paris: Larousse, 1979.

BIBLIOGRAPHY

Origo, Iris. *Tribune of Rome: A Biography of Cola di Rienzo*. London: Hogarth Press, 1938.

Papencordt, Felix. *Cola di Rienzo und seine Zeit*. Hamburg and Gotha: A. Perthes, 1841.

Partner, Peter. *The Lands of St. Peter. The Papal State in the Middle Ages and the Early Renaissance*. London: Methuen; Berkeley: University of California Press, 1972.

Perroy, Edouard. *The Hundred Years War*. New York: Capricorn Books, 1965.

Piur, Paul. *Cola di Rienzo*. Vienna: L.W. Seidel, 1931; Italian trans., Jeanne Chabod Rohr. Milan, 1934.

Porta, Giuseppe. "La lingua della 'Cronica' di Anonimo romano." In Tullio de Mauro, ed. *Il romanesco ieri e oggi*. Rome: Bulzoni, 1989, 13-26.

—. "Un nuovo manoscritto della 'Cronica' di Anonimo romano." *Studi medievali*, ser. 3, 25.1 (1984): 445-48.

Pozzi, Mario. "Appunti sulla 'Cronica' di Anonimo romano." *Giornale storico della letteratura italiana* 99 (1982): 481-504.

Preston, H.W., and L. Dodge. "Cola di Rienzo." *Atlantic Monthly* 71 (January 1893): 62-78.

Previté-Orton, C.W. *The Shorter Cambridge Medieval History*. 2 vols. New York: Cambridge University Press, 1966.

Proctor, Robert E. "The Revolution of Cola di Rienzo." *Speculum* 82 (1988): 254-57.

Reale, Ugo. *Vita di Cola di Rienzo*. Rome: Editori Riuniti, 1982.

—. *Cola di Rienzo: La straordinario vita del tribuno che sogno riportare Roma all'antico valore....* Rome: Newton Compton, 1991.

Reeves, Marjorie. *The Influence of Prophecy in the Later Middle Ages*. Oxford: Clarendon Press, 1969.

—. *Joachim of Fiore and the Prophetic Future*. London: SPCK, 1976.

Renouard, Yves. *The Avignon Papacy 1305-1403*. Denis Bethell, trans. Hamden, CT: Archon, 1970.

Ricci, Pier Giorgio. "Il commento di Cola di Rienzo alla *Monarchia* di Dante." *Studi medievali*, ser. 3, 6 (1965): 665-708.

Rodocanachi, Emmanuel. *Cola di Rienzo*. Paris: A. Lahure, 1888.

Romani, Mario. *Pellegrini e viaggiatori nell' economia di Roma dal XIV al XVII secolo*. Milan: Vita e pensiero, 1948.

BIBLIOGRAPHY

Sanfilippo, Mario. "Dell' Anonimo e della sua e altrui nobilità." *Quaderni medievali* 9 (1980): 121-28.

Schmidinger, Heinrich. "Die Antwort Clemens' vi. an die Gesandschaft der Stadt Rom vom Jahre 1343." In *Miscellanea in onore di Monsignor Martino Giusti*. 2 vols. Vatican City: BAV, 1978, 2:323-65.

Schwarz, Amy. "Images and Illusions of Power in Trecento Art: Cola di Rienzo and the Ancient Roman Republic." Ph.D. Diss. Binghamton: SUNY, 1994.

Segrè, Carlo. *Studi petrarcheschi*. Florence: Le Monnier, 1903.

Seibt, Gustav. *Anonimo romano: Geschichtsschreibung in Rom an der Schwelle Renaissance*. Stuttgart: Klett-Cotta, 1992.

Small, Carola M. "The District of Rome in the Early Fourteenth Century, 1300 to 1347." *Canadian Journal of History/Annales Canadiennes d'Histoire* 16 (1981): 193-213.

Sonnay, Philippe. "La politique artistique de Cola di Rienzo (1313-1354)." *Revue de l'art* 55 (1982): 35-43.

Sordi, Marta. "Cola di Rienzo e le Clausole mancanti della 'lex de imperio Vespasiani.'" In *Studi in onore di Edoardo Volterrra* 2. Milan: A. Giuffre, 1971, 303-11.

Steiner, Carlo. "La fede nell'impero e il concetto della patria italiana nel Petrarca." *Giornale dantesco* 14 (1906): 8-34.

Tanturli, Giuliano. "La Cronica di Anonimo romano." *Paragone* 31.368 (Oct. 1980): 84-93.

Tatham, E.H.R. *Francesco Petrarca, The First Modern Man of Letters*. 2 vols. London: Sheldon Press, 1925-26.

Toppani, Innocente. "Petrarca, Cola di Rienzo e il mito di Roma." *Atti dell' Istituto Veneto di scienze, lettere ed arti. Classe di scienze morali, lettere ed arti* 135 (1977): 155-72.

Torraca, Francesco. "Cola di Rienzo e la canzone *Spirto gentil* di Francesco Petrarca." In *Discussioni e ricerche letterarie*. Livorno: Vigo, 1888, 1-87.

Trifone, Pietro. "Aspetti dello stile nominale nella Cronica trecentesca di Anonimo romano." *Studi linguistici italiani* 12 (1986): 217-39.

Ullmann, Walter. *The Growth of Papal Government in the Middle Ages*. London: Methuen, 1970.

BIBLIOGRAPHY

Waley, Daniel. *The Papal State in the Thirteenth Century.* New York: St. Martin's Press, 1961.

Weiss, Roberto. "Barbato da Sulmona, il Petrarca e la rivoluzione di Cola di Rienzo." *Studi petrarcheschi.* Carlo Calcaterra, ed. Bologna: Minerva, 1950, 13-22.

Wilkins, Ernest Hatch. *Studies in the Life and Work of Petrarch.* Cambridge, MA: Medieval Academy of America, 1955.

——. *Petrarch's Correspondence.* Padua: Antenore, 1960.

——. *Life of Petrarch.* Chicago: University of Chicago Press, 1963.

Zeller, Jacques S. *Les tribuns et les revolutions en Italie.* Paris: Didier, 1874, 147-259.

Ziegler, Philip. *The Black Death.* New York: Penguin Books, 1969.

Zumbini, Buonaventura. *Studi sul Petrarca.* Florence: Le Monnier, 1895.

INDEX

INDEX

INDEX

INDEX

G

Gaetani, family 67, 88
Ganges River 76
Garamant 100
Gascony 162, 163
Gaul 174
Gauls 156, 159; Senonian 110
Gellius 31
Genazzano 142
Genoa 41, 98, 101-2, 143
Germans 156
Germany 76, 123, 127, 134, 141
Ghibellines 25, 79, 86, 126-27, 144, 175
Gillias, shepherd 92
Giordano del Monte 143
Giovanna, queen of Naples 29, 89, 121
Giovanni, bishop of Spoleto 128
Giovanni, Messer, Cola's messenger 48-52, 71, 77
Gracchus, Tiberius 22
Greece 46, 141
Greeks 156, 159
Gregorian Reform 138
Gregorovius, Ferdinand 24, 27, 38, 78, 120, 127, 138, 148, 161, 176
Guelphs 25, 29, 79, 86, 127, 144, 175
Gui de Boulogne, cardinal 121-22, 142, 149, 165

H

Hannibal 2, 13, 25, 35, 143, 161
Harpalon, Hugo 168-70
Hebrews 124
highways 39, 49
Holy Roman Emperors 25
Holy Roman Empire xi, 83
Homer 141
Horace 124, 135, 140
Hostilius, C. 165
Hugue de Charlus 128
Hungarian soldiers 90
Hungary 121

I

India 62, 67, 100
Innocent VI 140, 146, 149, 168-69, 170-72

J

Jacques d'Euse, see John XXII
Jean de Hesdin 174
Jeanne d'Auvergne 121
Jerusalem 68, 82
Jews, of Rome 172
Joachimism 119
Joachites 119, 120
Johann von Neumark, chancellor 86
John XXII 1, 161-62
John, king of France 121
Jubilee of 1350 106, 120, 123
Juvenal 25

K

Kempen, Ludwig von (Socrates) 97, 122, 124

L

Laelius, see Cosecchi, Lello di Pietro di Stefano dei
Latins 111, 161
Latium 64, 111
Laura xi, xviii
Laurentii, Nicholas, see Cola di Rienzo
Leonine City 6
Lewis of Bavaria, Holy Roman Emperor 51, 126
Ligurians 61
Limoges 142, 146
Livy, Titus, as source for Petrarch 14, 26, 30, 31, 41, 114; influence on Cola xvi, 2, 129; Petrarch's work on xviii; references to 25, 32, 43, 82, 125, 165
Louis I of Hungary 42, 89, 98

195

INDEX

INDEX

INDEX

This Book Was Completed on October 8, 1995 at Italica Press,
New York, New York. It Was Set In Dante. This
Printing is on 60-lb Acid-Free, Natural,
Paper by LightningSource
U. S. A. / E. U.
★   ★

★

Printed in the USA
CPSIA information can be obtained
at www.ICGtesting.com
LVHW091910211123
764566LV00002B/258

9 780934 977005